GAME PROGRAMMING WITH
VISUAL BASIC®.NET

player 1

GRAEME SUMMERS

THOMSON

NELSON

Australia · Canada · Mexico · New Zealand · Singapore · Spain · United Kingdom · United States

Level 7, 80 Dorcas Street
South Melbourne, Victoria Australia 3205

Email nelson@thomsonlearning.com.au
Website http://www.thomsonlearning.com.au

First published in 2006
10 9 8 7 6 5 4 3 2 1
10 09 08 07 06

National Library of Australia
Cataloguing-in-Publication data

Summers, Graeme.

    Game Programming with Visual Basic.Net.

    1st ed.
    Includes index.
    For secondary school students, years 10-12
    ISBN-10 0 17 013125 4.
    ISBN-13 978 0 17 013125 4.

    1. Microsoft Visual BASIC
    2. Computer games - Programming
    1. Title

794.81526

Publishing editor Eleanor Gregory
Cover designer Sue Dani
Designed and typeset by Graeme Summers
Illustrated by Reiner Prokein and Michael Hirsch
Production controller Deepa Travers
Printed in China by C&C Offset Printing Co. Ltd.

This title is published under the imprint of Nelson School.
Nelson Australia Pty Limited ACN 058 280 149 (incorporated in Victoria)
trading as Thomson Learning Australia.

Any URLs contained in this publication were checked for currency during
the production process. Note, however, that the publisher cannot vouch
for the ongoing currency of URLs.

Contents

1   Serious fun (what makes a good game)   1
    Check what you have learnt   4

2   Let's get it started (introduction to moving objects)   5
    Viper cycle   5
    Points to note   7
    Check what you have learnt   9
    Spaceship   9
    Points to note   11
    Check what you have learnt   12
    Fairy flying   12
    Points to note   14
    Check what you have learnt   15
    Explode   16
    Points to note   17
    Check what you have learnt   18

3   Heading in the right direction (moving objects)   19
    Tank aiming   21
    Points to note   22
    Check what you have learnt   23
    Follow me   24
    Points to note   26
    Check what you have learnt   27

4   Meet and greet (splash and entry forms)   29
    Splash   29
    Entry   33
    Points to note   35
    Check what you have learnt   36

5   Controlling the bugs (using GDI+ for moving objects)   37
    Wolf running   37
    Points to note   39
    Check what you have learnt   40
    Flying insects   42
    Points to note   44
    Check what you have learnt   45

6   Sound advice (background music and sound effects)   47
    Audio players   49
    Points to note   54
    Check what you have learnt   55

7   Collision decisions (dealing with colliding objects)   57
Space   58
Points to note   61
Check what you have learnt   62
Leap and land   62
Points to note   65
Check what you have learnt   65
Paddle ball   66
Points to note   70
Check what you have learnt   70

8   An array of hope (collections and arrays of objects)   71
Enemy attack   72
Points to note   74
Check what you have learnt   75
Double trouble   75
Points to note   77
Check what you have learnt   78

9   I see the earth move (moving backgrounds)   79
Helicopter patrol   80
Points to note   82
Check what you have learnt   83
Endless road   84
Points to note   88
Check what you have learnt   90

10 Telephones and tophats (board games)   91
Power of 2   94
Points to note   97
Check what you have learnt   98
Snakes and ladders   99
Points to note   103
Check what you have learnt   104

11 Blocks and dots (games involving mazes)   107
Mouse maze   107
Points to note   111
Check what you have learnt   113
Dot eater   114
Points to note   120
Check what you have learnt   122

12 How to be sharp (techniques in creating card games)   123
Want a hand?   124
Points to note   126
Check what you have learnt   127
Pontoon   128
Points to note   138
Check what you have learnt   139

13 Objects on the fly (creating objects at run-time)   **141**
Snake   142
Points to note   146
Check what you have learnt   147
Tetraminos   147
Points to note   156
Check what you have learnt   157

14 Space hero   **159**
Points to note   166
Check what you have learnt   167

15 Deployment benefits (deploying games for distribution)   **169**
Points to note   175
Check what you have learnt   176

Appendix 1 (modules)   177

Appendix 2 (subclasses)   185

Answers (to 'Check what you have learnt' questions)   190

Index   199

Chapter 1

Serious fun

Animals at play

Who hasn't been entertained watching young animals at play? Puppies will play by stalking, pouncing, biting, shaking objects from side to side and, of course, running and fetching. Zoologists believe that when animals play, as well as having fun, they are practicing the skills that they will need in their adult life. Along with their hunting and predatory skills they are developing social bonding with the 'pack' and their communication skills.

Are human beings so different? Our young have the longest juvenile period in the animal kingdom and are certainly no less playful. Chasings, Hide-and-Seek and wrestling are children's games that go back into pre history. How important have they been to the hunting, social and communication skills of human beings?

The development of manufactured games

Two and a half thousand years ago, the Greek philosopher Plato believed that Greek children should be provided with toys that would help develop the skills they would need in their adult life. In all early civilisations, as well as weaponry, architecture, literature and science, games were also developed for both children and adults. Backgammon, checkers, chess, card and dice games are all over one thousand years old. Snakes and ladders came from India, dominos from China, backgammon and checkers from Iraq, chess from Afghanistan, card games from somewhere in central Asia. The basis of each of these games was a reflection of the society from which it came. The types of games that people played said as much about their society as their art or literature. All these ancient games have been modified in form and structure over the centuries.

The twentieth century saw the mass production and spread of modern board games including Monopoly, Scrabble, Cluedo and Trivial Pursuit. A multitude of these and other board games still exist today for the home market.

It was in the 1930s when the coin operated fun parlours began to spring up across the United States. Pinball machines appeared not long afterwards and dominated this type of entertainment for the next three decades.

The most rapid development in games arrived with the electronic age. In the 1970s the essentially mechanical games of the fun parlours were transformed into a new generation of arcade games led by Pong and later Space Invaders. Soon after, with the availability of personal computers and home game consoles, the floodgates were opened to what was referred to as video games.

The developments of the next three decades could be summarised by the names of milestones like Pac Man, Donkey Kong, Tetris, Sim City, Super Mario Bros., Wolfenstein 3D, Doom, Quake, Ultima V, Unreal1, Final Fantasy VII, Grand Theft Auto, MotoGP…

In 2005 the game industry in Australia turned over $100 million while, in the United States, it was estimated to have an impact of $18 billion on its economy. Are games just an extremely expensive waste of time? Are they producing a generation of robotic screen gazers? What would Plato say? If they are an embedded part of our society, how do we identify those with the most positive impact?

What are the benefits?

There are more games and a greater range of games available today than at any other time in history. If we make the best possible choices from those available, what are the benefits? Clearly the games that we choose are those that give us the most fun. It is unlikely that we will try to analyse what is 'good' for us and then choose accordingly. But it may well be that those games that are the most fun are those that also benefit us the most.

Fun games are not passive activities. They engage us and stir our competitive spirits. They challenge us to solve problems and entice us to attempt solutions with increasing levels of difficulty. Fun games appeal to our sense of adventure and stimulate our imagination. They sharpen our hand-eye coordination and our reflexes. In the real world we may seek monitory reward for our efforts, but in playing a game we enjoy the reward is intrinsic.

Game playing is callisthenics for the brain. Fun is our motivation to keep doing it.

What makes a good game?

A good idea

All good games start with someone's good idea. The idea doesn't have to be filled with complexities. Some of the most enduring games have an ingeniously simple structure. Take games like Checkers, Scrabble or Tetris as examples. The overall concept of each can be grasped in a couple of minutes. Yet for the many enthusiasts of these games they are obsessively interesting. They have some indefinable 'hook' that grabs the player. Even though the idea is simple, there are an almost infinite number of permutations. Each time the game is played it is different from every other time it was played.

The good idea may just be a variation of something already in place. Advent was the first of the MUD (Multi User Dungeon) adventure games. This allowed a large number of players to interact online. There were many 'shoot-em-up' games before Wolfenstein 3D. But it was the first to introduce the concept of the first person player.

The value of a new idea ultimately is a matter of personal taste. However there are features of games that are not based purely on personal preference and can be assessed objectively.

Music, sound effects

Background music can set the mood as it does in movies. Ideally the music is sensitive to the rise and fall of tension and changes in pace. Sound effects can add to the realism, alert the player to a critical event or even provide an element of humour.

Animation

Almost all games require a certain level of movement or animation. This does not necessarily mean a lifelike realism. Some of the most absorbing games have very simple graphics and animation. It is important that the animation used suits the genre of the game and there is a match of graphical components.

Levels

The option of being able to choose a level of difficulty is a good way of introducing a player to a game. If the player feels there is no hope of winning there will be an immediate loss of interest. There must always be a sense of some chance of being able to win. If there is no option for an entry level the game should progressively move through levels of difficulty.

Rewards

Rewards should match the good decisions made by the player. If rewards are meagre the player will not be motivated to strive for them. At the same time, rewards should not be so great that the player loses interest because he becomes unbeatable. Achieving the right balance of rewards is the aim of a game writer. When rewards are taken the player should understand why this has occurred so he can plan better strategies to avoid this. It must be noted however that in the playing of some games the rewards are intrinsic, the good play is rewarded by a successful outcome.

Anticipation

To maintain an interest level the player must feel the game is going somewhere. Like a movie that gives subtle hints as to the possible direction of the plot, there has to be some indications of progression and a movement towards something better.

Interesting decisions

Players will enjoy a game when they are interested in the decisions they are required to make. The decisions that are made have to be of some consequence or the player will lose interest. A good decision has to be coupled with a suitable reward. The player will stay connected if the decisions are paced in a way that doesn't produce frustration or hopelessness.

Humanise the opponent

Players like to have an opponent that seems to have some intelligence. For game writers this may be the greatest challenge. Humanising the opponent means, not only intelligence, but also personality, weaknesses and strengths. The opponent must also display a determination to win.

Randomness

Randomness can provide the element of surprise. Players don't want to repeatedly play a game that is exactly the same each time. However players must have the ability to have influence on the progression of the game through the good decisions that they make.

What next?

Hopefully we have some ideas about what makes a good game and what is challenging and interesting. However an even more challenging task is not the playing of a game, it is the construction of a game. The focus of this book will be the mastering of techniques to develop simple but well-constructed games using a mainstream development environment, Visual Basic.NET. Enjoy!

Serious fun – check what you have learnt

1   Why do zoologists believe that the play of young animals is critical to their survival?

2   As well as the acquired hunting skills, what other important skills does play develop in young animals?

3   Why did Plato advocate play for young Greek children?

4   In what way are games a reflection of the society they are from?

5   It is stated that fun games are not passive activities. What types of leisure activities do you regard as passive?

6   It is stated that game playing is callisthenics for the brain. Give your own definition of game playing.

7   Give your own definition of fun.

8   Some of the games with simple yet original ideas have been listed. What is a game, with which you are familiar, that you believe has a simple yet original 'hook'?

9   List three objective features of a good game that you regard as the most important. State your reasons.

10 It is said that some people play games as a release or escape from reality. Do you believe that the fantasy aspect of games is a feature that should have been included in our list?

Chapter 2

Let's get it started

The first movement

Movement is fundamental to the progression of all games. Movement may be the change in location of an object or changes in pictures that provide an animated sequence.

The location of an object on a form is defined by the Left and Top properties. They measure the number of pixels an object is from the left and top borders of a form respectively.

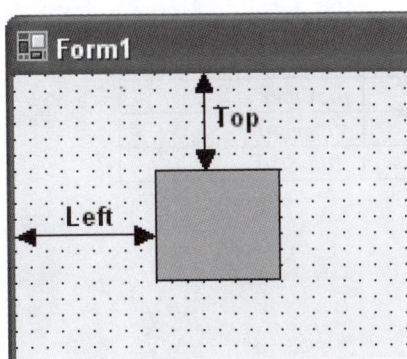

The Left and Top properties are not found in the properties window. Rather they are shown as the Location property (Left, Top).

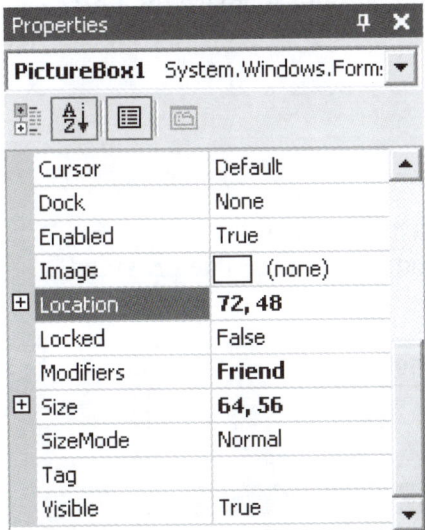

Program example: Viper cycle

Create a new Windows application with the name *Viper cycle*. This example will demonstrate how changing the value of the Left property can produce movement of an object.

Create the interface

■ Add a picture box and a timer to the form as shown on the following page. You can double-click or drag these controls from the toolbox. The timer will automatically be added to the **component tray** below the form.

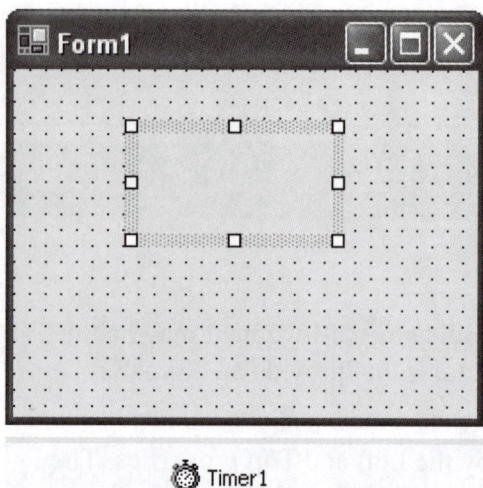

Timer1

■ Single-click on each of the objects then set the following properties. Leave all other properties with their default values.

Form1

BackColor	255, 255, 192
Icon	(you choose)
Text	Viper Cycle

PictureBox1

Name	picViper
Image	Viper.gif
SizeMode	AutoSize

Timer1

Name	tmrMove
Enabled	True
Interval	50

Write the code and add comments

■ Double-click the timer to bring up the code window. Type the single line of code in the provided template. Each tick of the timer will increase the Left property of the picture box by 2 pixels.

```
Private Sub tmrMove_Tick(ByVal sender As System.Object, ByVal e As _
System.EventArgs) Handles tmrMove.Tick
    picViper.Left += 2 ' move 2 pixels right
End Sub
```

■ From inside the code window select the *picViper* object and the *LocationChanged* event. Enter the following code in the template provided.

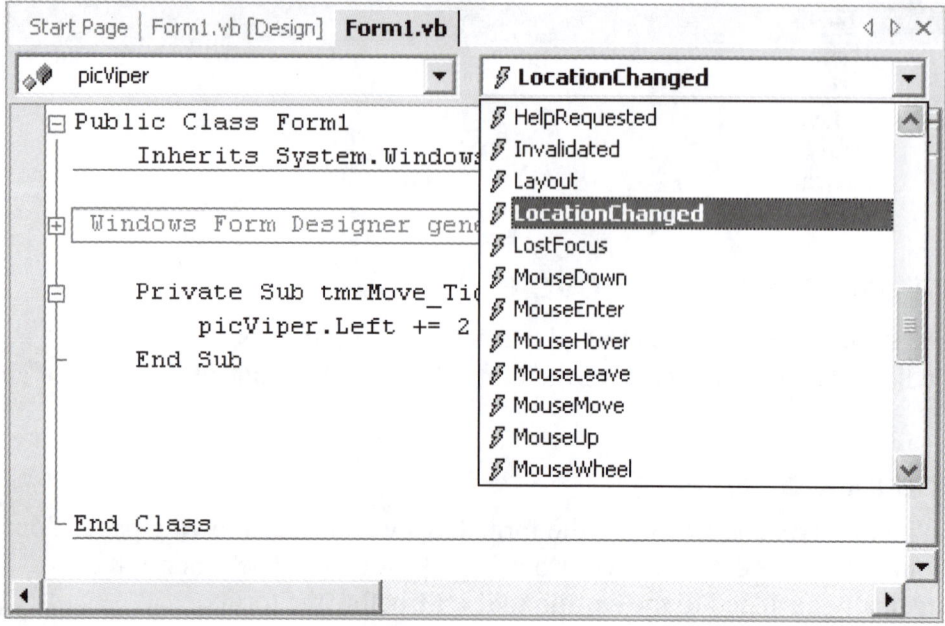

```
Private Sub picViper_LocationChanged(ByVal sender As Object, ByVal e As _
System.EventArgs) Handles picViper.LocationChanged
    If picViper.Left >= Me.Width Then ' off the right side of form
        picViper.Left = -picViper.Width ' move to left side of form
    End If
End Sub
```

Try it out

Pressing the **Start button** on the toolbar will launch the application.

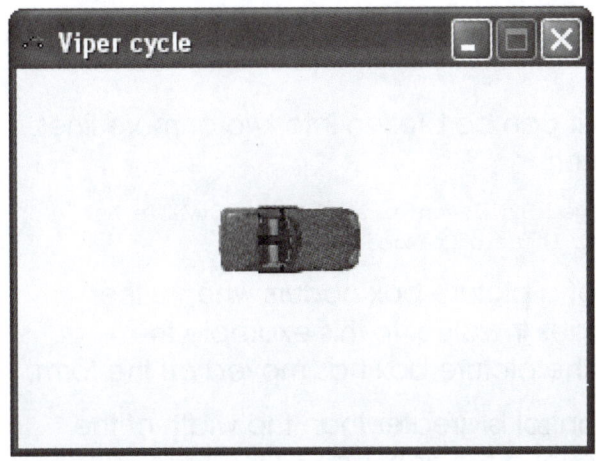

Viper cycle – points to note

■ When naming controls the three letter prefix will describe the type of object. The remaining letters describe its function. So we have used the prefixes *pic* for picture box and *tmr* for timer.

■ The **Left** property of a control measures the number of pixels the left side of a control is from the left side of the form. The **Top** property of a control measures the number of pixels the top side of a control is from the top of the form.

■ The **Location** property of a control contains both the left and top measurements. **Location.X** is the same as the Left property, **Location.Y** is the same as the Top property.

■ In all of the code written in this book there are some lines of code that don't fit the width of the page. A line of code can be extended to a second line using an **underscore** character.

```
Private Sub tmrMove_Tick(ByVal sender As System.Object, ByVal e As _
System.EventArgs) Handles tmrMove.Tick
```

■ Changes in the Left and Top properties produce movement.

```
picViper.Left += 2 ' move 2 pixels right
```

This line of code adds 2 pixels to the existing Left property.

■ Certain controls, that are not seen at run-time, automatically place themselves in the form's **component tray**. The timer is one of these controls.

- The **Interval** property of a timer determines how often it 'ticks'. A setting of 1000 is a tick rate of 1 per second. A setting of 50 is a tick rate of 1 per $1/20$th second. It determines how often its event procedure runs.

- A timer will start 'ticking' if its **Enabled** property is set to *True* or if the **Start** method is applied. Similarly it will stop ticking if the Enabled property is set to False or the **Stop** method is applied.

- The **SizeMode** property of a picture box determines how it treats its image. A setting of **AutoSize** will make the picture box resize itself to fit the size of the image.

- It is important to include **comments** in code to document the logic. Comments are preceded by a single quote.

```
picViper.Left += 2 ' move 2 pixels right
```

- If a line of code gets too long it can be broken into two or more lines using the **underscore** character:

```
Private Sub picViper_LocationChanged(ByVal sender As Object, ByVal e As _
System.EventArgs) Handles picViper.LocationChanged
```

- The **LocationChanged** event of a picture box occurs when either Location.X or Location.Y changes in value. In this example the procedure is used to check if the picture box has moved off the form.

- When The Left property of a control is greater than the width of the form (Me.Width) it has gone beyond the right side of the form. When this occurs in the Viper cycle example the picture box is put on the other side of the form. So it appears to cycle.

```
If picViper.Left >= Me.Width Then ' off the right side of form
    picViper.Left = -picViper.Width ' move to left side of form
End If
```

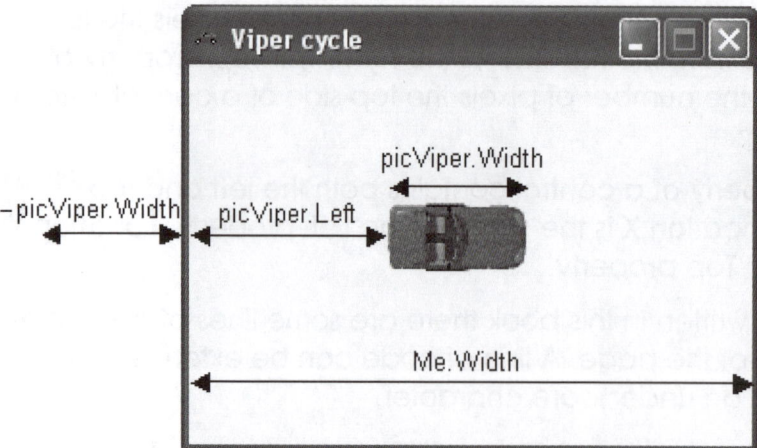

- An **If Then** statement is referred to as **two-way branching**. It provides two alternative actions. In this case the tone of the actions is to move the picture box to the left side of the form, the other is to do nothing.

Viper cycle – check what you have learnt

1   Other prefixes used for controls are btn for Button, lbl for Label and iml for ImageList. Suggest suitable names for:

    a   a button used to start a race

    b   a label used to keep score

    c   an image list used to hold a deck of cards

2   What are the Left and Top properties of an object whose Location is given as 48, 120?

3   What assignment would need to be made to move a picture box named *picRocket* 8 pixels to the left?

4   What is common to all controls that are placed in a form's component tray?

5   How often does a timer tick that has had its Interval property set to 200?

6   What property of a timer determines whether it is ticking or not?

7   What is the advantage in including comments in your code?

8   Events are said to be 'raised'. What causes the LocationChanged event to be raised?

9   What is true of the Left property of a control if it is off the form on the left side?

10 The height and width of a form are stored in the properties Me.Height and Me.Width. Write the small portion of code that checks the location of a picture box named *picRocket* that is moving down the form. If the picture box goes off the bottom of the form it is to return to a location above the top of the form.

Program example: Spaceship

Create a new Windows application with the name *Spaceship*.

Create the interface

- Add a picture box and an image list to the form

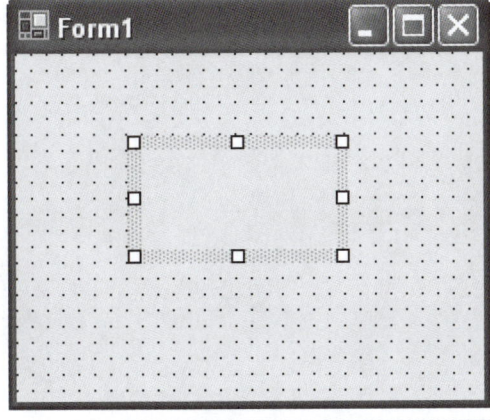

ImageList1

■ Set the following properties:

Form1

BackColor	Black
Icon	(you choose)
KeyPreview	True
MaximizeBox	False
Text	Spaceship

PictureBox1

Name	picShip
Image	Spaceship up.bmp
SizeMode	AutoSize

ImageList1

Name	imlSpaceships
ImageSize	64, 64

Label1

ForeColor	White
Text	Use the cursor keys to move

■ The image list must have these four bitmaps loaded into its Images collection.

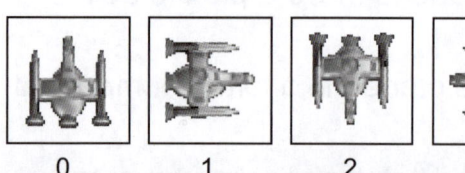

0   1   2   3

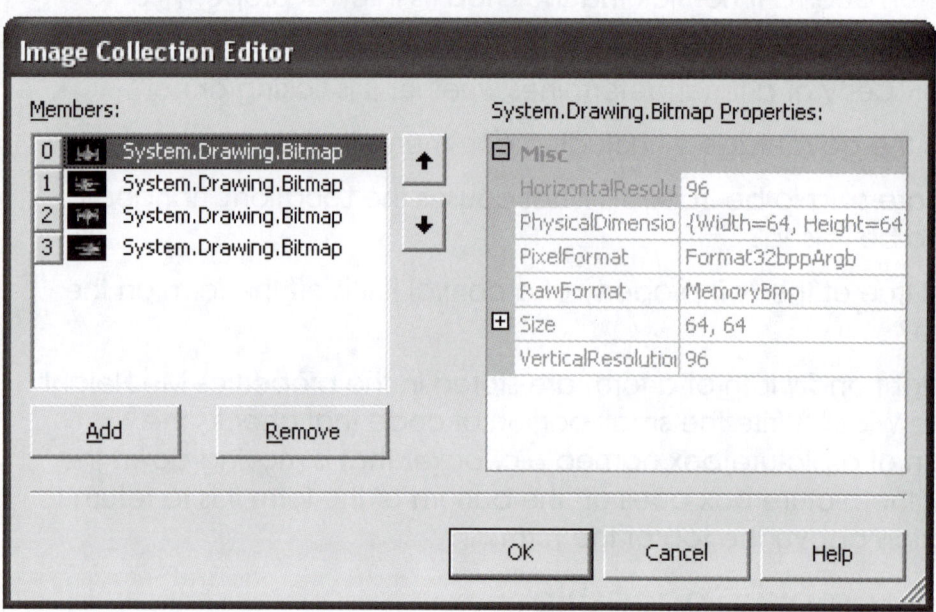

Write the code and add comments

■ Open the code window by pressing the **View Code** button in the **solution explorer**.

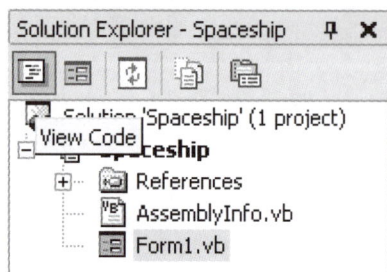

- Select (Form1 events) and the **KeyDown** event from the drop down lists then enter the following code. When a key is pressed the code of the key is passed into this procedure. This procedure uses **multiple branching**.

```
Private Sub Form1_KeyDown(ByVal sender As Object, ByVal e As _
System.Windows.Forms.KeyEventArgs) Handles MyBase.KeyDown
    ' load appropriate image then move spaceship
    Select Case e.KeyCode
        Case Keys.Up
            picShip.Image = imlSpaceships.Images.Item(0)
            picShip.Top -= 4
        Case Keys.Down
            picShip.Image = imlSpaceships.Images.Item(2)
            picShip.Top += 4
        Case Keys.Right
            picShip.Image = imlSpaceships.Images.Item(1)
            picShip.Left += 4
        Case Keys.Left
            picShip.Image = imlSpaceships.Images.Item(3)
            picShip.Left -= 4
    End Select
End Sub
```

Try it out

Spaceship – points to note

- When an image list is added to a form it automatically places itself in the **component tray**.

- An image list is used to store images needed at different times in an application.

- All images in an image list should be the same size. This size must be specified (in pixels) in the **ImageSize** property before images are added to the Images collection. The maximum size for an image is 256, 256.

- Each item in a **collection** is referred to as a **member**. Each member in a collection has an **Index**, starting with 0. All collections in Visual Basic are **zero based**.

- The form's **KeyDown** event occurs when a key is pressed down. When making use of this event the form's **KeyPreview** property should be set to *True*.

- All **event procedures** (or **event handlers**) have two arguments: **sender** and **e**. The sender is the object that has experienced the event; e contains a number of event arguments. For the KeyDown event an important argument is which key was pressed down.

- A **Select Case** structure in Visual Basic is otherwise known as **multiple branching**. It is used when you have a number of alternative actions. In this case four different actions corresponding to the four **cursor keys**.

```
Case Keys.Up
    picShip.Image = imlSpaceships.Images.Item(0)
    picShip.Top -= 4
```

For the Up key the first image in the image list is put into the picture box, then the picture box is moved up by reducing the Top property by 4 pixels.

Spaceship – check what you have learnt

1 What are image list controls used for?

2 What is the unit of measure for Location and Size?

3 a What is the maximum size for an image stored in an image list?

   b What is the default value for ImageSize?

4 What is meant by a collection being zero-based?

5 What property setting should be made of a form if you intend using the KeyDown event?

6 What are the two arguments of an event procedure?

7 What property of e was used to identify which cursor key was pressed?

8 a What is meant by two-way branching?

   b What is meant by multiple branching?

9 Why don't we retain the default control names like PictureBox1?

10 Add an **If Then** statement to each of the **Case** statements, similar to that found in Viper cycle, to enable the spaceship to cycle around the form (both horizontally and vertically).

Program example: Fairy flying

Create a new Windows application with the name *Fairy flying*.

Create the interface

- Add a picture box, a timer and an image list to the form as shown on the following page.

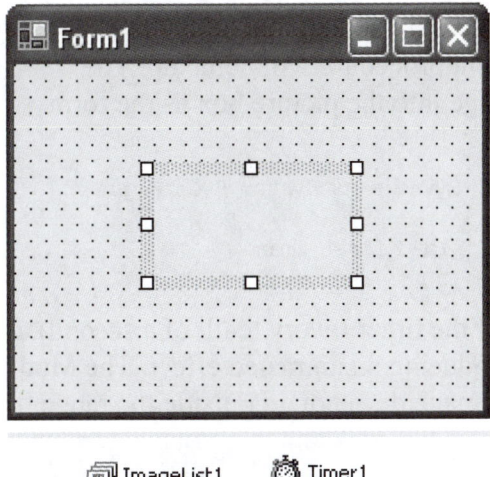

- Set the following properties:

Form1

BackColor	192, 255, 255
MaximizeBox	False
Text	Fairy flying

PictureBox1

Name	picFairy
Size	96, 96

ImageList1

Name	imlFairies
ImageSize	96, 96
TransparentColor	Gray

Timer1

Name	tmrMoveWings
Enabled	True
Interval	100

- The image list now must have the following nine bitmaps loaded into its Images collection starting with *fairy flying east 0.bmp* and ending with *fairy flying east 8.bmp*.

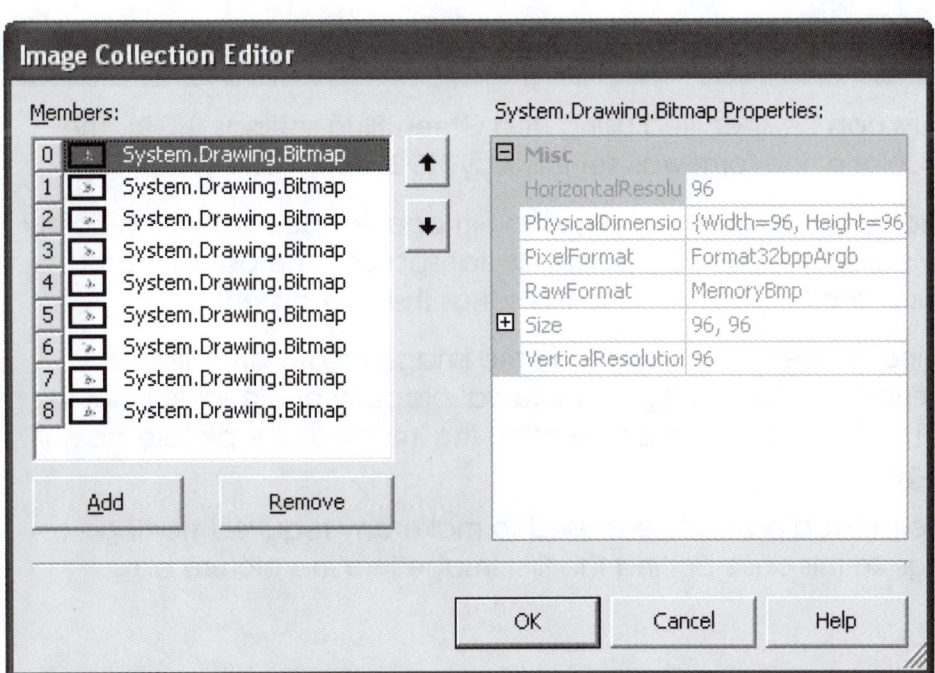

Write the code and add comments

- Double-Click the form and its default event procedure will come up. The following code will put the first fairy image into the picture box as the form loads.

```
Private Sub Form1_Load(ByVal sender As Object, ByVal e As System.EventArgs) _
Handles MyBase.Load
    picFairy.Image = imlFairies.Images.Item(0) ' load first image
End Sub
```

- Double-Click the timer. With each tick of the timer (every tenth of a second) a new bitmap is put into the picture box producing an animated effect. The Mod operator ensures that the variable WhichImage does not go outside the range 0 to 8.

```
Private Sub tmrMoveWings_Tick(ByVal sender As System.Object, ByVal e As _
System.EventArgs) Handles tmrMoveWings.Tick
    Static WhichImage As Integer = 0
    WhichImage += 1 ' next image index
    WhichImage = WhichImage Mod 9 ' must be 0 to 8
    picFairy.Image = imlFairies.Images.Item(WhichImage) ' load next image
End Sub
```

Try it out

Fairy flying – points to note

- Colours can be specified using Red Green Blue settings (RGB). The BackColor of the form was set this way (192, 255, 255).

- The TransparentColor property of an image list specifies which colour in the stored images will appear as transparent. The background colour of the fairies is gray, so it is set as the transparent colour.

- The nine images (0 to 8) stored in the image list are an animated sequence of a fairy flying. The Interval property of the timer is set to 100 (1/10th second). This is how often the image in the picture box changes.

- The Form Load procedure is used to make any required starting settings. In this case putting the first image into the picture box.

- An **Integer variable** is declared in the timer's procedure:

  ```
  Static WhichImage As Integer = 0
  ```

  It is declared and immediately given a value of 0. The **Static** statement means that the value of WhichImage will be 'remembered' the next time the procedure runs.

- With every tick of the timer two things happen to the variable WhichImage:

  Its value is increased by 1

  ```
  WhichImage += 1
  ```

  Its value will be kept in the 0 to 8 range using the **Mod** operator.

  ```
  WhichImage = WhichImage Mod 9
  ```

Fairy flying – check what you have learnt

1   Which two properties of an image list should be set before images are loaded in?

2   If an image list has eight images in its Images collection what is the first and last Index?

3   Using an upper case character in the middle of a word like picFairy or tmrMoveWings is known as **camel casing**. Given that spaces are not allowed in object names why do you think camel casing is used?

4   **Mod** is sometimes known as **remainder division** because it gives the remainder after a division is performed. Calculate the following remainders:

   a   19 Mod 5   b   20 Mod 7   c   32 Mod 4

5   What are the only possible results with Mod 9?

6   What type of numbers are Integers?

7   What is the default event of a timer?

8   What does it mean if an object's Left property is a negative number?

9   Where is an object if its location property is 0, 0?

10   Add the facility to Fairy flying to be able to move her about the form with the cursor keys.

Program example: Explode

Create a new Windows application with the name *Explode.*

Create the interface

■   Add a picture box, a button, a timer and an image list to the form.

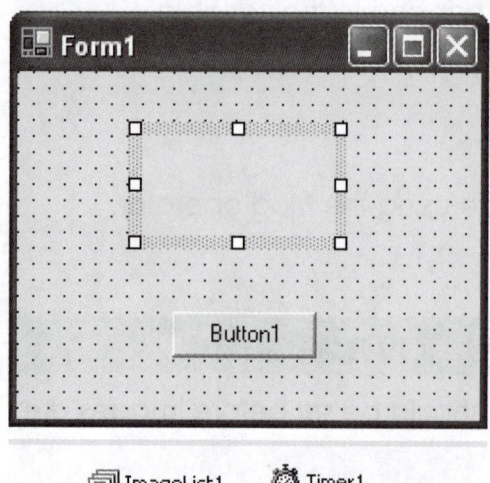

■   Set the following properties:

Form1

BackColor	64, 64, 64
Icon	(you choose)
Text	Explode

PictureBox1

Name	picExplode
Image	Explosion 0.gif
SizeMode	Autosize
Visible	False

ImageList1

Name	imlFrames
ImageSize	60, 50

Timer1

Name	tmrSequence
Enabled	False

Button1

Name	btnDoIt
Text	Do It

■   The image list now must have the following eleven bitmaps loaded into its Images collection: *Explosion 0.gif* to *Explosion 10.gif.* Before bitmaps are added to the Images collection both the **ImageSize** and **TransparentColor** properties should be set. These bitmaps are **GIF** files that already have a transparent background.

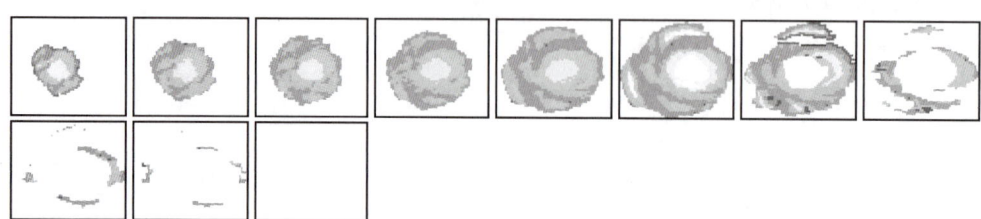

Write the code and add comments

■ With each tick of the timer (every tenth of a second) the following procedure is run. The timer keeps ticking until it gets to the last image in the sequence. Then it stops itself.

```
Private Sub tmrSequence_Tick(ByVal sender As System.Object, ByVal e As _
System.EventArgs) Handles tmrSequence.Tick
    Static Frame As Integer = 0
    picExplode.Image = imlFrames.Images.Item(Frame) ' show the image
    Frame += 1 ' advance to next frame
    If Frame > 10 Then ' all frames used
        tmrSequence.Stop() ' stop the explosion
        picExplode.Visible = False ' hide picture box
        Frame = 0 ' ready for next time
    End If
End Sub
```

■ When the button is clicked it starts the timer that makes the explosion animation.

```
Private Sub btnDoIt_Click(ByVal sender As System.Object, ByVal e As _
System.EventArgs) Handles btnDoIt.Click
    picExplode.Visible = True ' show picture box
    tmrSequence.Start() ' start the explosion
End Sub
```

Try it out

Explode – points to note

■ The **Visible** property of the picture box is set to *False*. So when the application starts it cannot be seen.

■ The default event for a **button** is the **Click** event. Every control has a default event. The code template for this event appears in the code window when the control is double-clicked in design mode.

■ The **event handler** (or event procedure) for the Click event of the button performs two simple tasks: make the picture box visible, start the timer.

```
picExplode.Visible = True ' show picture box
tmrSequence.Start() ' start the explosion
```

- This timer does not keep ticking. When the animation sequence is complete it stops itself.

```
If Frame > 10 Then ' all frames used
    tmrSequence.Stop() ' stop the explosion
```

Stop is a **method** of the timer control. Similarly **Start** is a method of the timer control. Methods are actions that act upon an object.

- An **Integer variable** is declared in the timer's procedure:

```
Static Frame As Integer = 0
```

It is declared and immediately given a value of 0. The **Static** keyword means that the value of Frame will be 'remembered' the next time the procedure runs.

Explode – check what you have learnt

1 a How do you make a control 'disappear' from a form?

   b How do you make the control reappear?

2 Every control has a default event. For example, the default event of a button is Click. What do you think is particularly special about the default event?

3 What are two important methods of a timer control?

4 What are the names of some properties that you've noticed belong to more than one control?

5 What is the other name for an 'event handler'?

6 What is the two-way branching statement used in this programming example?

7 Two-way branching always begins with a condition that is either *True* or *False*. What is the condition used in this example?

8 In the following line of code:

```
Frame = 0 ' ready for next time
```

What is meant by the comment 'ready for next time'?

9 a What is the default Interval of a timer?

   b What length of time is this?

10 What sort of effects do you think would add to the realism of the explosion?

Chapter 3

Heading in the right direction

Position and direction on a form

The X and Y locations

All locations on a form have the syntax X, Y. The two Integers measure the horizontal and vertical distances (in pixels) from the top left corner. So this corner has the Location 0, 0. Any movement to the right increases the X coordinate while any movement downwards increases the Y coordinate.

The figure below summarises movement in any direction. Four quadrants have been labelled. In quadrant 1 both X and Y movement is positive; in quadrant 2 the X movement is negative while the Y movement is positive etc. While the orientation is not the same, these quadrants correspond to the four quadrants taught in most Junior Mathematics courses.

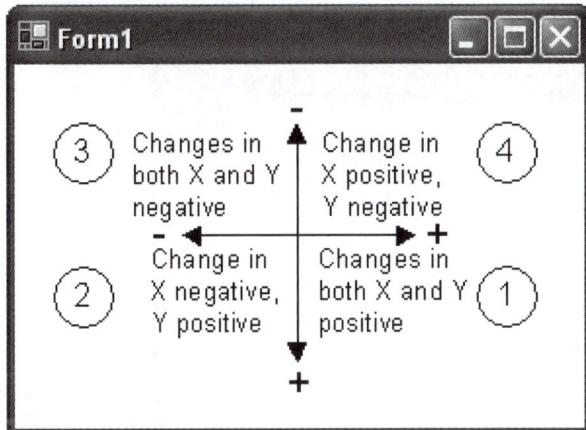

Changes in the Left and Top properties bring about corresponding changes in the read-only properties Location.X and Location.Y.

Using angles to specify direction

While movement in a direction can be stated in terms of changes in X and Y, it can also be simply expressed as an angle in degrees. The connection between the two methods can be made with simple Trigonometry as shown below.

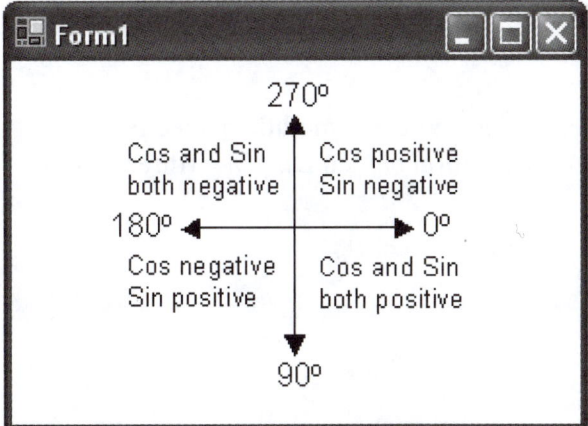

We will soon learn that changes in X can be calculated with Cosines and changes in Y can be calculated with Sines.

When objects need to be pointing in different directions it is most convenient to Index the Collection of Images starting with 0, pointing to the right, and increasing as you move clockwise. The Index 0 corresponds to the angle of 0°.

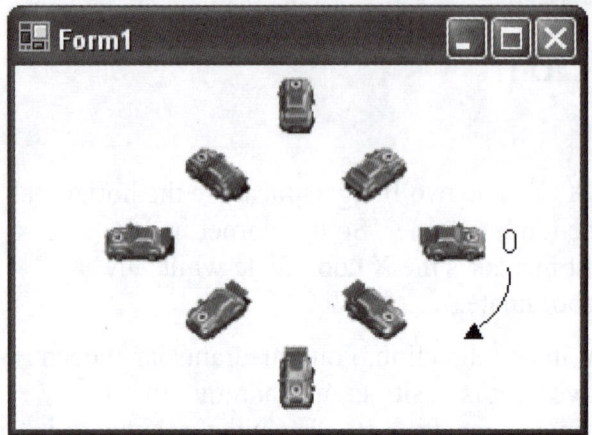

The eight images of the car, with indexes 0 to 7, are shown below in the collection editor of an image list control.

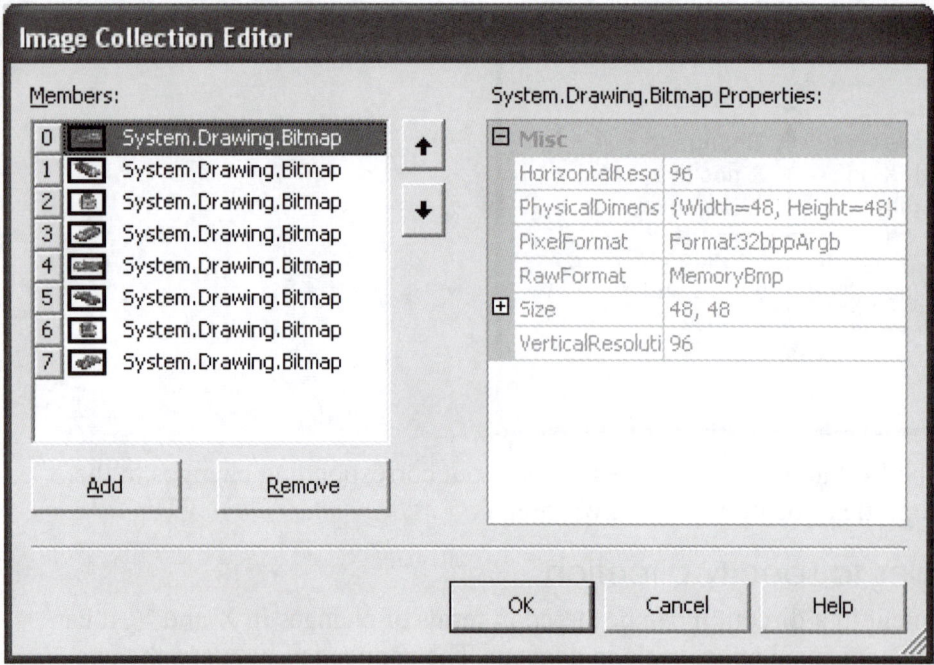

These eight images only allow direction changes in multiples of 45°. With more images smaller angle changes are possible.

Some very useful functions

On the accompanying CD, in the modules folder, there is a module named *Bearing.vb* (See Appendix 1). It has four **overloads** of a function named *DirnDeg* (direction in degrees).

```
Public Overloads Function DirnDeg(ByVal FromObj As Object, _
ByVal ToObj As Object) As Double
Public Overloads Function DirnDeg(ByVal FromPoint As Point, _
ByVal ToPoint As Point) As Double
Public Overloads Function DirnDeg(ByVal FromPoint As Point, _
ByVal ToObj As Object) As Double
Public Overloads Function DirnDeg(ByVal FromObj As Object, _
ByVal ToPoint As Point) As Double
```

Each function provides a very simple way of determining what direction it is (in degrees) from one object to another or from a point to an object etc. There are another four functions in the same module that calculate a direction in radians. The **radian** is another unit of angular measurement. It has the relation π radians $= 180^{\circ}$.

The following small program examples illustrate how these functions can be very useful in a gaming environment.

Program example: Tank aiming

Create a new Windows application with the name *Tank aiming*.

Create the interface

■ Add a picture box and an image list to the form.

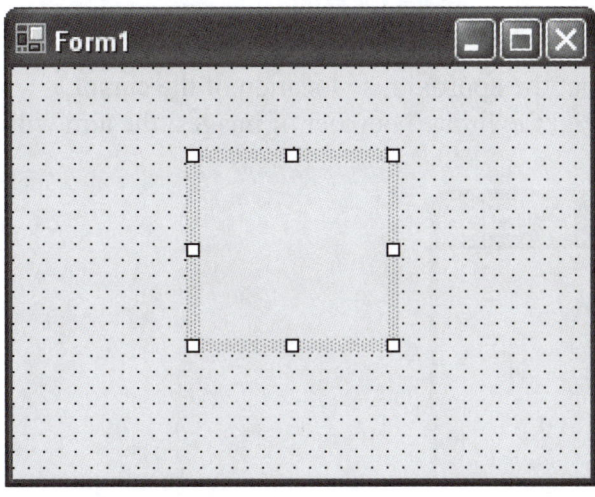

ImageList1

■ Set the following properties:

Form1

BackColor	255,255,192
Cursor	Cross
Text	Tank Aiming

ImageList1

Name	imlUpper
ImageSize	160,160
TransparentColor	Transparent

PictureBox1

Name	picTank
BackColor	Transparent
BackgroundImage	groundpart 8.gif
Image	upperpart 8.gif
SizeMode	Autosize

■ Add the 32 images (0 to 31) to the Images collection of *imlUpper*. Add them in the order *upperpart 0.gif, upperpart 1.gif ... upperpart 31.gif*. These images have rotational differences that divide 360° into 32 equal parts. Thank you to Reiner Prokein for all the tank images.

Write the code and add comments

- From the Project menu choose Add Existing Item…. Browse to the *Modules* folder on the accompanying CD and select the module *Bearing.vb* (see Appendix 1). This is the module that has the direction calculating functions.

- Choose the MouseMove event of Form1 then enter the following code:

```
Private Sub Form1_MouseMove(ByVal sender As Object, ByVal e As _
System.Windows.Forms.MouseEventArgs) Handles MyBase.MouseMove
    ' find the direction (in degrees) - tank centre to cross
    Dim Direction As Integer = DirnDeg(picTank, New Point(e.X, e.Y))
    ' calculate which image to use (0 to 31)
    Dim WhichImage As Integer = CInt(Direction / 360 * 32) Mod 32
    picTank.Image = imlUpper.Images.Item(WhichImage)
End Sub
```

Try it out

The upper part of the tank should seek out the approximate location of the cursor. Because of rounding in the calculation and the limited number of images, the aim will not always be perfect.

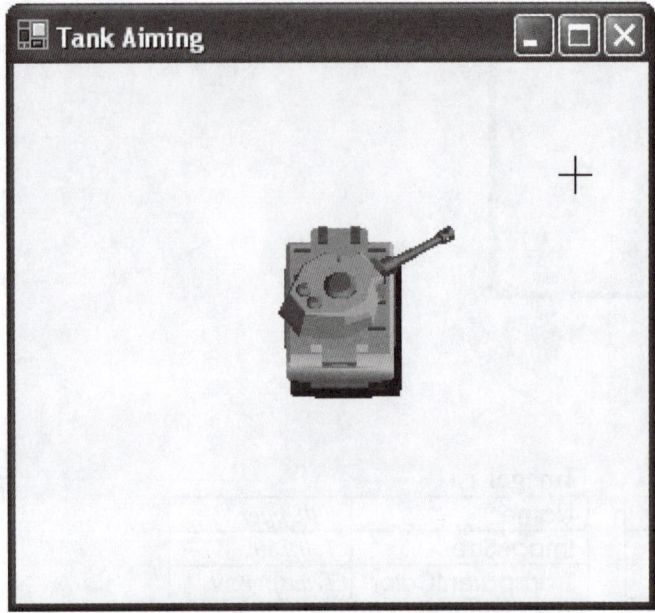

Tank aiming – points to note

- Colours can be defined by their **Red-Green-Blue** (RGB) composition. For example the **BackColor** of the form was entered as 255, 255, 192. These numbers must each be in the range 0-255.

- Before adding images to the Images collection of an image list the **ImageSize** and **TransparentColor** properties must be set.

- Direction and WhichImage are the only variables used in this example. Both are **Integers** and are declared locally. **Integers** are whole numbers that can be positive or negative or zero. **Local variables** are variables that are only used in the procedure in which they are declared. If the same variable is needed in more than one procedure it has to be declared at **form level**.

- Two of the properties of the mouse event argument are **e.X** and **e.Y**. They hold the location of the cursor on the form, measured in **pixels**. `New Point(e.X, e.Y)` is a point created from the location of the cursor.

- DirnDeg is a function that has been **user-defined**. When a function is required that is not already a part of the Visual Basic language the user can define a custom made function to meet particular requirements. User defined functions that may be needed in other projects are most conveniently packaged in a **code module** (in this case Bearing.vb).

- The version of the function DirnDeg, used in this example, accepts two **arguments** — FromObj, the object from which to start, and ToPoint, the point to where it is directed. DirnDeg then makes a calculation of the direction in degrees. The accuracy is that of a **Double** but this value has to be rounded to a whole number from 0 to 359.

- **CInt** converts a number to an Integer and rounds to the nearest whole number.

- Once the angle has been calculated (0° to 359°) one of the 32 upper part images is chosen (0 to 31). The 32 images are divided in proportion to the size of the angle. For example, if the angle calculated was 50° then the image to use is calculated as:

```
CInt(50 / 360 * 32) Mod 32
= CInt(4.44) Mod 32
= 4 Mod 32
= 4
```

So Image 4 would be used. **Mod** 32 is applied in case CInt calculates a value of 32. In which case it would evaluate to 0.

- In this example the **BackgroundImage** of the picture box remains constant while the **Image** property varies with the position of the cursor.

- The Images collection of an image list is **zero-based**, meaning the first index is zero.

Tank aiming – Check what you have learnt

1 In what way can numbers be used to specify colour? Eg BackColor of a form.

2 Show the working that calculates which image (0 to 31) that would be loaded when Direction = 128.

3 A picture box can simultaneously hold two images. What are the two properties for these images?

4 Which two properties of an image list must be set before adding images to the Images collection?

5 The Cross cursor was chosen for this example. What are some other cursors that can be used?

6 In the MouseMove event of a form, what two properties of the MouseEventArgs specify the position of the cursor?

7   What is the difference between variables declared at form level and variables declared locally in a procedure?

8   Why do we package useful functions and procedures in a code module?

9   Mod is sometimes called 'remainder division' because it divides then returns the remainder as the result. For example 17 Mod 3 = 2. With Mod 3 the only possible results are 0, 1 and 2.

      What are the only possible results when Mod 32 is applied?

10 To periodically fire a bullet from the tank would require three additional controls: a picture box and two timers. One timer is needed to set the frequency of the firing (eg once every 2 seconds), the other to make the bullet move. To correctly position the bullet for firing some Mathematics with Cos and Sin will be needed. You will need to include an Imports statement at the top of the code window:

```
Imports System.Math
```

You will need to use Sin and Cos to calculate where the bullet will start moving from. Then its movement will also be controlled by Sin and Cos.

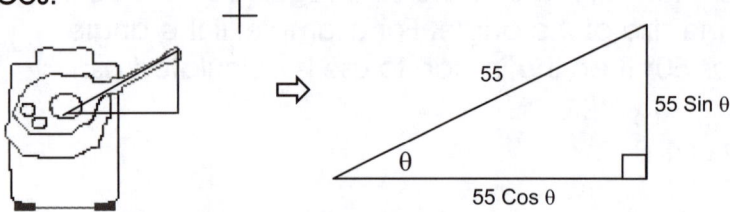

Apply this to the 'Tank aiming' example.

Program example: Follow me

Create a new Windows application with the name *Follow me*.

Create the interface

-     Add a picture box, an image list and a timer to the form.

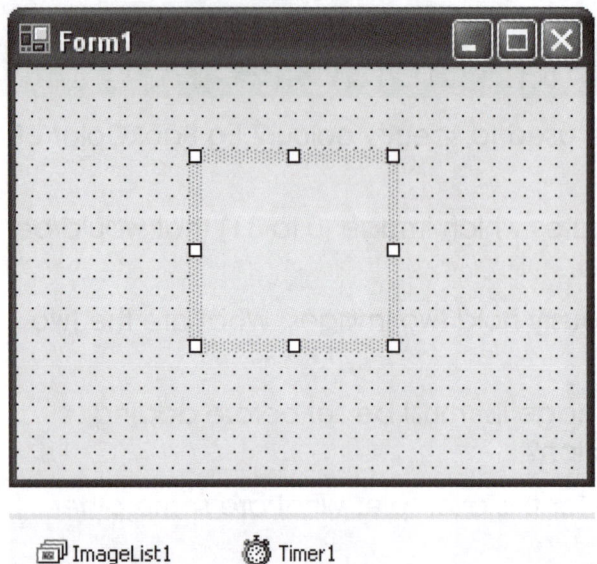

- Set the following properties:

Form1

BackColor	255,225,192
Cursor	Cross
Text	Follow Me

ImageList1

Name	imlRallyCar
ImageSize	48, 48
TransparentColor	97, 68, 43

PictureBox1

Name	picCar
SizeMode	AutoSize

Timer1

Name	tmrMove
Enabled	True

- Add the 32 images (0 to 31) of the small blue rally car to the Images collection of the image list. Add them in the order *small blue rally car 0.bmp,* *small blue rally car 1.bmp, … small blue rally car 31.bmp*. Thank you to Reiner Prokein for the rally car images.

Write the code and add comments

- From the Project menu choose Add Existing Item…. Browse to the *Modules* folder on the accompanying CD and select the module *Bearing.vb* (see Appendix 1). This is the module that has the direction calculating functions.

- Include the following **Imports** statement at the top of the code window. System. Math is required because of the use of functions Sin and Cos, and the constant PI.

```
Imports System.Math
```

- Declare the following form level variable. Variables are declared at form level when they are used in more than one procedure.

```
Dim Direction As Double = 0
```

- When the form is loaded the starting image of the car is put in the picture box.

```
Private Sub Form1_Load(ByVal sender As Object, ByVal e As System.EventArgs) _
Handles MyBase.Load
    ' start with the car in the zero direction
    picCar.Image = imlRallyCar.Images.Item(0)
End Sub
```

- As the mouse moves this procedure calculates the direction from the car to the cursor in degrees. Having the direction in degrees is convenient to calculate the image.

```
Private Sub Form1_MouseMove(ByVal sender As Object, _
ByVal e As System.Windows.Forms.MouseEventArgs) Handles MyBase.MouseMove
    ' calculate the direction from the car to the cursor
    Direction = DirnDeg(picCar, New Point(e.X, e.Y))
End Sub
```

- The timer procedure calculates the correct image for the direction in which the car is moving then moves the car in this direction. Direction has been calculated in degrees. It has to be converted into radians to use Sin and Cos.

```
Private Sub tmrMove_Tick(ByVal sender As System.Object, _
ByVal e As System.EventArgs) Handles tmrMove.Tick
    ' calculate and load the correct image
    Dim WhichImage As Integer = CInt(Direction / 360 * 32) Mod 32
    picCar.Image = imlRallyCar.Images.Item(WhichImage)
    ' use Cos and Sin to calculate the change in location
    picCar.Left += 4 * Cos(Direction / 180 * PI)  ' angle in radians
    picCar.Top += 4 * Sin(Direction / 180 * PI)   ' angle in radians
End Sub
```

Try it out

The car will seek out the location of the cursor and move towards it.

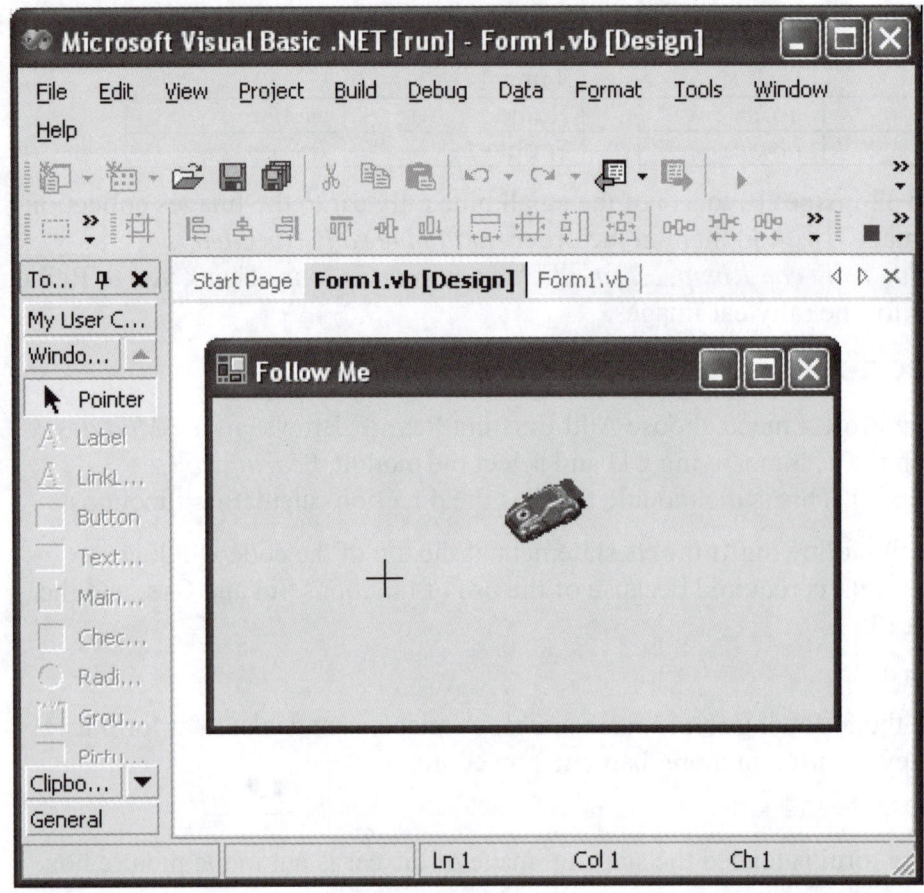

Follow me – points to note

- The **System.Math** namespace contains functions useful for certain Mathematical calculations. In this example it was imported so that **Sin** and **Cos** were available.

  A form level variable was declared. It is numeric. It was declared **Double** (numbers with a decimal point). Numbers with a decimal point can be declared Single or Double. Double has more precision than Single.

  ```
  Dim Direction As Double = 0
  ```

- Direction is a variable that is declared at **form level** because it is used in more than one procedure.

- DirnDeg has several **overloads** (or versions). The overload used in this example calculates the direction from the centre of an object to a point.

- The value of WhichImage is calculated as it was in the 'Tank aiming' example. Note that this variable is **declared** and **instantiated** (given a value) in the one line of code.

```
Dim WhichImage As Integer = CInt(Direction / 360 * 32) Mod 32
```

  The 32 images are divided in proportion to the size of the angle.

- The function **CInt** converts the expression in the brackets to an Integer. It rounds the calculated value to the nearest Integer.

```
Dim WhichImage As Integer = CInt(Direction / 360 * 32) Mod 32
```

- **Sin** is associated with the Y or vertical direction, **Cos** is associated with the X or horizontal direction.

- **PI** is a constant that is included in the System.Math namespace.

- To convert degrees into **radians** you have to divide by 180 and multiply by PI:

```
Direction / 180 * PI
```

Follow me – Check what you have learnt

1 What functions and which constant was used from the System.Math namespace?

2 What angles (in degrees) produce
   a only horizontal movement
   b only vertical movement

3 What is the difference (in degrees) between each of the rotational positions of the rally car images?

4 The DirnDeg function in this example calculates the direction from the car to the cursor. What is the difference (in degrees) if the calculation was made from the cursor to the car?

5 What is the only unit of angular measurement accepted by the Sin and Cos functions?

6 Use your calculator to find how many radians is equivalent to 240°.

7 What range of angles has both horizontal and vertical movements negative?

8 What does the CInt function do to a number?

9 What are the overloads of a function?

10 To make the 'Follow me' example more of a challenge the car could gradually increase speed. What two alternative strategies can be applied to increase speed? Apply either of these to this example.

Chapter 4

Meet and greet

The first thing you see

When an application starts up there may be several reasons for displaying a **Splash form** for a few seconds:

- To simply give a flashy introduction to your application.
- To allow time for necessary data to be loaded.
- To give information about you and your product.
- To display copyright or user registration information.

What we will refer to as an **Entry form** is one that collects some necessary information from the user before continuing. The information may or may not be security related. In a particular application it may be appropriate to have one or both of Splash and Entry forms.

Program example: Splash

This would normally be done as an addition to an existing application rather. However this example will be put together as a simple demonstration that will stand on its own.

Create a new Windows application with the name *Splash*.

Create the interface

The first form, Form1, will be the form from which most of the application will run. In this case it is merely present to test the functioning of the splash form. A label with the text shown below has been added just to clearly identify the form.

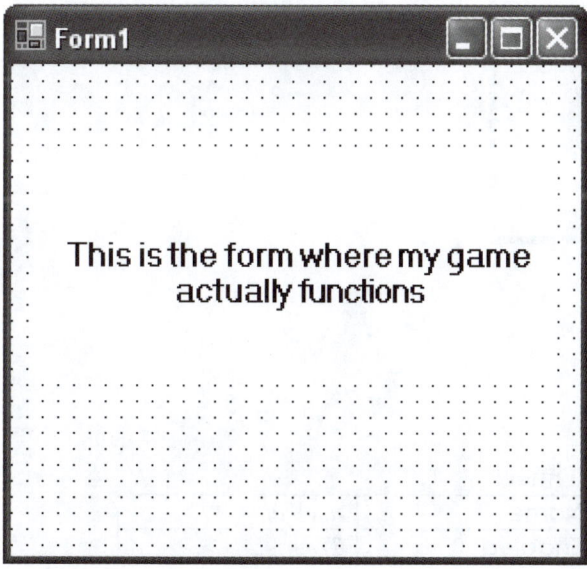

- From the Project menu select Add Windows Form. This will add a second form to the project. It will be the splash form.

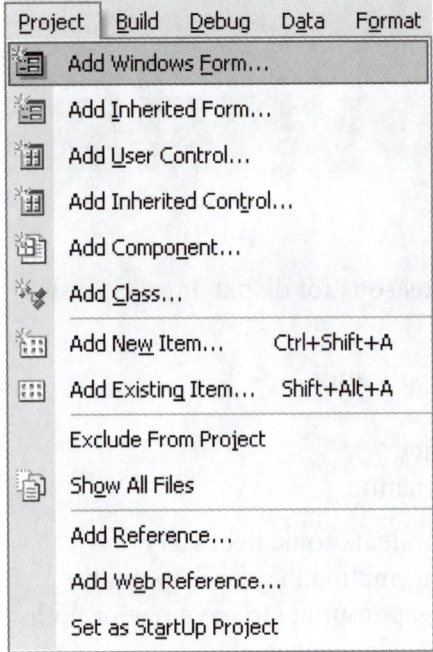

By default this form will have the name *Form2*.

■ The controls you add to this form will depend on your own design choices. Typically there will be labels and picture boxes. However as a part of its functionality you must add a timer.

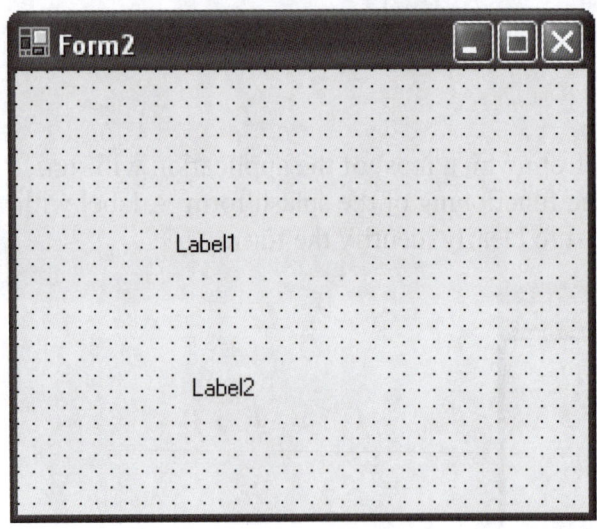

 Timer1

■ Set the following properties:

Form2

FormBorderStyle	*None*
StartPosition	*CenterScreen*

Timer1

Name	*tmrWait*
Enabled	*True*
Interval	*3000*

■ The properties of the various labels and picture boxes will be your choice.

Write the code and add comments

■ Enter this code for the Tick event of your timer:

```
Private Sub tmrWait_Tick(ByVal sender As System.Object, ByVal e As _
System.EventArgs) Handles tmrWait.Tick
   Me.Close() ' this form is no longer required
End Sub
```

An additional item

■ Add a code **module**. This is also done through the Project menu:

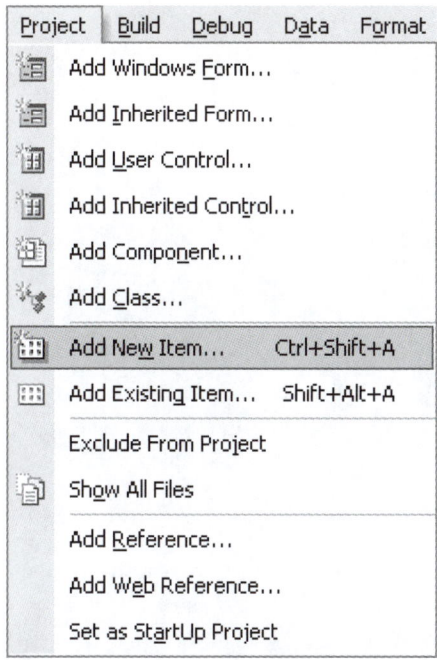

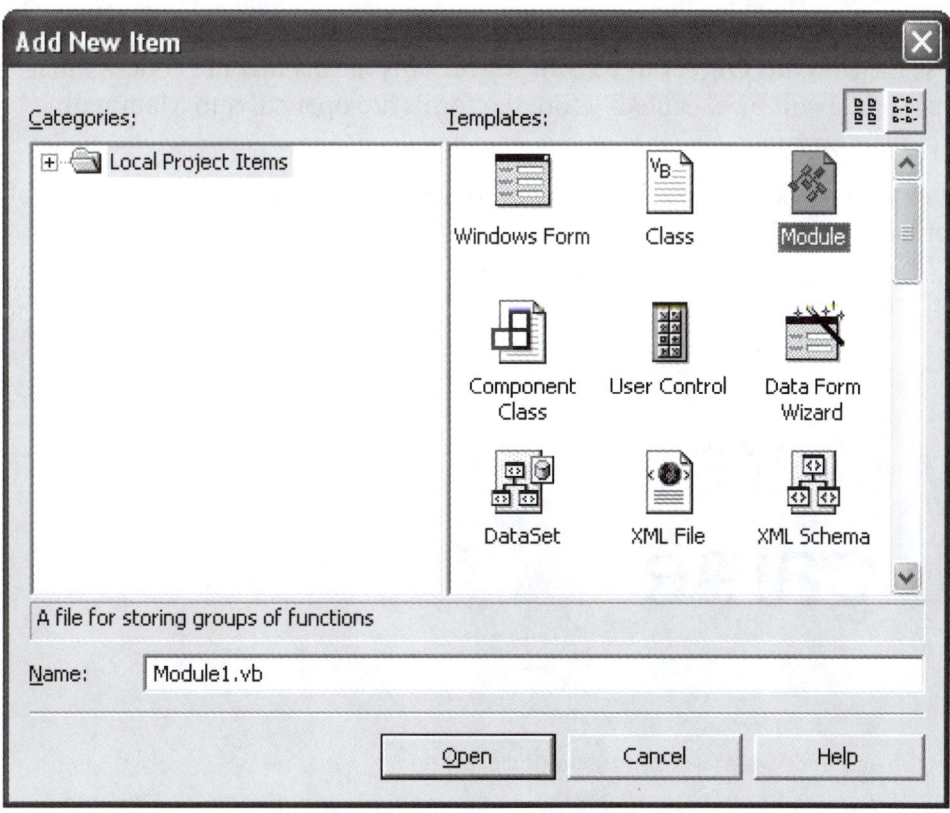

- Open this code module (Module1.vb) by double-clicking it in the Solution Explorer. Enter the code as shown below:

```
Module Module1

    Public Sub Main()
        Dim Form1 As New Form1()
        Dim Form2 As New Form2()
        Form2.ShowDialog() ' splash form
        Form1.ShowDialog() ' main form
    End Sub

End Module
```

- Right-Click on your Solution, select Properties.

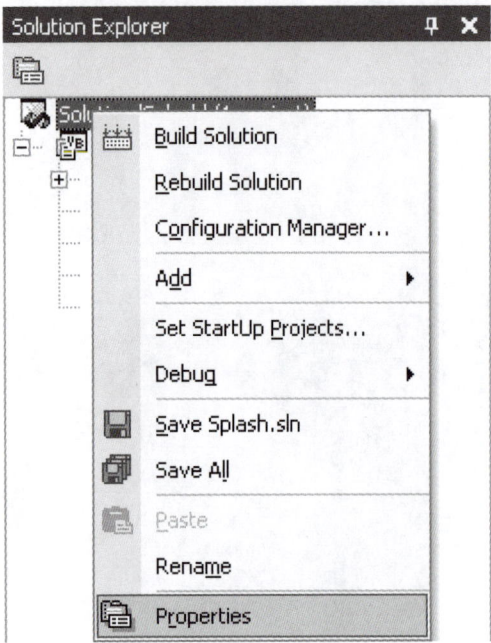

- Choose the **Startup Object** to be **Sub Main**. This means that the code written on the module will be executed before the forms are opened. Sub Main will control their opening.

All the rest of your work will now be done on Form1, which is where the main part of your project will be.

Try it out

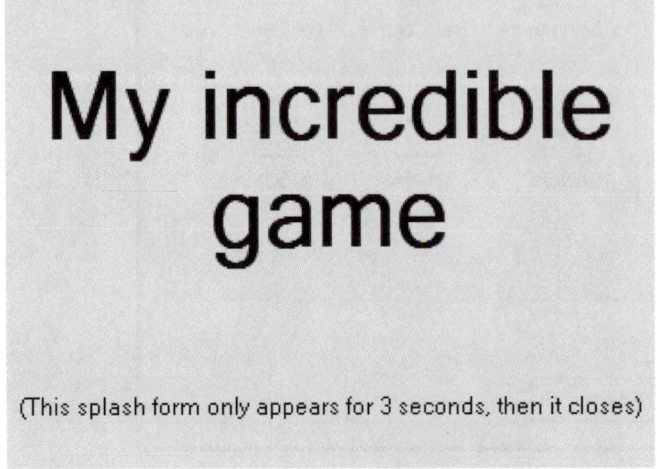

(This splash form only appears for 3 seconds, then it closes)

Program example: Entry

Like *Splash* this programming example is merely an outline of the types of structures required for your own applications. In this example the user's name is passed from the entry form to the main form.

Create a new Windows application with the name *Entry*.

Create the interface

For this example Form1 will be the entry form. The user will be able to enter his/her name in the text box then move on to the next form where the name will be transferred.

■   Set up your Entry form with controls to collect the information you need. In the form shown below two labels, a text box and a button have been added.

■   The text box is named *txtName* and the button *btnOpen*.

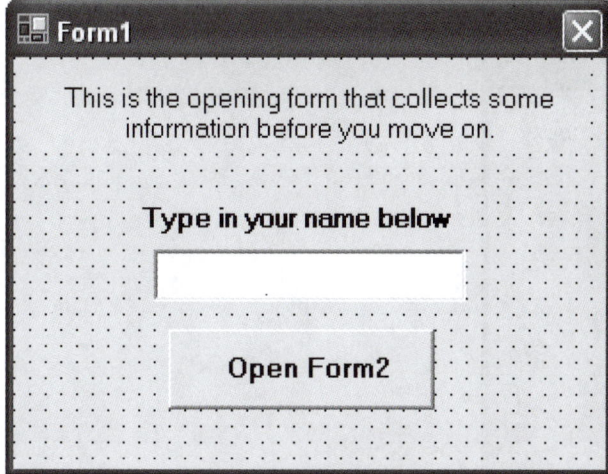

■   From the Project menu Add a Windows Form. This will be the main working form.

■   Add two labels to Form2. The blank label is to have the name *lblName*.

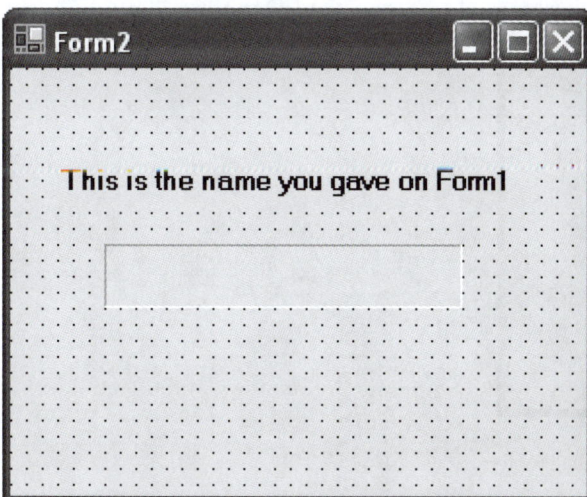

Write the code and add comments

■　　Double-click on the button *btnOpen* on Form1. Add the following code:

```
Private Sub btnOpen_Click(ByVal sender As System.Object, ByVal e As _
System.EventArgs) Handles btnOpen.Click
    Dim Form2 As New Form2()
    Form2.lblName.Text = txtName.Text ' give the label the name from Form1
    Form2.Show() ' open Form2
    Me.Hide   ' hide Form1
End Sub
```

■　　Open the code window on Form2. Add the following code:

```
Private Sub Form2_Closed(ByVal sender As Object, ByVal e As System.EventArgs) _
Handles MyBase.Closed
    End ' closing Form2 is the end of the application
End Sub
```

Try it out

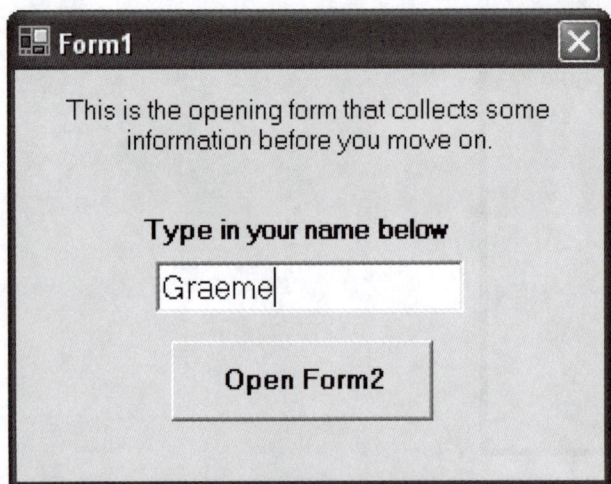

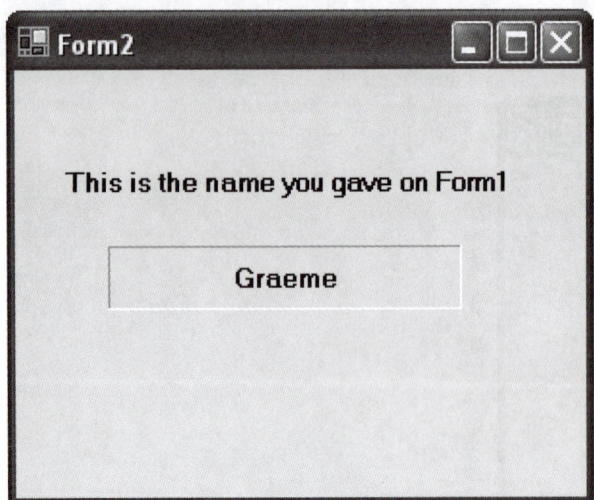

Meet and greet – points to note

- A **splash form** can be added to any application not only to provide some pizzazz but also to display relevant information.

- **Entry forms** have the strictly practical purpose of gathering information from the user.

- By default the **startup object** of a project is Form1. The startup object can be set to **Sub Main**, a procedure in a code module. In Splash, Sub Main controls the sequence of the forms.

```
Public Sub Main()
    Dim Form1 As New Form1()
    Dim Form2 As New Form2()
    Form2.ShowDialog() ' splash form
    Form1.ShowDialog() ' main form
End Sub
```

- A difficult concept to grasp is Form1 the **variable** and Form1 the **class**. If we were to make the comparison

```
Dim MyPic As New PictureBox
```

MyPic is the variable and PictureBox is the class.

- The **ShowDialog** method (rather than **Show**) used in *Splash* ensures that the form must be closed (or disposed) before one can move focus to another. A form with this characteristic is called a **modal** form.

- The way focus is moved from Form1 to Form2 in the *Entry* example could be applied to any application requiring multiple forms.

```
Dim Form2 As New Form2()
Form2.lblName.Text = txtName.Text ' give the label the name from Form1
Form2.Show() ' open Form2
Me.Hide   ' hide Form1
```

There is no particular requirement that Form1 be hidden.

- Entry forms can be used to receive a password. Text boxes have a property to disguise password entries, **PasswordChar**. This is usually set as *.

    Enter your user name

    | graemebs |

    Enter your password

    | ******** |

- In the *Entry* example Form1 is the startup object. Closing Form2 is not going to end the application. Hence the specific command must be given when Form2 closes:

```
Private Sub Form2_Closed(ByVal sender As Object, ByVal e _
As System.EventArgs) Handles MyBase.Closed
    End ' closing Form2 is the end of the application
End Sub
```

Meet and greet – check what you have learnt

1   What are some reasons for having a splash form?

2   What are some of the features a splash form should possess?

3   What is the specific purpose of an entry form?

4   How could an entry form act as a security device?

5   In the following declaration

    ```
    Dim PassWrd As TextBox
    ```

    Which is the variable and which is the class?

6   If a project has two forms, Form1 and Form2, what are the three options for a startup object?

7   When acting on forms, what is the difference between the Show method and the ShowDialog method?

8   In the Splash example what determined the length of time the splash form was displayed?

9   In a timer procedure is the code executed before or after the time period of the tick?

10 Adding splash or entry forms (or both) will be optional exercises for all your programming tasks.

Chapter 5

Controlling the bugs

What, no picture boxes?

In all the previous programming examples the moving objects have almost all been picture boxes. Changing the Image and Location properties has produced a variety of satisfactory animation effects. However difficulties can arise when it is necessary to have some overlapping or layering. An alternative is to draw an image directly onto the form. This can be achieved by applying the *DrawImage* method to a graphics object.

The DrawImage method

DrawImage is a part of the **GDI+** (Graphics Device Interface) of Visual Basic .NET. GDI+ is a class-based system that allows an application to produce graphics for both the video display and printer. It is an extensive system with a huge capacity to produce all sorts of graphics effects.

Successive calls of *DrawImage* will produce a trail of images as shown with the running wolf below.

For an animated effect an old image has to be erased before the new image is drawn. This is achieved by drawing a small part of the form background over the old image.

Program example: Wolf running

Create a new Windows application with the name *Wolf running*.

Create the interface

- Add a label and an image list. The image list will automatically be placed in the form's component tray. The running wolf will take its animation images from the image list.

⬛ ImageList1

■ Set the following properties:

Form1

BackColor	White
Form BorderStyle	FixedSingle
KeyPreview	True
Size	390, 120
Text	Wolf running

Label1

Text	Press the right arrow key to make the wolf run

ImageList1

Name	imlWolf
ImageSize	96, 96
TransparentColor	111, 79, 51

■ There are eight bitmaps of the running wolf, found on the accompanying CD. Load these, starting with *Wolf running east 0.bmp*, into the Images collection of the image list. The TransparentColor defined above, using its Red Green Blue composition, is the dark brown background colour in each of the bitmaps. Thank you to Reiner Prokein for these images.

Write the code and add comments

■ Declare some variables to be used across several procedures.

```
Dim objBackground As Graphics ' declare a graphics object
Dim X As Integer = 0, Y As Integer = 10 ' starting coordinates
```

■ A graphics object is created on the form after the form loads. The first image of the wolf is drawn on the graphics object.

```
Private Sub Form1_Paint(ByVal sender As Object, ByVal e As _
System.Windows.Forms.PaintEventArgs) Handles MyBase.Paint
    objBackground = Me.CreateGraphics ' create a graphics object on the form
    ' show first image of wolf
    objBackground.DrawImage(imlWolf.Images.Item(0), X, Y)
End Sub
```

■ When the right arrow key is pressed the previous image of the wolf is covered over by a rectangle that is the same colour as the form; then the next image is drawn.

```
Private Sub Form1_KeyDown(ByVal sender As Object, ByVal e As _
System.Windows.Forms.KeyEventArgs) Handles MyBase.KeyDown
    Static WhichImage As Integer = 0 ' starting image
    If e.KeyCode = Keys.Right Then
        ' cover up previous image before displaying the next one
        Dim RectCopy As New Rectangle(X, Y, 96, 96)
        objBackground.FillRectangle(New SolidBrush(Me.BackColor), RectCopy)
        X += 16 ' move wolf forward 16 pixels
        WhichImage = (WhichImage + 1) Mod 8 ' advance to next image (0-7)
        ' display new image
        objBackground.DrawImage(imlWolf.Images.Item(WhichImage), X, Y)
        If X >= Me.Width Then ' off the right side of the form
            X = -96 ' back to left side of the form
        End If
    End If
End Sub
```

Try it out

■ Press the right arrow key repeatedly or hold it down to auto repeat.

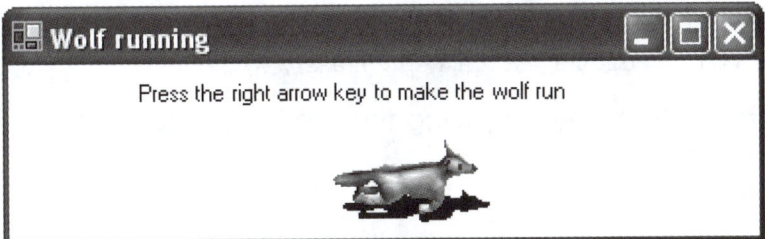

Wolf running – points to note

■ The RGB value required for the TransparentColor property of an image list can be determined using Windows Paint. For the wolf images the RGB values are 11, 79, 51.

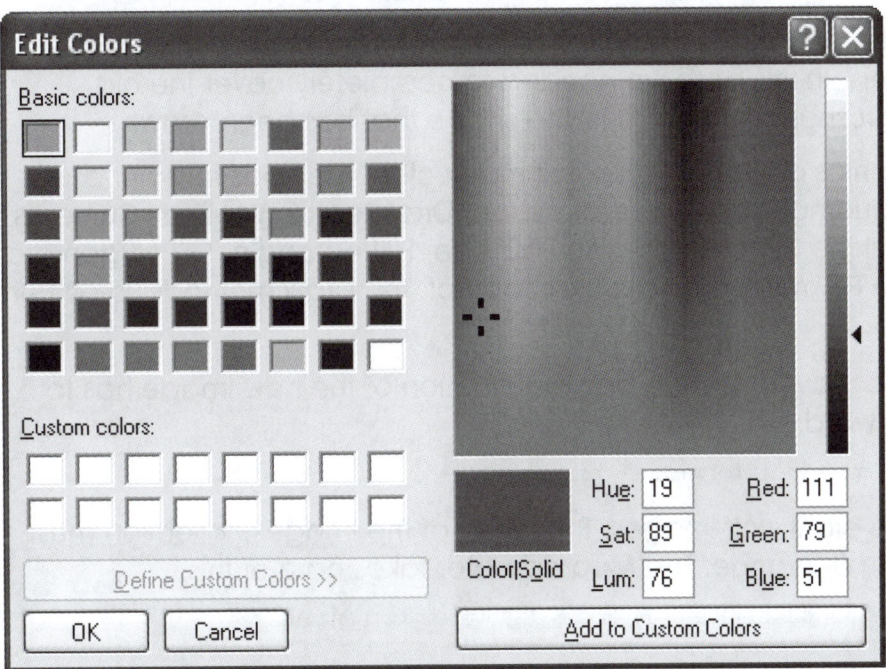

■ **GDI+** (Graphics Device Interface) is the part of .NET that allows a developer to produce a wide variety of graphical effects on both the video display and printer.

■ The **DrawImage** method acts upon a **Graphics** object. Typically graphics objects are created on forms, picture boxes and printers, however they can be created on other objects such as labels and buttons etc.

■ If a graphics object is to be created on a form it must be done after the form loads.

```
objBackground = Me.CreateGraphics ' create a graphics object on the form
```

Once a graphics object has been created it can then be drawn on.

- The DrawImage method has thirty **overloads**. This means there are thirty different sets of arguments that can be used. We have used just one of the overloads. It requires an image and the top left coordinates of where the image is to be drawn.

```
objBackground.DrawImage(imlWolf.Images.Item(WhichImage), X, Y)
```

- A **Rectangle** can be defined by supplying the top left coordinates and its width and height.

```
Dim RectCopy As New Rectangle(X, Y, 96, 96)
```

This is the area of the form where the last wolf was drawn.

- **FillRectangle** is a method that draws a rectangle on a graphics object. The overload used in this example requires a **SolidBrush** object of a particular colour and the rectangle specifying where it is to be drawn. In this case the colour is the BackColor of the form.

```
objBackground.FillRectangle(New SolidBrush(Me.BackColor), RectCopy)
```

- Brushes come in a few varieties: **SolidBrush**, **HatchBrush**, **TextureBrush** and others. In this case we needed to completely cover the old image. Brushes are used to fill the shape that has been drawn.

- The Graphics object in GDI+ has many other methods to paint and draw including **DrawEllipse**, **DrawLine**, **DrawRectangle**, **DrawCurve** as well as all the 'Fill' methods like **FillEllipse**, **FillRectangle**, **FillPolygon** etc. While the Fill methods use a Brush object, the Draw methods use a **Pen** object.

- Just like a moving picture box the location of the new image has to move forward:

```
X += 16 ' move wolf forward 16 pixels
```

- There are eight wolf images. The index of the images collection must stay in the 0-7 range. The **Mod** operator takes care of this.

```
WhichImage = (WhichImage + 1) Mod 8 ' advance to next image (0-7)
```

Wolf running – check what you have learnt

1   What would need to be true about the choice of colour to be used to act as the transparent colour?

2   a   Typically which objects would commonly use the CreateGraphics method?

    b   Write a line of code that will create a graphics object objCanvas on a picture box named picPaint.

3   Why do you suppose the CreateGraphics method cannot be used in a Form Load procedure, but can be used in a Form Paint procedure?

4   a   Which two graphics object methods are used in this programming example?

    b   What are some of the other graphics objects methods?

5   Why would one use GDI+ for animation instead of picture boxes?

6   What is the difference between the FillRectangle method and the DrawRectangle method?

7   What are the three arguments for the DrawImage method, as used in the Wolf running example?

8   The rectangle shown below has the name MyArea. Make a declaration of this variable assigning its location and size.

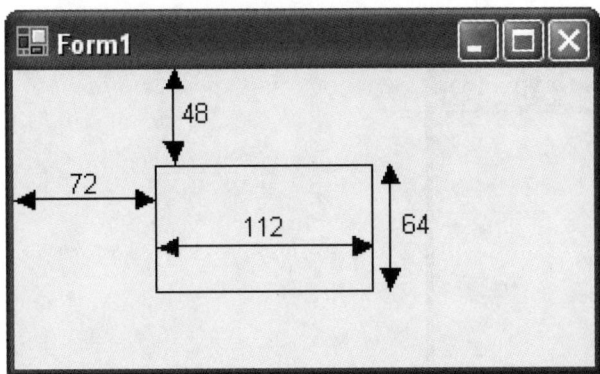

9   Rewrite some of the previous programming examples that used moving picture boxes. Make use of the DrawImage method. Programs like Fairy flying, Explode or Follow me would be suitable.

10 Write a program that will make Elsa walk to the east or to the west using the cursor keys. Images of Elsa walking are provided on the accompanying CD. Note that the background colour of each of the images has an RGB value of 106, 76, 48.

Program example: Flying insects

Create a new Windows application with the name *Flying insects*.

Create the interface

■ Add two image lists and three timers. They will automatically be placed in the form's component tray.

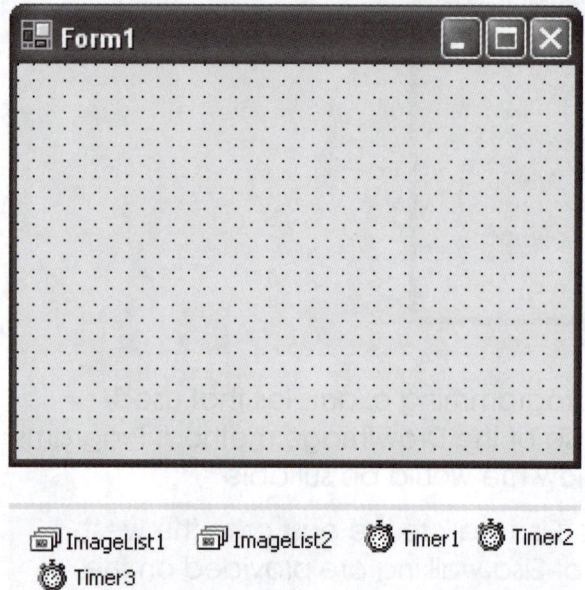

 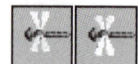

■ Set the following properties:

Form1

BackgroundImage	Magicbus.bmp
FormBorderStyle	Fixed Single
Icon	Butterfly.ico
MaximizeBox	False
Text	Flying insects

Timer1

(Name)	tmrButterfly
Enabled	True
Interval	300

ImageList1

(Name)	imlButterflies
ImageSize	32,32
TransparentColor	Gray

ImageList2

(Name)	imlDragonflies
ImageSize	32,32
TransparentColor	Gray

Timer2

(Name)	tmrDragonfly
Enabled	True
Interval	100

Timer3

(Name)	tmrPause
Enabled	True
Interval	2000

■ Add the seven butterfly images to *imlButterflies* from *blue butterfly east 0.bmp* to *blue butterfly east 6.bmp*.

■ Add the two dragonfly images to *imlDragonflies*

■ Thank you to Michael Hirsch for the graphic used on the BackgoundImage and Reiner Prokein for the insect images.

Write the code and add comments

■   Declare two form level variables that are used in several procedures.

```
Dim objCanvas As Graphics ' declare a graphics object
Dim DragonflyMove As Integer = 5 ' the starting move for dragonfly
```

■   A graphics object is created on the form after the form loads.

```
Private Sub Form1_Paint(ByVal sender As Object, ByVal e As _
System.Windows.Forms.PaintEventArgs) Handles MyBase.Paint
    objCanvas = Me.CreateGraphics   ' create graphics object on form
End Sub
```

■   This timer procedure produces a new image of the butterfly. The previous image
     of the butterfly is covered with a copy of a rectangular section of the form's
     BackgroundImage.

```
Private Sub tmrButterfly_Tick(ByVal sender As System.Object, ByVal e As _
System.EventArgs) Handles tmrButterfly.Tick
    Randomize()
    Static WhichButterfly As Integer = 0     ' start with image 0
    Static bX As Integer = -10 ' start butterfly on left side of form
    ' start butterfly at a random height
    Static bY As Integer = Me.Height * 0.25 + (Me.Height * 0.5 * Rnd())
    ' section of background to copy is the rectangle behind the butterfly
    Dim RectCopy As New Rectangle(bX, bY, 32, 32)
    ' draw this section over the last butterfly image
    objCanvas.DrawImage(Me.BackgroundImage, bX, bY, RectCopy, GraphicsUnit.Pixel)
    bX += 20 + Int(Rnd() * 11)    ' random increment in X from 20 to 30
    bY += -30 + Int(Rnd() *61)    ' random increment in Y from -30 to 30
    If bX > Me.Width Then ' if butterfly is off the right side of form
        bX = 0  ' go back to left side of form
        bY = Me.Height * (0.25 + 0.5 * Rnd())   ' new random height
    End If
    ' show image of butterfly
    objCanvas.DrawImage(imlButterflies.Images.Item(WhichButterfly), bX, bY)
    WhichButterfly = (WhichButterfly + 1) Mod 7 ' total of 7 images: 0, 1, 2, ... 6
End Sub
```

■   The dragonfly flies with more regularity. The previous image of the dragonfly is
     covered with a copy of a rectangular section of the form's BackgroungImage. It
     pauses every two seconds.

```
Private Sub tmrDragonfly_Tick(ByVal sender As System.Object, ByVal e As _
System.EventArgs) Handles tmrDragonfly.Tick
    Randomize()
    Static WhichDragonfly As Integer = 0     ' start with image 0
    Static dX As Integer = Me.Width ' start dragonfly on right side of form
    ' start dragonfly at a random height
    Static dY As Integer = Me.Height * 0.25 + (Me.Height * 0.5 * Rnd())
    ' section of background to copy is rectangle behind the dragonfly
    Dim RectCopy As New Rectangle(dX, dY, 32, 32)
    ' draw this section over the last dragonfly image
    objCanvas.DrawImage(Me.BackgroundImage, dX, dY, RectCopy, GraphicsUnit.Pixel)
    dX -= DragonflyMove ' reduce X coordinate (or remain still if zero)
    If dX < -32 Then     ' if dragonfly is off the left side of form
        dX = Me.Width    ' go to right side of form
        dY = Me.Height * (0.25 + 0.5 * Rnd())   ' new random height
    End If
    ' draw image of dragonfly
    objCanvas.DrawImage(imlDragonflies.Images.Item(WhichDragonfly), dX, dY)
    WhichDragonfly = (WhichDragonfly + 1) Mod 2  ' only 2 images: 0 and 1
End Sub
```

- With every two second tick of this timer the value of the variable DragonflyMove alternates between 0 and 5.

```
Private Sub tmrPause_Tick(ByVal sender As System.Object, ByVal e As _
System.EventArgs) Handles tmrPause.Tick
    ' alternates between 0 and 5 pixels
    DragonflyMove = (DragonflyMove + 5) Mod 10
End Sub
```

Try it out

Flying insects – points to note

- Note the **Interval** property has different settings on tmrButterfly and tmrDragonfly. This is to simulate the different 'flutter rates' of their wings.

- Note that the graphics object is **declared** at form level, **instantiated** (the giving of a value) in the Form Paint procedure and **applied** in the timer procedures.

  ```
  Dim objCanvas As Graphics ' declare a graphics object

  objCanvas = Me.CreateGraphics    ' create graphics object on form

  objCanvas.DrawImage(imlButterflies.Images.Item(WhichButterfly), bX, bY)
  ```

- To give the butterfly simulated erratic movement random numbers were used for the changes in both X and Y coordinates:

  ```
  bX += 20 + Int(Rnd() * 11)    ' random increment in X from 20 to 30
  bY += -30 + Int(Rnd() *61)    ' random increment in Y from -30 to 30
  ```

- The butterfly also enters the form at a random position.

  ```
  bY = Me.Height * (0.25 + 0.5 * Rnd())    ' new random height
  ```

- Another overload of the **DrawImage** method is used to draw a part of the form's BackgroundImage over the previously drawn butterfly:

```
Dim RectCopy As New Rectangle(bX, bY, 32, 32)
' draw this section over the last butterfly image
objCanvas.DrawImage(Me.BackgroundImage, bX, bY, RectCopy, GraphicsUnit.Pixel)
```

  This **overload** is used if only a part of an image is to be drawn on the graphics object. An argument is supplied to specify a rectangle. In this case it is the rectangle where the last butterfly was drawn. Even though an image has been drawn on the form the **BackgroundImage** remains as is. The same idea is applied to both insects.

- The **event handler** (or event procedure) for *tmrPause* changes the value of a variable used in the event handler for *tmrDragonfly*. For blocks of two seconds *tmrDragonfly* alternates between moving the image 0 or 5 pixels.

```
DragonflyMove = (DragonflyMove + 5) Mod 10
```

  The variable DragonflyMove can only ever have a value of 0 or 5. However the procedure still continues to cycle through the animation images.

- The variable DragonflyMove has been declared at form level. This is because it is used in two procedures. Whenever a variable is used in more than one procedure it is declared at **form level**. As a general principle you should try to keep variables **local**. That is, contained in the one procedure.

- An effective use of random numbers and timers has allowed the simulation to express the different behaviours of the two insects. Also note that the butterfly cycles through seven images whereas the dragonfly has only two.

Flying insects – check what you have learnt

1   How often does the butterfly change its image?

2   Write the line of code that instantiated the graphics object.

3   Why are both the following variables declared with Static?

```
Static WhichDragonfly As Integer = 0     ' start with image 0
Static dX As Integer = Me.Width ' start dragonfly on right side of form
```

4   The Y coordinate of the butterfly is incremented by a random number. What does the butterfly do if the random number calculates to:

   a   -30   b   0   c   30

5   DragonflyMove is a variable that determines how many pixels the dragonfly moves with each tick of its timer. Show how this variable alternates between 0 and 5.

```
DragonflyMove = (DragonflyMove + 5) Mod 10
```

6   What is the noticeable effect if the following line of code is omitted?

```
objCanvas.DrawImage(Me.BackgroundImage, bX, bY, RectCopy, GraphicsUnit.Pixel)
```

7 What range of values is possible with the following expression?

```
Me.Height * (0.25 + 0.5 * Rnd())
```

8 What is meant by an overload of a method?

9 **a** How do the behaviours of the butterfly and the dragonfly differ?

    b How has this been achieved?

10 Use the DrawImage method to make a program that is a race of three rally cars. You can decide how many laps they must race.

Chapter 6

Sound advice

Sound effects

Windows uses a number of familiar alerts to help identify particular **system events**. These are small WAV files with names like *chimes.wav*, *chord.wav* and *ding.wav*. Similarly sound effects are a necessary part of any gaming application.

To play a small **WAV** file using the least resources we will use the **Windows API** (Application Programming Interface). API programming makes use of the libraries of functions in **Dynamic Link Libraries** (DLLs). A module named *Playwave.vb* (see Appendix 1) is included on the accompanying CD. The library file *winmm.dll* (Windows multi-media) is accessed for its sound playing facility. *Playwave.vb* contains a very simple procedure named *PlayWaveFile*. The declaration of that procedure is shown below:

```
Public Sub PlayWaveFile(ByVal FileName As String, Optional ByVal SoundFlags As _
PlaySoundFlags = PlaySoundFlags.SND_FILENAME Or PlaySoundFlags.SND_ASYNC Or _
PlaySoundFlags.SND_NODEFAULT)
```

After adding the module to a project the use of *PlayWaveFile* is typically a simple single command. For example:

```
If Collision(Car1, Car2) Then
   PlayWaveFile("Crash.wav")
End If
```

If the WAV file is in the same folder as the application (EXE file) then a path does not need to be included in the file specification.

Note the list of **play sound flags** that can be optionally customised. To keep it simple the most common choices have been set as the defaults (name is a file name, play asynchronously and silence if the sound is not found). Playing asynchronously means the procedure returns immediately after beginning the sound.

A small demonstration application that includes the use of *PlayWaveFile* follows later in this chapter.

Background music

If you want continuous background music *PlayWaveFile* will not do. It is only suitable for a few seconds of sound. Two alternatives for playing sounds of indefinite length will be described, using **DirectX** and using the **Windows media player**.

DirectX

DirectX is a collection of APIs and technologies created by Microsoft. It was originally released in 1996 to assist game programmers access the multimedia features of their computers. The libraries of current versions of DirectX can be accessed with the .NET languages. There are fourteen separate libraries associated with computer graphics, handling input, generating sounds and music and communication between clients and servers in a multi-user environment. In this chapter we will be looking at just one of those libraries – Microsoft.DirectX.AudioVideoPlayback.

- In order to have the latest version of DirectX available to you on your computer you should go to the downloads page of Microsoft.com.

  http://www.microsoft.com/downloads/search.aspx?displaylang=en

- Choose DirectX from the Download Categories:

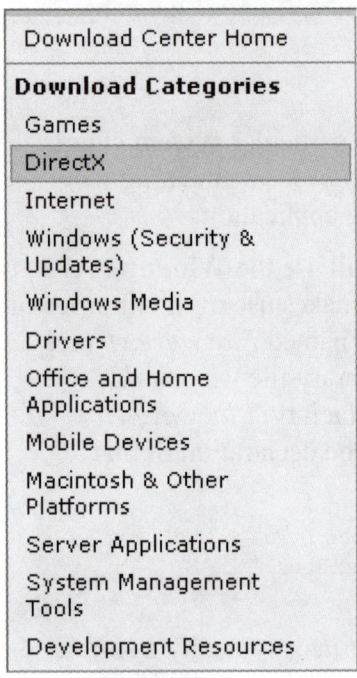

- Be certain to select a DirectX download that is specified 'For Software Developers'.

Once DirectX has been installed on your computer a **reference** must be made to a .NET component to make use of its classes in a Visual Basic .NET project.

The Windows media player

- To have the latest media player available go to the downloads page of Microsoft.com then choose Windows Media from the download categories:

  http://www.microsoft.com/downloads/search.aspx?displaylang=en

- Choose the latest version of the Windows media player.

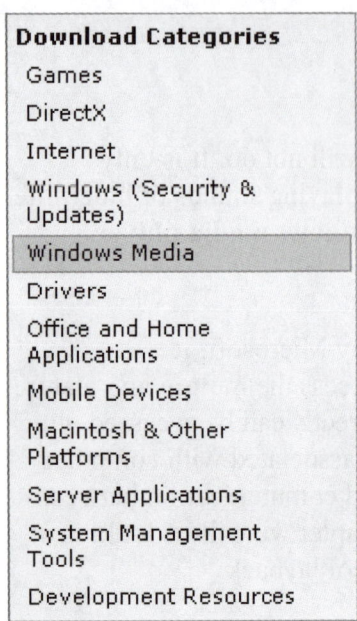

Once Windows media player has been installed on your computer a **reference** must be made to this COM component to use make use of its classes in a Visual Basic .NET project.

The media player control can be added to the toolbox by browsing to *wmp.dll*. When added to a form the control has the familiar functions available on the media player application.

However, if background music is all that is required, a media player object can be utilised without the need for the control. So instead of placing the control on a form, all the required properties and methods are available after making a simple declaration. For example:

```
Dim WmpSound As WindowsMediaPlayerClass
```

After which a property can be assigned like:

```
WmpSound.URL = SoundFile
```

Or methods applied:

```
WmpSound.play()
```

```
WmpSound.Stop()
```

Program example: Audio players

Create a new Windows application with the name *Audio players.*

Create the interface

■   Add three radio buttons, three buttons, four labels, a checkbox, a timer and an Open file dialog to the form.

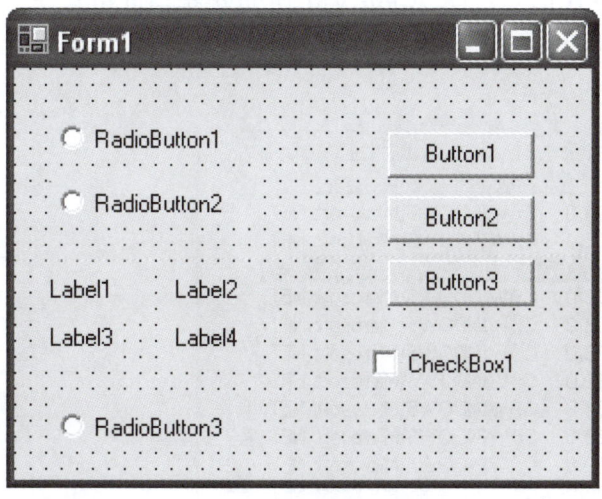

- Set the following properties:

Form1

Icon	(you choose)
MaximizeBox	False
Text	Audio players

RadioButton1

Name	rdbDirectX
Checked	True
Text	DirectX

RadioButton2

Name	rdbWmp
Text	Windows media player

RadioButton3

Name	rdbAPI
Text	Windows API (short WAV sounds)

Button1

Name	btnOpen
Text	&Open

CheckBox1

Name	chkLoop
Text	Loop

Button2

Name	btnPlay
Enabled	False
Text	&Play

Button3

Name	btnStop
Enabled	False
Text	&Stop

Label1

Text	Current position

Label2

Text	Duration

Label3

Name	lblPos
BorderStyle	Fixed3D
Text	0
TextAlign	MiddleCenter

Label4

Name	lblDuration
BorderStyle	Fixed3D
Text	0
TextAlign	MiddleCenter

Timer1

Name	tmrPlaying
Interval	1000

OpenFileDialog1

Name	dlgOpen
Filter	Sound files (*.wav;*.mp3)|*.wav;*.mp3
Title	Open a sound file

Write the code and add comments

- Both DirectX and the Windows media player must be installed for this example. **References** to these audio devices must be added:

- From the Project menu choose Add Reference.

- Firstly make a reference to Microsoft.DirectX.AudioVideoPlayback on the .NET tab.

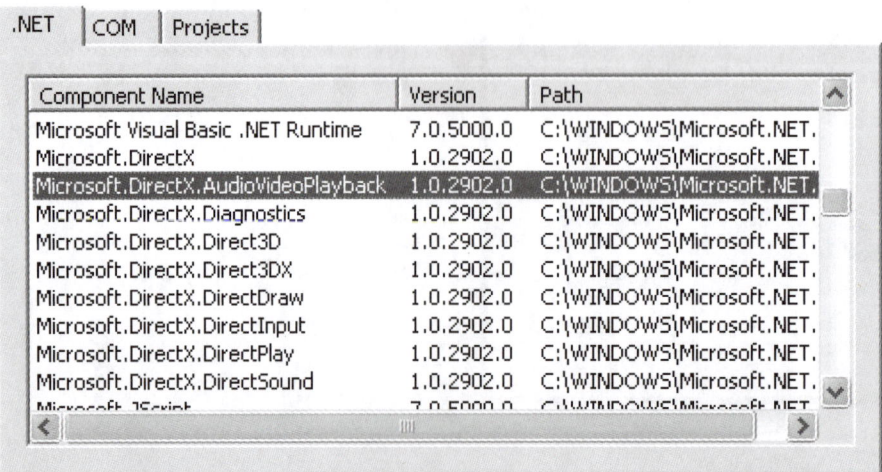

■ Now make a reference to the Windows media player on the **COM** tab.

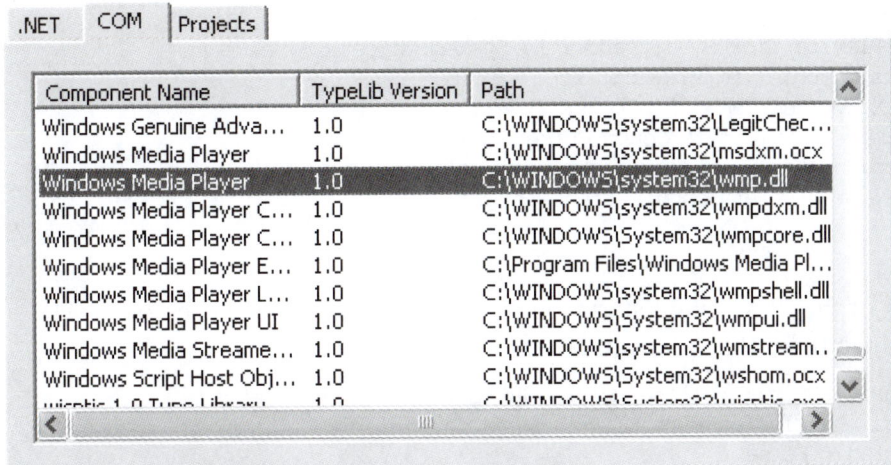

■ From the Project menu choose Add Existing Item.... Browse to the Modules folder on the accompanying CD and select the module *PlayWave.vb*.

■ Include the following **Imports** statements at the top of the code window.

```
Imports Microsoft.DirectX.AudioVideoPlayback
Imports WMPLib
```

■ Declare the following form level variables. Note that we will be using event handlers for the audio players, so they have been declared **WithEvents**.

```
Dim WithEvents DirectXSound As Audio
Dim WithEvents WmpSound As WindowsMediaPlayerClass
Dim SoundFile As String
```

■ This is the Reset procedure that brings all controls to the starting point. This is a **general procedure** that is called by five other procedures.

```
Private Sub Reset()
    tmrPlaying.Stop() ' stop timer
    lblPos.Text = 0 ' set position back to zero
    lblDuration.Text = 0 ' set duration to zero
    btnOpen.Enabled = True  ' enable open button
    btnStop.Enabled = False ' disable stop button
    btnPlay.Enabled = False ' disable play button
    ' enable all 3 radio buttons
    rdbDirectX.Enabled = True
    rdbWmp.Enabled = True
    rdbAPI.Enabled = True
End Sub
```

■ An Open dialog is used to select an audio file to be played.

```
Private Sub btnOpen_Click(ByVal sender As System.Object, ByVal e As _
System.EventArgs) Handles btnOpen.Click
    If dlgOpen.ShowDialog() = DialogResult.OK Then
        SoundFile = dlgOpen.FileName
        btnPlay.Enabled = True ' enable the play button
        If rdbDirectX.Checked Then  ' DirectX
            DirectXSound = New Audio(SoundFile)
        ElseIf rdbWmp.Checked Then  ' Windows media player
            WmpSound = New WindowsMediaPlayerClass
            WmpSound.autoStart = False ' waits for the Play method
            WmpSound.URL = SoundFile ' assign the file to play
        End If
    End If
    btnStop.Enabled = False ' disable the stop button
End Sub
```

■ The following event procedure checks the progress of the audio file being played.

```
Private Sub tmrPlaying_Tick(ByVal sender As System.Object, ByVal e As _
System.EventArgs) Handles tmrPlaying.Tick
    If rdbDirectX.Checked Then   ' DirectX
        lblPos.Text = CInt(DirectXSound.CurrentPosition)
    ElseIf rdbWmp.Checked Then   ' Windows media player
        lblPos.Text = CInt(WmpSound.currentPosition)
    End If
End Sub
```

■ The Click of the Play button starts the sound playing for the chosen object. It also starts the timer that keeps track of the playing progress.

```
Private Sub btnPlay_Click(ByVal sender As System.Object, ByVal e As _
System.EventArgs) Handles btnPlay.Click
    btnPlay.Enabled = False
    btnOpen.Enabled = False
    btnStop.Enabled = True
    If rdbDirectX.Checked Then   ' DirectX
        rdbWmp.Enabled = False ' disable other radio buttons
        rdbAPI.Enabled = False
        DirectXSound.Play() ' start playing
        lblDuration.Text = CInt(DirectXSound.Duration) ' show total play time
        tmrPlaying.Start()' start timer
    ElseIf rdbWmp.Checked Then   ' Windows media player
        rdbDirectX.Enabled = False ' disable other radio buttons
        rdbAPI.Enabled = False
        WmpSound.play() ' start playing
        lblDuration.Text = CInt(WmpSound.currentItem.duration) ' show total play time
        tmrPlaying.Start() ' start timer
    Else ' Windows API
        rdbWmp.Enabled = False ' disable other radio buttons
        rdbDirectX.Enabled = False
        If chkLoop.Checked Then ' if looping
            PlayWaveFile(SoundFile, PlayWave.PlaySoundFlags.SND_FILENAME Or _
            PlayWave.PlaySoundFlags.SND_ASYNC Or PlayWave.PlaySoundFlags.SND_LOOP)
        Else ' play once
            PlayWaveFile(SoundFile)
            Reset()
        End If
    End If
End Sub
```

■ This procedure demonstrates the simple way playing can be terminated for each player.

```
Private Sub btnStop_Click(ByVal sender As System.Object, ByVal e As _
System.EventArgs) Handles btnStop.Click
    If rdbDircctX.Checked Then   ' DirectX
        DirectXSound.Stop()
    ElseIf rdbWmp.Checked Then   ' Windows media player
        WmpSound.stop()
    Else     ' Windows API
        PlayWaveFile(vbNullString, 0)
    End If
    Reset()
End Sub
```

- The timer and other controls have to be reset if a radio button is changed.

```
Private Sub rdbAPI_CheckedChanged(ByVal sender As Object, _
ByVal e As System.EventArgs) Handles rdbAPI.CheckedChanged, _
rdbDirectX.CheckedChanged, rdbAPI.CheckedChanged
    Reset()
End Sub
```

- This event handler responds to DirectX reaching the end of the sound file, then checks to see if it has to play again.

```
Private Sub DirectXSound_Ending(ByVal sender As Object, ByVal e As _
System.EventArgs) Handles DirectXSound.Ending
    If chkLoop.Checked Then ' if looping
        DirectXSound.CurrentPosition = 0 ' go back to start, play again
    Else
        Reset()
    End If
End Sub
```

- This event handler responds to the media player reaching the end of the sound file, then checks to see if it has to play again.

```
Private Sub WmpSound_PlayStateChange(ByVal NewState As Integer) _
Handles WmpSound.PlayStateChange
    If NewState = 1 Then ' if reached end
        If chkLoop.Checked Then ' if looping
            WmpSound.play() ' play again
        Else
            Reset()
        End If
    End If
End Sub
```

Try it out

Open a large mp3 or wav file with DirectX. Play it once. Do the same with Windows Media Player. Try a short wav sound effect with the API player. Try out the looping capability of all three.

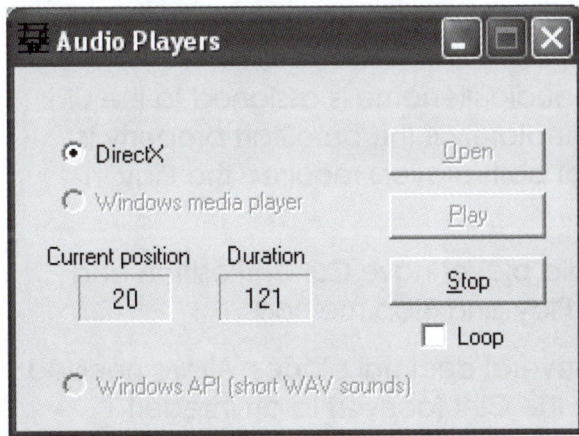

Audio players – Points to note

- The **Filter** property of an **Open file dialog** has two parts separated by a vertical bar. The first part is simply the file type(s) description and can be expressed however you choose. The second part, however, specifically defines the file types and must be expressed using the syntax shown. Each extension must be preceded by a **wildcard character**, and the file types must be separated by semi-colons.

Filter	Sound files (*.wav; *.mp3)|*.wav; *.mp3

- **DirectX** is a **.NET** component while the Windows media player is a **COM** component. For this reason alone DirectX is a preferable option for playing background music.

- The two **Imports** statements make the audio classes and their associated properties and methods available.

- The Reset is not an event procedure. It is called from inside other procedures. Because the code is required in several different places it has been written separately as a **general procedure**. This reduces and simplifies the code.

- When code becomes more complex **comments** are more important than ever. They provide **internal documentation** for the programmer as well as helping others understand the logic.

```
DirectXSound.CurrentPosition = 0 ' go back to start, play again
```

- A sound file is assigned when a new DirectX audio object is created. For the media player a sound file can be assigned after the new object is created:

```
DirectXSound = New Audio(SoundFile)

WmpSound = New WindowsMediaPlayerClass
WmpSound.URL = SoundFile
```

  For the media player when an audio filename is assigned to the **URL** property it will start playing immediately if the **autoStart** property is True. This was set to False so that both players required the **Play** method to start playing.

- Both DirectX and Windows media player have **CurrentPosition** and **Duration** properties. Both have **Play** and **Stop** methods.

- The CurrentPosition is given to several decimal places. All we needed to see was a whole number, so the **CInt** (convert to an Integer) function was applied:

```
lblPos.Text = CInt(DirectXSound.CurrentPosition)
```

- **If Then** statements are known as **two-way branching**.

```
If rdbDirectX.Checked Then  ' DirectX
   lblPos.Text = CInt(DirectXSound.CurrentPosition)
ElseIf rdbWmp.Checked Then  ' Windows media player
   lblPos.Text = CInt(WmpSound.currentPosition)
End If
```

- When DirectX finishes playing an audio file the **CurrentPosition** property stops at the end of the file. When Windows media player finishes playing it's CurrentPosition property returns to the start of the file (a value of 0). So to repeat playing requires a slightly different technique for each:

For DirectX assigning the CurrentPosition to 0 will start a replay.

```
DirectXSound.CurrentPosition = 0
```

For the media player the **Play** method will start a replay.

```
WmpSound.play()
```

- To detect the end of an audio file both the DirectX and media player objects were declared **WithEvents**. The **Ending** event was used for DirectX and the **PlayStateChange** was used for the media player. The only **NewState** we needed to detect was ending which has a value of 1.

- PlayWaveFile is distinctly different for **playing**, **looping** and **stopping** compared to DirectX and the media player. All three operations are achieved by calling the same procedure but by using different arguments:

```
PlayWaveFile(SoundFile)

PlayWaveFile(SoundFile, PlayWave.PlaySoundFlags.SND_FILENAME Or _
PlayWave.PlaySoundFlags.SND_ASYNC Or PlayWave.PlaySoundFlags.SND_LOOP)

PlayWaveFile(vbNullString, 0)
```

Audio players – Check what you have learnt

1   In what way are sounds desirable additions to gaming applications?

2   What are two distinct limitations of the API sound player that makes it suitable only for sound effects?

3   What are the PlaySoundFlags defaults used with the PlayWaveFile procedure?

4   What is the constant vbNullString? What role does it have in stopping the playing of a WAV file?

5   a   What is the purpose of the Reset procedure in the program example?

    b   Why separate this code into its own procedure?

6   a   DirectX has a number of libraries for game development. Which library was used in this program example?

    b   What are some of the other libraries used for?

7   What is the value of the CurrentPosition property when an audio file has finished playing if the object is
    a   DirectX audio
    b   Windows media player

8   By default the Windows media player will start playing as soon as the URL property is set to the name of a sound file. What property setting overrides this?

9   The Windows media player is not a .NET component. What is the distinct difference in the event procedure arguments between a .NET component and a COM component?

10   To have continuous music playing behind an application using DirectX or the Windows media player you need to
   i   declare an audio object
   ii   start the music playing
   iii ensure that it keeps repeating

   Take an application you have already created and apply these steps to provide suitable background music.

Chapter 7

Collision decisions

Things that go bump

In the gaming context a collision is not necessarily such a bad thing. In fact a large number of games have things that bump or come in contact in some way:
- a character picking up an item of value
- a ball bouncing against a bat
- crossing over a finish line
- shooting a basketball into a basket
- a missile colliding with an enemy spacecraft
- a character landing on a platform

Likewise it may be important when certain objects cease to be in contact:
- a character dropping an object
- a ball leaving a basket
- a character leaping from a platform

Included on the accompanying CD is a module to be used specifically for collision (or non-collision) detection. The *Collision* module, has a **function** *Collision* with five **overloads** (see Appendix 1). Have a close look at the declaration of the first overload:

```
Public Overloads Function Collision(ByVal Obj1 As Object, ByVal Obj2 As Object, _
Optional ByVal HorizTolerance1 As Integer = 0, Optional ByVal VertTolerance1 As _
Integer = 0, Optional ByVal HorizTolerance2 As Integer = 0, _
Optional ByVal VertTolerance2 As Integer = 0) As Boolean
```

It has two mandatory **arguments** and four that are optional. Used with just the first two arguments it simply checks if two objects are touching or overlapping, the four tolerance arguments taking their default values of zero. The two objects shown below in the first diagram would return a *True* value for the function, while the two objects in the second diagram would return *False*.

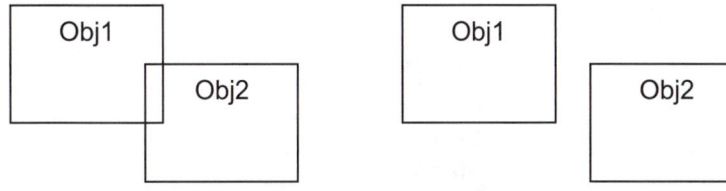

The additional arguments allow the entry of horizontal and vertical tolerances (in pixels) for one or both objects. These tolerances are shown with broken lines on the figures below.

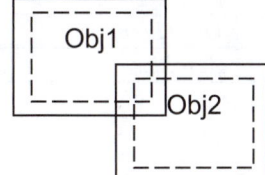 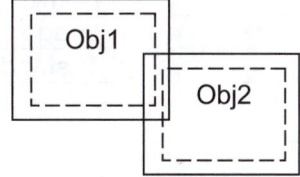

In the first diagram *Collision* is *True*, in the second *Collision* is *False*.

Most often its use is very simple:

```
If Collision(picCar1, picCar2) Then
```

The remaining four overloads of *Collision* provide detection for a Rectangle and an Object, a Rectangle and a Rectangle, a Point and an Object, and a Point and a Rectangle.

A big step forward

The following three programming examples demonstrate applications of the *Collision* function. All three represent a big step forward, especially when it comes to the coding. Careful attention must be given to all the described steps, the points to note and the check questions that follow each example.

Program example: Space

Create a new Windows application with the name *Space*.

Create the interface

■   Add two labels, four picture boxes, one image list and three timers to a form.

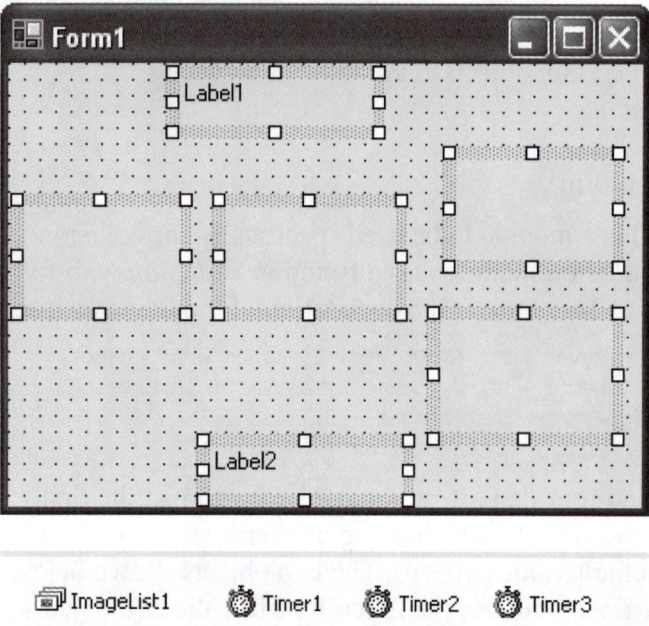

■   Set the following properties:

Form1

BackColor	*Black*
BackgroundImage	*Stars.bmp*
Icon	*(you choose)*
KeyPreview	*True*
Text	*Space*

PictureBox1

Name	*picExplosion*
Image	*Explosion 0.gif*
SizeMode	*AutoSize*
Visible	*False*

PictureBox2

Name	*picShip*
Image	*Spaceship.bmp*
SizeMode	*AutoSize*

PictureBox3

Name	*picUFO*
Image	*UFO2.bmp*
SizeMode	*AutoSize*

PictureBox4

Name	picMissile
Image	Missile.bmp
SizeMode	AutoSize

Label1

Name	lblScore
BackColor	Black
BorderStyle	Fixed3D
Font	MS Sans Serif Bold 12
ForeColor	White
Text	0
TextAlign	MiddleCenter

Label2

BackColor	Black
ForeColor	White
Text	Use the cursor keys to move up and down, spacebar to fire a missile

Timer1

Name	tmrUFO
Enabled	True
Interval	100

Timer2

Name	tmrMissile
Enabled	False
Interval	100

Timer3

Name	tmrExplosion
Enabled	False
Interval	100

ImageList1

Name	imlExplosion
ImageSize	60, 50
TransparentColor	Transparent

Thank you to Reiner Prokein for the spaceship graphic.

- Add the eleven explosion images (0 to 10) to the Images collection of *imlExplosion*.

Write the code and add comments

- From the Project menu choose Add Existing Item…. Browse to the *Modules* folder on the accompanying CD and select the module *Positioning.vb*. This module has a centering function (see Appendix 1). W will also need to add the modules *Collision.vb* for collision detection and *PlayWave.vb* for sounds.

- Copy the wave file *destroy.wav* to the Bin folder.

- The KeyDown event triggers the code to move the spaceship and fire a missile.

```
Private Sub Form1_KeyDown(ByVal sender As Object, ByVal e As _
System.Windows.Forms.KeyEventArgs) Handles MyBase.KeyDown
    Select Case e.KeyCode
        Case Keys.Up    ' move spaceship up
            picShip.Top -= 10
        Case Keys.Down  ' move spaceship down
            picShip.Top += 10
        Case Keys.Space ' fire a missile
            CentreOn(picShip, picMissile)
            picMissile.Visible = True
            tmrMissile.Start()
    End Select
End Sub
```

- The event procedure for this timer causes the movement of the UFO.

```
Private Sub tmrUFO_Tick(ByVal sender As Object, ByVal e As System.EventArgs) _
Handles tmrUFO.Tick
    picUFO.Top += 8 ' move the UFO down the form
End Sub
```

- This event procedure checks if the change in Location of the UFO has put it off the form.

```
Private Sub picUFO_LocationChanged(ByVal sender As Object, ByVal e As _
System.EventArgs) Handles picUFO.LocationChanged
    If picUFO.Top > Me.Height Then ' UFO off form?
        picUFO.Top = -picUFO.Height ' move UFO to top of form
    End If
End Sub
```

- The explosion is an animation that goes through 11 frames (0 to 10). Once all 11 frames have been displayed the timer is turned off.

```
Private Sub tmrExplosion_Tick(ByVal sender As System.Object, ByVal e As _
System.EventArgs) Handles tmrExplosion.Tick
    Static Frame As Integer = 0
    picExplosion.Image = imlExplosion.Images.Item(Frame) ' show image
    Frame = (Frame + 1) Mod 11      ' next frame must be 0 to 10
    If Frame = 0 Then    ' explosion over
        picExplosion.Visible = False
        tmrExplosion.Enabled = False
    End If
End Sub
```

- This event procedure causes the movement of the missile.

```
Private Sub tmrMissile_Tick(ByVal sender As System.Object, ByVal e As _
System.EventArgs) Handles tmrMissile.Tick
    picMissile.Left += 20    ' move missile to right
End Sub
```

- This event procedure checks on the Location of the missile. Has it collided with the UFO or has it left the form?

```
Private Sub picMissile_LocationChanged(ByVal sender As Object, ByVal e As _
System.EventArgs) Handles picMissile.LocationChanged
    ' if there is a collision between the missile and the UFO
    If Collision(picUFO, picMissile) Then
        picMissile.Visible = False
        picExplosion.Location = picUFO.Location ' move explosion to UFO
        picExplosion.Visible = True
        PlayWaveFile("destroy.wav") ' explosion sound
        picUFO.Top = -picUFO.Height ' move UFO to top of form
        tmrExplosion.Start() ' start explosion animation
        lblScore.Text += 1  ' increase score
        ' if missile has gone off the form then stop
    ElseIf picMissile.Left >= Me.Width Then
        picMissile.Visible = False
        tmrMissile.Stop()
    End If
End Sub
```

Try it out

- Use the cursor keys to move up and down, fire a missile with the spacebar.

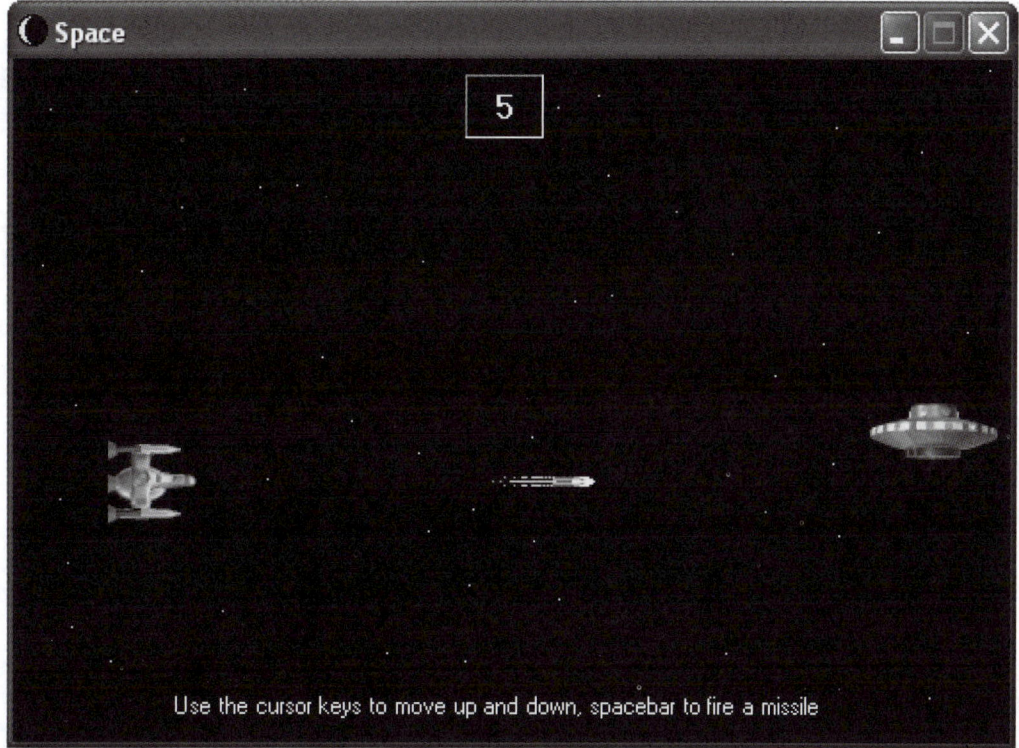

Space – points to note

- **Timers** have been used to control the **movement** of the missile and UFO, as well as controlling the explosion **animation**.

- The **ImageSize** and **TransparentColor** properties of an image list must be set before adding images to the Images collection.

- Setting the **KeyPreview** property of a form to True ensures the form processes the keystroke before it goes to a control.

- Two very useful **modules** are used in this example. *Positioning.vb* contains a procedure *CentreOn*. It centres one object on another. It is used to centre the missile on the spaceship.

    ```
    CentreOn(picShip, picMissile)
    ```

    Collision.vb is the other module that has already been described.

- The use of Collision is very simple in this example. Has the missile hit the UFO?

    ```
    If Collision(picMissile, picUFO) Then
    ```

- The **overloads** of a function are its different versions. In the case of Collision each overload has a different set of arguments.

- The procedure *tmrExplosion_Tick* controls the explosion animation. The animation progresses through its eleven frames then stops. A variable Frame is declared with the **Static** statement. Declaring a local variable with Static ensures its value is held for the next time the procedure is run (for this procedure, in $^1/_{10}$ second). If declared with Dim the previous value would be lost.

1   Give some examples of situations in games where a collision occurs.

2   Under what circumstances might you need to check for a non collision?

3   What is the purpose of each of the three timers in this example?

4   What methods turn a timer on or off?

5   The Interval of tmrExplosion is set at 100. How long does it take for the whole explosion animation to occur?

6   What possible values result from the operation Mod 11?

7   Checking for a collision of one object with another is just one overload of the Collision function. What do the other four overloads check?

8   Draw a simple diagram to show where the UFO is when

    `picUFO.Top = -picUFO.Height`

9   Suggest ways in which this program could become more challenging as it progresses.

10 The regularity of the appearance of the UFO makes it fairly easy to hit. Altering its speed or that of the missile would increase the difficulty. Implement this and/or your suggested modifications from question 9.

Program example: Leap and land

Create a new Windows application with the name *Leap and land.*

Create the interface

■   Add one label, two picture boxes, two image lists and two timers to a form.

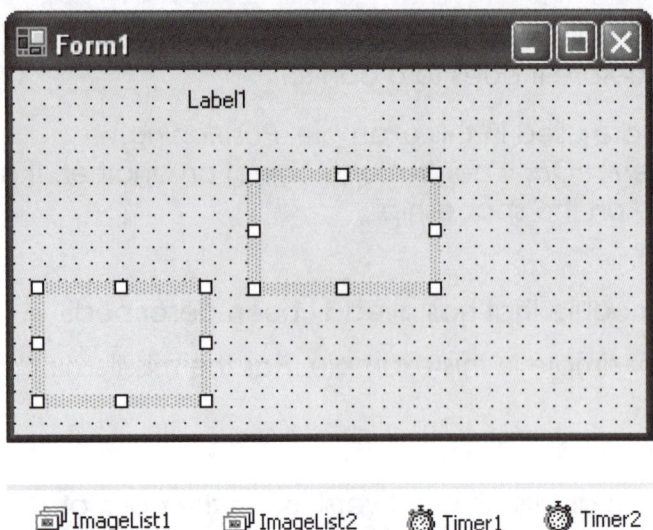

■ Set the following properties:

Form1

BackColor	255, 224, 192
MaximizeBox	False
Text	Leap and land

Label1

Text	Use the cursor keys to move left and right, spacebar to jump

PictureBox1

Name	picChar
Size	18,24

PictureBox2

Name	picPlatform
Image	Platform.bmp
SizeMode	AutoSize

ImageList1

Name	imlWalkRight
ImageSize	18, 24

ImageList2

Name	imlWalkLeft
ImageSize	18, 24

Timer1

Name	tmrLeap
Enabled	False
Interval	100

The character graphics are from a StarChar strip in a resource pack composed by True Predator.

■ Position *picChar* at the bottom of the form. This will be its base.

■ Add the character images *char_left_0.gif* to *char_left2.gif* to the Images collection of *imlWalkLeft* and *char_right_0.gif* to *char_right2.gif* to the Images collection of *imlWalkRight*.

Write the code and add comments

■ From the Project menu choose Add Existing Item…. Browse to the *Modules* folder on the accompanying CD and select the module *Collision.vb*.

■ This **enumeration**, declared at form level is a clear way of identifying the character's state of movement.

```
Private Enum Movement
    Leaping = 0
    Returning = 1
    Falling = 2
    Horizontal = 3
End Enum
```

■ Three **form level variables** are required. All these variables are needed in more than one procedure. The **constants** BASETOP, PLATFORMTOP and LEAPTOP represent the Top property of the character in three different positions. The locations of the character and the platform on the form will need to be adjusted to match these. Alternatively adjust these values to suit your form layout.

```
Dim WhichImage As Integer = 0    ' can be 0, 1 or 2
Dim LeapDist As Integer   ' alternates between +4 and -4
Const BASETOP As Integer = 112 ' Top of character at base level
Const PLATFORMTOP As Integer = 48 ' Top of character at platform level
Const LEAPTOP As Integer = 24 ' Top of character at his maximum height
Dim CurrentState As Movement = Movement.Horizontal
```

- The KeyDown event procedure allows the user to move the character left, right or make a leap.

```
Private Sub Form1_KeyDown(ByVal sender As Object, ByVal e As _
System.Windows.Forms.KeyEventArgs) Handles MyBase.KeyDown
    Select Case e.KeyCode
        Case Keys.Right
            WhichImage = (WhichImage + 1) Mod 3 ' must be 0 to 2
            picChar.Image = imlWalkRight.Images(WhichImage)
            picChar.Left += 2   ' move left
        Case Keys.Left
            WhichImage = (WhichImage + 1) Mod 3 ' must be 0 to 2
            picChar.Image = imlWalkLeft.Images.Item(WhichImage)
            picChar.Left -= 2   ' move right
        Case Keys.Space
            CurrentState = Movement.Leaping
            LeapDist = -4 ' on way up
            tmrLeap.Start() ' start a leap
    End Select
End Sub
```

- When the timer is enabled the character will move either up or down.

```
Private Sub tmrLeap_Tick(ByVal sender As System.Object, _
ByVal e As System.EventArgs) Handles tmrLeap.Tick
    picChar.Top += LeapDist ' move up/down
End Sub
```

- This procedure checks each new position of the character to see if its movement needs to change.

```
Private Sub picChar_LocationChanged(ByVal sender As Object, _
ByVal e As System.EventArgs) Handles picChar.LocationChanged
    Select Case CurrentState
        Case Movement.Returning ' returning back down from a leap
            'if character has hit the bottom or the platform
            If picChar.Top = BASETOP Or (Collision(picChar, picPlatform) _
            And picChar.Top = PLATFORMTOP) Then
                CurrentState = Movement.Horizontal
                tmrLeap.Stop()
            End If
        Case Movement.Falling ' falling after dropping from platform
            If picChar.Top = BASETOP Then
                CurrentState = Movement.Horizontal
                tmrLeap.Stop()
            End If
        Case Movement.Leaping ' leaping upwards
            'if character has reached top of leap
            If picChar.Top <= LEAPTOP Then
                LeapDist = 4
                CurrentState = Movement.Returning
            ' if character has hit the platform while leaping
            ElseIf Collision(picChar, picPlatform) Then
                LeapDist = 4
                CurrentState = Movement.Falling
            End If
        Case Movement.Horizontal ' neither leaping, returning or falling
            ' if character has walked off the platform
            If picChar.Top = PLATFORMTOP And Not Collision(picChar, picPlatform) Then
                LeapDist = 4
                CurrentState = Movement.Falling
                tmrLeap.Start()
            End If
    End Select
End Sub
```

Try it out

Jump the character up to the platform. Have him walk right and left. Leap from the platform. Try to leap at the platform from underneath.

Leap and land – points to note

■ In the **Form_KeyDown** procedure each keystroke advances the character to its next image as well as moving him either right or left.

■ In this example the Collision function is used to detect when the character makes contact with the platform and when it loses contact with the platform.

```
If Collision(picChar, picPlatform) Then ' hit platform

' check if no contact with platform
If CurrentTop < BASETOP And Not Collision(picChar, picPlatform) Then
```

■ The *tmrLeap_Tick* procedure controls both the rising and falling of the character. When the variable LeapDist is positive *picChar* will rise, when LeapDist is negative *picChar* will fall.

```
LeapDist = 4   ' on way up

LeapDist = -4 ' on way down
```

■ It is very important to include clear **comments** in your coding, particularly when procedures become more complex.

■ The **Constant** LEAPTOP was set at 24. This limits the top of the leap.

■ *tmrFall_Tick* is a much simpler procedure. The movement is only in one direction continuing until it reaches the base level.

Leap and land – check what you have learnt

1 What are the three constants representing?

2 How does the KeyDown procedure make the character walk?

3 Why are variables declared at form level? Use the variable CurrentState as an example.

4 Which form level variable appears in every procedure?

5 What line of code ensures that WhichImage can only take on one of the values 0, 1 or 2?

6 LeapDist is a variable that alternates between the values +4 and −4. What is the purpose of having these two values?

7 What line of code checks to see if the character is still in contact with the platform?

8 What are the optional arguments of Collision? What are their default values?

9 If you didn't want the user to be able to start a leap while one was already under way, What alterations would you make to the existing code?

10 Putting in an additional platform does present some challenges (having more than two would be better dealt with using arrays later). Alterations would need to be made to both tmrLeap_Tick and tmrFall_Tick. Also LEAPTOP can no longer be a constant as its value depends on where the leap started.

Modify this program to include two platforms on different levels.

Program example: Paddle ball

Create a new Windows application with the name *Paddle ball*.

Create the interface

■ Add six labels, one picture box and one timer to a form.

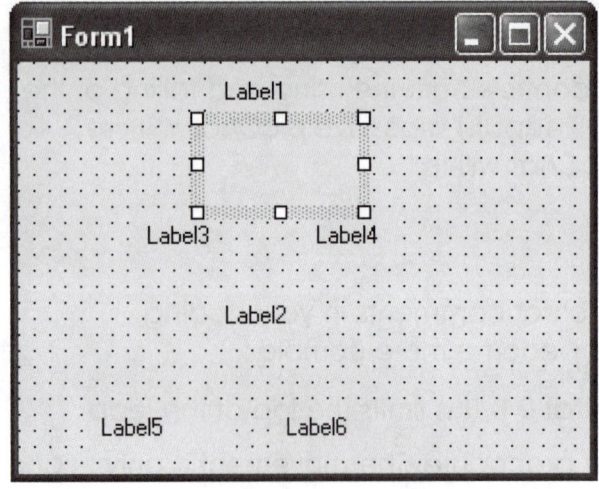

 Timer1

- Set the following properties:

Form1

BackColor	Bisque
KeyPreview	True
MaximizeBox	False
MinimizeBox	False
Text	Paddle ball

PictureBox1

Name	picBall
Image	Redball.gif
SizeMode	AutoSize

Timer1

Name	tmrBall
Interval	10

Label1

Text	Press A and S to move Green, K and L to move Blue

Label2

Name	lblGo
Text	Press G to Go

Label3

Name	lblGreenScore
BackColor	PapayaWhip
BorderStyle	Fixed3D
ForeColor	Lime
Text	0
TextAlign	MiddleCenter

Label4

Name	lblBlueScore
BackColor	PapayaWhip
BorderStyle	Fixed3D
ForeColor	Blue
Text	0
TextAlign	MiddleCenter

Label5

Name	lblGreenPaddle
BackColor	Lime
BorderStyle	FixedSingle
Size	48,8
Visible	False

Label6

Name	lblBluePaddle
BackColor	Blue
BorderStyle	FixedSingle
Size	48,8
Visible	True

Write the code and add comments

- From the Project menu choose Add Existing Item…. Browse to the *Modules* folder on the accompanying CD and select the module *Collision.vb*. Also add the module *PlayWave.vb*.

- Copy the wave files *boing.wav* and *thud.wav* to the Bin folder.

- These five **form level variables** are used in multiple procedures.

```
Dim IncX As Integer = 2     ' X increment of the bouncing ball
Dim IncY As Integer = 2     ' Y increment of the bouncing ball
Dim XPos As Integer         ' X position of the ball
Dim YPos As Integer         ' Y position of the ball
Dim MaxX As Integer         ' maximum X position for ball
```

- The Form Load initialises some of the form level variables.

```
Private Sub Form1_Load(ByVal sender As Object, ByVal e As _
System.EventArgs) Handles MyBase.Load
    XPos = picBall.Left ' starting position of ball
    YPos = picBall.Top
    MaxX = Me.DisplayRectangle.Width - picBall.Width
End Sub
```

- Restart is a **general procedure** that sets the players scores back to zero

```
Private Sub Restart()
    lblBlueScore.Text = 0
    lblGreenScore.Text = 0
End Sub
```

■ These keystrokes control the movement of the paddles and starts each new rally.

```
Private Sub Form1_KeyDown(ByVal sender As Object, ByVal e As _
System.Windows.Forms.KeyEventArgs) Handles MyBase.KeyDown
    Select Case e.KeyCode
        Case Keys.A   ' Green move left
            If lblGreenPaddle.Visible Then
                lblGreenPaddle.Left -= 8
            End If
        Case Keys.S   ' Green move right
            If lblGreenPaddle.Visible Then
                lblGreenPaddle.Left += 8
            End If
        Case Keys.K   ' Blue move left
            If lblBluePaddle.Visible Then
                lblBluePaddle.Left -= 8
            End If
        Case Keys.L  ' Blue move right
            If lblBluePaddle.Visible Then
                lblBluePaddle.Left += 8
            End If
        Case Keys.G  ' Go
            If Not tmrBall.Enabled Then  ' ball must have stopped
                Randomize()
                XPos = Int(Rnd() * MaxX)    ' random start
                YPos = 16
                tmrBall.Start()  ' start ball moving
                lblGo.Visible = False    ' hide Go message
            End If
    End Select
End Sub
```

■ This procedure controls the movement of the ball including the striking of the paddles and bouncing off the walls.

```
Private Sub tmrBall_Tick(ByVal sender As System.Object, ByVal e As _
System.EventArgs) Handles tmrBall.Tick
    Randomize()
    XPos += IncX        ' calculate new X and Y positions
    YPos += IncY
    If YPos > Me.Height Then    ' ball off form, somebody missed
        tmrBall.Stop() ' stop ball
        lblGo.Visible = True     ' show Go message
        If lblGreenPaddle.Visible Then  ' Green missed
            lblBlueScore.Text += 1  ' Blue gets point
            Swap_Paddles()
        Else     ' Blue missed
            lblGreenScore.Text += 1 ' Green gets point
            Swap_Paddles()
        End If
    Else ' ball still in play
        If XPos <= 0 Or XPos >= MaxX Then ' ball hits side wall
            PlayWaveFile("boing.wav")
            IncX *= -1   ' opposite X direction
        End If
        If YPos <= 0 Then    ' ball hits back wall
            PlayWaveFile("boing.wav")
            IncY *= -1   ' opposite Y direction
        End If
        picBall.Location = New Point(XPos, YPos) ' move ball to new position
    End If
End Sub
```

■ This **general procedure** (as opposed to an event procedure) reverses the value of the Visible property of each paddle – one becomes visible while the other becomes not visible. Swap_Paddles is used in other event procedures.

```
Private Sub Swap_Paddles()
    lblGreenPaddle.Visible = Not lblGreenPaddle.Visible
    lblBluePaddle.Visible = Not lblBluePaddle.Visible
End Sub
```

■ Checking for a collision with either of the paddles is done in this procedure.

```
Private Sub picBall_LocationChanged(ByVal sender As Object, ByVal e As _
System.EventArgs) Handles picBall.LocationChanged
    If Collision(picBall, lblBluePaddle) Or Collision(picBall, lblGreenPaddle) Then
        PlayWaveFile("thud.wav")
        Swap_Paddles()
        IncY *= -1    ' opposite Y direction
    End If
End Sub
```

■ A change in the blue score triggers this check for a winner.

```
Private Sub lblBlueScore_TextChanged(ByVal sender As Object, ByVal e As _
System.EventArgs) Handles lblBlueScore.TextChanged
    If lblBlueScore.Text = 10 Then
        MessageBox.Show("Blue wins!", "Paddle ball", MessageBoxButtons.OK, _
        MessageBoxIcon.Information)
        Restart()
    End If
End Sub
```

■ A change in the green score triggers this check for a winner.

```
Private Sub lblGreenScore_TextChanged(ByVal sender As Object, ByVal e As _
System.EventArgs) Handles lblGreenScore.TextChanged
    If lblGreenScore.Text = 10 Then
        MessageBox.Show("Green wins!", "Paddle ball", MessageBoxButtons.OK, _
        MessageBoxIcon.Information)
        Restart()
    End If
End Sub
```

Try it out

■ You will need a partner to play. Pressing 'G' will start a rally. Blue goes first. Use the 'A', 'S', 'K' and 'L' keys to move the paddles. The first player to scores 10 wins.

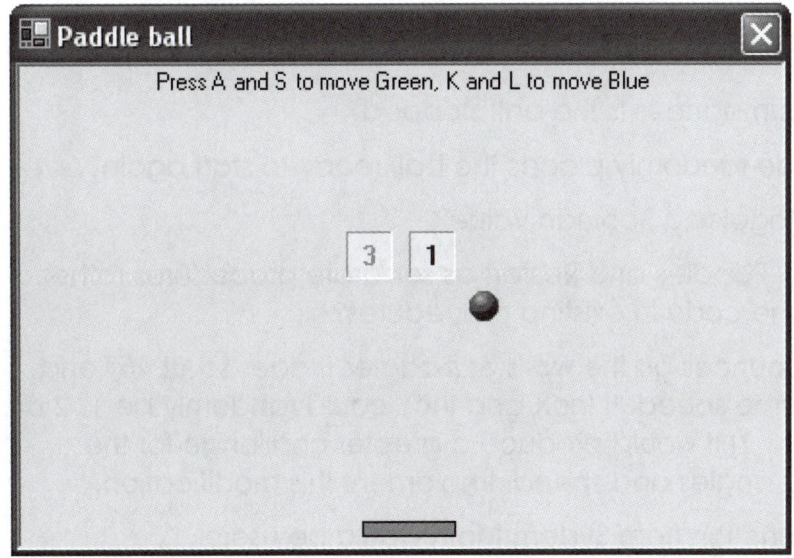

Paddle ball – points to note

- The variables IncX and IncY determine the direction of movement of the ball. To reverse the X direction, change the sign of IncX.

  ```
  IncX *= -1    ' opposite X direction
  ```

  To reverse the Y direction, change the sign of IncY.

  ```
  IncY *= -1    ' opposite Y direction
  ```

  When the ball hits one of the sides reverse the X direction, when the ball hits a paddle or the top wall reverse the Y direction.

- Each time the 'G' key is pressed the ball starts moving again. It is first moved to a **random** X location so that each rally does not start the same.

  ```
  XPos = Int(Rnd() * MaxX)     ' random start
  ```

- The collision that is to be detected is between the ball and each of the paddles.

  ```
  If Collision(picBall, lblBluePaddle) Or _
  Collision(picBall, lblGreenPaddle) Then    ' ball hits paddle
  ```

  Note also that for Collision to be True both object arguments have to be visible.

- The **Visible** property has a **Boolean** value – True or False. The **Not** operator toggles its current value.

  ```
  lblGreenPaddle.Visible = Not lblGreenPaddle.Visible
  lblBluePaddle.Visible = Not lblBluePaddle.Visible
  ```

Paddle ball – check what you have learnt

1   What line of code actually puts the ball in a new location?

2   In calculating MaxX why do you suppose the DisplayRectangle.Width property is used rather than just the Width property?

3   Which way is the ball moving if both IncX and IncY are negative?

4   How is a 'bounce' achieved with IncX and IncY?

5   Throughout the program what conditions are used to check which player's turn it is?

6   Under what circumstances is the ball stopped?

7   What line of code randomly places the ball ready to start again?

8   What operator toggles a Boolean value?

9   Why have Swap_Paddles and Restart as separate procedures rather than including the code in existing procedures?

10⌨ When the ball bounces off the walls or paddles it does so at 45° and always at the same speed. If IncX and IncY could randomly be 1, 2 or 3 (rather than just 2) it would produce a greater challenge for the players, altering angles and speed. Implement this modification.

  Using the **Sign** function from System.Math would be useful.

Chapter 8

An array of hope

Visual Basic .NET arrays

Arrays are groups of objects from the same class. You can have an array of Integers, an array of Pictureboxes, an array of Buttons, an array of Labels etc.

- Each object in an array is called an **element** of the array. Like any other variables each element can be assigned a value. Integers are assigned to Integer arrays, picture boxes are assigned to PictureBox arrays etc.
- Every element in an array has the same **Name**.
- Each element has a unique **Index** (or number of Indexes). In this way it is distinguishable from each of the other elements in the array.
- Every array is **zero-based**. This means the first Index is 0, followed by 1, 2, 3 etc. For example, the picture boxes below belong to an array named *Enemy*. The Name and Index of each is shown.

 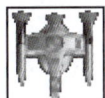 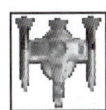   

Enemy(0) Enemy(1) Enemy(2) Enemy(3) Enemy(4) Enemy(5)

- The effective use of arrays simplifies and reduces the code in an application.
- From this point all of the games in this book will make use of at least one array.

Declaring an array of controls

In earlier versions of Visual Basic arrays of controls could be created at design time. With Visual Basic .NET an array of controls must be declared in code. This is extacly the same as the declaration of other arrays like arrays of Integers or arrays of Strings. For example:

```
Dim Rocket(9) As PictureBox ' declares an array of ten picture boxes
Dim Score(5) As Integer ' declares an array of five integers
Dim RallyCar(4) As PictureBox ' declares an array of five picture boxes
Dim Selector(7) As Button ' declares an array of eight buttons
Dim Player(3) As String ' declares an array of four strings
```

Assigning values to the elements

Once the array has been declared its elements can then be assigned values. If, for example, you have declared an array of picture boxes, you will need to have an equal number of picture boxes on the form that you have prepared as values. You could assign them one at a time:

```
RallyCar(0) = PictureBox1
RallyCar(1) = PictureBox2
RallyCar(2) = PictureBox3
RallyCar(3) = PictureBox4
RallyCar(4) = PictureBox5
```

But more typically a **loop** would be used to make the assignments. To isolate exactly which picture boxes you want to assign they need to be made identifiable. The multi-purpose **Tag property** can be used for this. In the above example the Tag property of the picture box controls could be given the value 'car'.

The following shows how each of the 'cars' can be assigned in a Form Load procedure. This procedure uses a **For Each** loop:

```
Private Sub Form1_Load(ByVal sender As Object, ByVal e As System.EventArgs) _
Handles MyBase.Load
    Dim obj As Object, I As Integer = 0
    For Each obj In Me.Controls ' all controls on the form
        ' only those picture boxes tagged with "car"
        If TypeOf obj Is PictureBox AndAlso obj.Tag = "car" Then
            RallyCar(I) = obj ' assign this picturebox to an element of the array
            I += 1 ' increase I by 1 ready for the next assignment
        End If
    Next obj
End Sub
```

Of course if five elements were declared in the array there would also need to be five picture boxes tagged "car" on the form.

Program example: Enemy attack

Create a new Windows application with the name *Enemy attack*.

Create the interface

■   Add one picture box and one timer to a form.

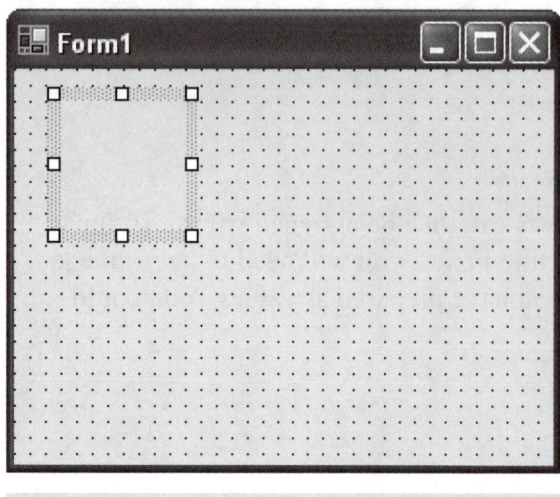

- Set the following properties:

Form1

BackColor	Black
Text	Enemy attack

PictureBox1

Image	Spaceship south.bmp
SizeMode	AutoSize
Tag	enemy

Timer1

Name	tmrMove
Enabled	True

- Copy and paste the picture boxes until you have a total of six.

Write the code and add comments

- Declare an array of picture boxes at form level.

```
Dim Enemy(5) As PictureBox ' an array of 6 picture boxes
```

- During the loading of the form the tagged picture boxes are assigned into the array. All the controls on the form are checked using a **For Each** loop.

```
Private Sub Form1_Load(ByVal sender As Object, ByVal e As System.EventArgs) _
Handles MyBase.Load
    Dim obj As Object, I As Integer = 0
    For Each obj In Me.Controls ' all controls on the form
        ' only those picture boxes tagged with "enemy"
        If TypeOf obj Is PictureBox AndAlso obj.Tag = "enemy" Then
            Enemy(I) = obj ' assign this picturebox to an element of the array
            I += 1 ' increase I by 1 ready for the next assignment
        End If
    Next obj
End Sub
```

- With each tick of the timer a random enemy picture box is moved.

```
Private Sub tmrMove_Tick(ByVal sender As System.Object, ByVal e As _
System.EventArgs) Handles tmrMove.Tick
    Randomize()
    Dim WhichEnemy As Integer = Int(Rnd() * 6) ' random number 0-5
    Enemy(WhichEnemy).Top += 4 ' move 4 pixels down
    If Enemy(WhichEnemy).Top > Me.Height Then ' gone off bottom of form
        Enemy(WhichEnemy).Top = -Enemy(WhichEnemy).Height ' send to top of form
    End If
End Sub
```

Try it out

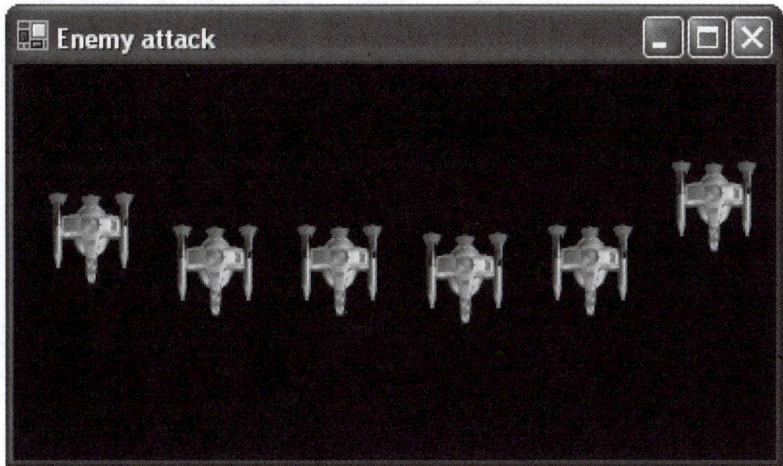

Enemy attack – points to note

- An **array** is a set of objects. Each object has the same **name** but has a unique **index**. When array is declared it is given a name, its largest index and the **class** it comes from.

```
Dim Enemy(5) As PictureBox ' an array of 6 picture boxes
```

- The array is declared at **form level** as it is used in more than one procedure.

- A **For Each** loop cycles through all the objects in a collection. If the collection is **Me.Controls** then the loop will cycle through all the controls on a form.

```
For Each obj In Me.Controls ' all controls on the form

Next obj
```

All that needs to be done inside the loop is to find the particular controls you are looking for. In Enemy attack we are looking for picture boxes that have a particular Tag.

```
If TypeOf obj Is PictureBox AndAlso obj.Tag = "enemy" Then
    Enemy(I) = obj ' assign this picturebox to an element of the array
    I += 1 ' increase I by 1 ready for the next assignment
End If
```

- There is a subtle difference between using

```
If TypeOf obj Is PictureBox AndAlso obj.Tag = "enemy" Then
```

as opposed to using

```
If TypeOf obj Is PictureBox And obj.Tag = "enemy" Then
```

In the first condition, if the object is not a picture box, the Tag will not even be looked at. In the second condition both the type of object and the Tag are looked at whether or not the object is a picture box.

- Declaring a variable with the keyword **Static** in a procedure ensures the value of the variable is 'remembered' the next time the procedure runs, whereas declaring a variable with **Dim** means the variable makes a 'fresh' start.

- The **Randomize** statement ensures that you don't get the same sequence of random numbers.

- The function **Rnd** produces a random number greater than 0 and less than 1. Rnd * 6 produces a random number greater than 0 and less than 6. The **Int** function discards the decimal part. So the set of numbers possible from the expression

```
Int(Rnd() * 6)
```
is 0, 1, 2, 3, 4, 5.

- To move the chosen array element down the form the Top property has to be increased:

```
Enemy(WhichEnemy).Top += 4 ' move 4 pixels down
```

- When the following assignment is made the picture box is located such that the bottom of it is sitting on the top border of the form.

```
Enemy(WhichEnemy).Top = -Enemy(WhichEnemy).Height ' send to top of form
```

1   Make the declaration for an array of eight picture boxes with the name RallyCar.

2   What is the first index of all arrays?

3   What is the advantage of using arrays in applications where a group of similarly functioning objects is required?

4   Why is a loop the most efficient way of assigning to an array?

5   What collection is Me.Controls?

6   Why was the array declared outside the two procedures (at form level)?

7   In the following line of code a picture box that is correctly tagged is being looked for:

```
If TypeOf obj Is PictureBox AndAlso obj.Tag = "enemy" Then
```

Suppose the object found in this instance was a label, would the Tag be checked?

8   What is the possible set of Integers obtained from the expression

```
Int(Rnd() * 10)
```

9   Why is the variable WhichEnemy declared with Dim rather than Static?

10 ⌨ As well as choosing a random spaceship, choose a random number of pixels it is to move. For example from 4 to 8 pixels.

Program example: Double trouble

Create a new Windows application with the name *Double trouble*.

Create the interface

■   Add two picture boxes and a timer to the form.

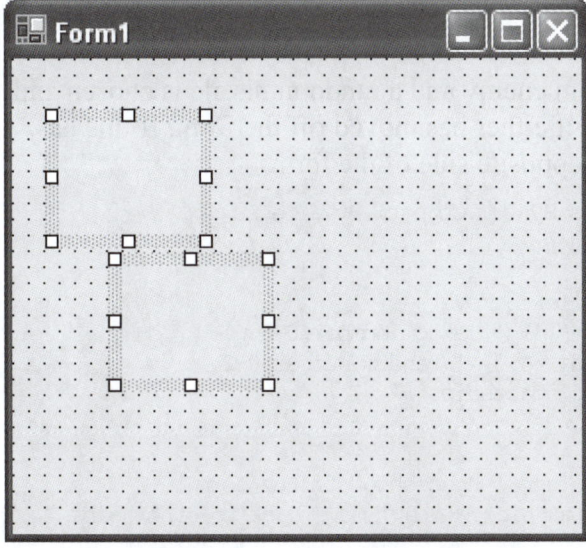

🕚 Timer1

■ Set the following properties:

Form1

BackColor	Black
Text	Double trouble

Timer1

Name	tmrMove
Enabled	True
Interval	15

PictureBox1

Image	Spaceship east.bmp
SizeMode	AutoSize
Tag	spaceship

PictureBox2

Image	Missile east.bmp
SizeMode	AutoSize
Tag	missile

■ Copy and paste the picture boxes until you have four spaceships and three missiles.

Write the code and add comments

■ Two arrays of picture boxes are declared at form level: one array for the spaceships, one array for the missiles.

```
Dim Enemy(3) As PictureBox ' an array of 4 picture boxes
Dim Missile(2) As PictureBox ' an array of 3 picture boxes
```

■ The **form load** procedure checks through all the controls on the form, finds the picture boxes, then assigns those tagged with "spaceship" to the enemy array and those tagged with "missile" to the missile array.

```
Private Sub Form1_Load(ByVal sender As Object, ByVal e As System.EventArgs) _
Handles MyBase.Load
    Dim obj As Object
    Dim I As Integer = 0, J As Integer = 0
    For Each obj In Me.Controls ' all controls on the form
        If TypeOf obj Is PictureBox Then ' only check for picture boxes
            If obj.Tag = "spaceship" Then
                Enemy(I) = obj ' add this object to the Enemy array
                I += 1 ' advance ready for next element
            ElseIf obj.Tag = "missile" Then
                Missile(J) = obj ' add this object to the Missile array
                J += 1 ' advance ready for next element
            End If
        End If
    Next obj
End Sub
```

■ With each tick of the timer a random enemy and a random missile is chosen and moved. The procedure also checks if either has moved off the form. If this has happened the control is put on the opposite side of the form.

```
Private Sub tmrMove_Tick(ByVal sender As System.Object, ByVal e As _
System.EventArgs) Handles tmrMove.Tick
    Randomize()
    ' choose a random spaceship and missile to move
    Dim WhichShip As Integer = Int(Rnd() * 4) ' random number 0-3
    Dim WhichMissile As Integer = Int(Rnd() * 3) ' random number 0-2
    ' missiles will move twice as fast as spaceships
    Enemy(WhichShip).Left += 1
    Missile(WhichMissile).Left += 2
    If Enemy(WhichShip).Left >= Me.Width Then ' spaceship off the form?
        Enemy(WhichShip).Left = -Enemy(WhichShip).Width ' move back to other side
    End If
    If Missile(WhichMissile).Left >= Me.Width Then ' missile off the form?
        ' move back to other side
        Missile(WhichMissile).Left = -Missile(WhichMissile).Width
    End If
End Sub
```

Try it out

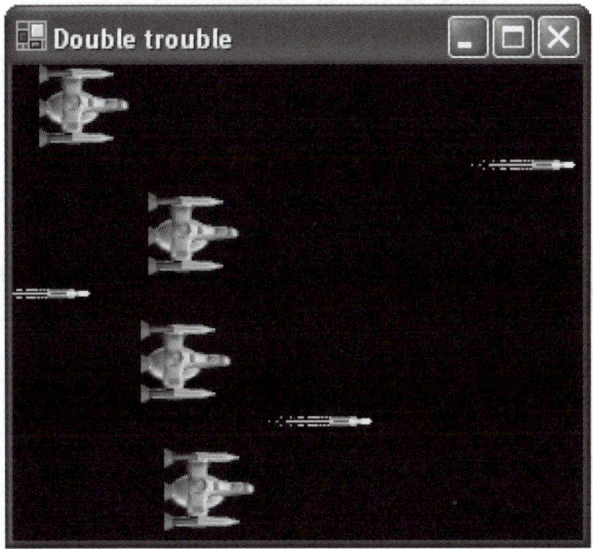

Double trouble – points to note

- When a value is assigned to a **variable** they must both belong to the same class. For example, if a variable is declared as an Integer then only an Integer should be assigned to it. Similarly, if a variable is declared a PictureBox then only a PictureBox should be assigned to it. That is why the following condition is used. **TypeOf** is checking what **class** the object is from:

  ```
  If TypeOf obj Is PictureBox Then ' only check for picture boxes
  ```

- The **Object class** is an exception to the above rule. It is the 'everything' class. A value belonging to any other class can be assigned to a variable declared Object. So when a **For Each** loop checks through all the controls on a form it is likely that several different classes will be encountered. For that reason the variable used in the loop must be declared Object.

- When there is to be two distinct arrays of picture boxes they have to tagged accordingly. In this case some are tagged "spaceship" and some are tagged "missile".

- All arrays are **zero based**. This means the first index is zero.

- The largest index is used in each array declaration:

  ```
  Dim Enemy(3) As PictureBox ' an array of 4 picture boxes
  Dim Missile(2) As PictureBox ' an array of 3 picture boxes
  ```

- Because two arrays are to be populated in the **Form Load** procedure two Integer variables have to be declared and set to 0.

  ```
  Dim I As Integer = 0, J As Integer = 0
  ```

- Likewise, when one of the elements is **randomly** selected from each of the arrays, two separate Integer variables are used:

  ```
  Dim WhichShip As Integer = Int(Rnd() * 4) ' random number 0-3
  Dim WhichMissile As Integer = Int(Rnd() * 3) ' random number 0-2
  ```

- There are two ways of making an object, controlled by a timer, move faster. Increase the number of pixels moved with each tick or decrease the value of the Interval property of the timer.

- A standard technique is used to check if a control has moved off the form:

```
If Enemy(WhichShip).Left >= Me.Width Then ' spaceship off the form?
    Enemy(WhichShip).Left = -Enemy(WhichShip).Width ' move back to other side
End If
```

Double trouble – check what you have learnt

1   In the following For Each loop

```
For Each obj In Me.Controls
```

why is the variable obj declared Object?

2   Why do you suppose the Tag property has been made to belong to the Object class?

3   Why are the picture box arrays declared at form level?

4   What is meant by the term zero-based?

5   Why are the PictureBox arrays populated in the Form Load procedure and not in some other procedure?

6   What range of values is possible with the following expression?

```
Int(Rnd() * 4)
```

7   If we had twenty enemy spaceships instead of four, what changes would be required to the code?

8   Why is the variable J increased by 1 each time a correctly tagged picture box is found in the loop?

```
J += 1
```

9   What are the two ways of making a moving object slow down?

10 Create an application that has a number of rally cars moving diagonally across the form. Both the Left and Top properties would have to change to achieve this.

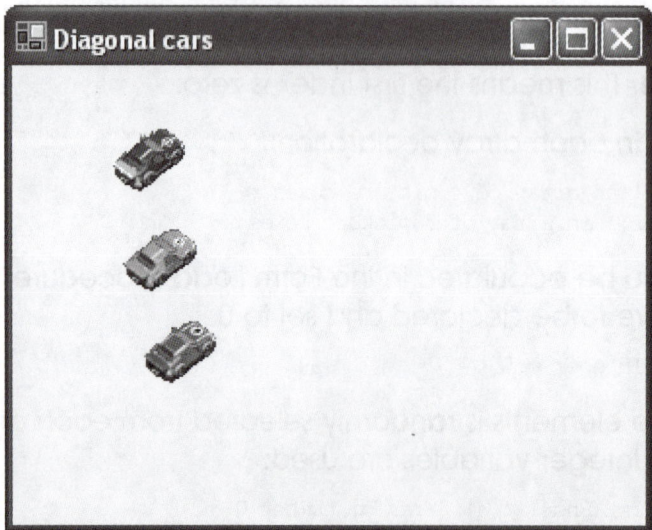

Chapter 9

I see the Earth move

It's all relative

Is the car moving on a stationary road, or is the road moving under a stationary car? We have seen how to make objects move across a form by changing their Location property. A method that can be more effective involves making changes to the **BackgroundImage** property of a form giving an object the illusion of movement.

Scrolling a single image

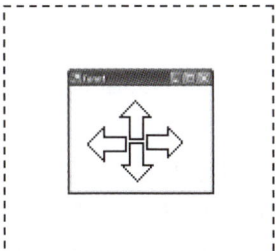

A large single image (considerably larger than the form) can be used to provide changing selections for the BackgroundImage. This would give the illusion that an object is roaming about a terrain that extends beyond the bounds of the form in all directions.

Rotating a series of images

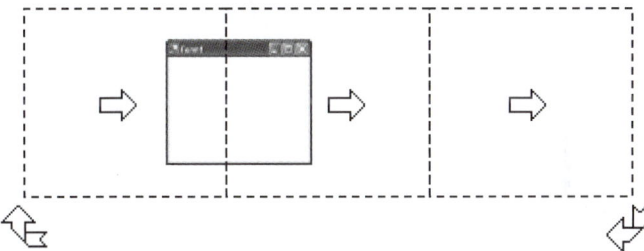

A continuous rotation of a series of images, horizontally or vertically, can provide an endless background for the journey of an object. Again, the illusion created is that of a moving object passing through a changing terrain. It is important that the background appears to be continuous; so the images have to be selected (or created) with seamless joins.

In the cityscape scene below there are two rotating images. The right hand side of one of the images matches the left hand side of the other and vice versa.

The Formbackground.vb module

Each of the following example applications makes use of the ready-made code module *Formbackground.vb* (see Appendix 1). It contains the procedures *ScrollBackground* and *RotateBackground*. These procedures allow you to achieve the previously described effects with ease. The module also contains a public enumeration *WhichWay* to provide a simple method of stating four directions.

ScrollBackground

```
ScrollBackground(ByVal WhichForm As Form, ByVal InputBitmap As Bitmap, ByVal _
PixelInc As Integer, ByVal Direction As WhichWay)
```

The arguments of *ScrollBackground* are the form being used, the bitmap that is the background image, how many pixels the background is to move and the direction it is to move.

RotateBackground

```
RotateBackground(ByVal WhichForm As Form, ByVal InputBitmapArray() As Bitmap, _
ByVal PixelInc As Integer, ByVal Direction As WhichWay)
```

The arguments of *RotateBackground* are the form being used, the array of bitmaps that is to form the background image, how many pixels the background is to move and the direction it is to move.

Program example: Helicopter patrol

Create a new Windows application with the name *Helicopter patrol*.

Create the interface

- Add two picture boxes, two timers and an image list to the form.

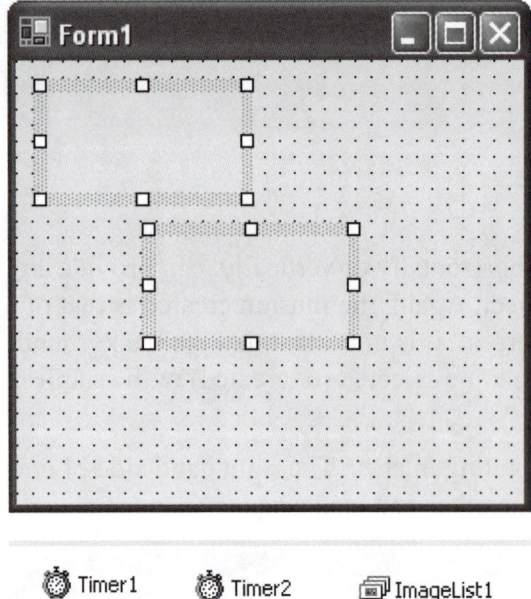

- Set the following properties:

Form1

FormBorderStyle	FixedSingle
KeyPreview	True
MaximizeBox	False
Text	Helicopter patrol

PictureBox1

Name	picHeli
BackColor	Transparent
Image	Helicopter0.gif
SizeMode	AutoSize

PictureBox2

Image	bwaerial.jpg
Tag	0
Visible	False

ImageList1

Name	imlHeli
Images	(see below)
ImageSize	52, 59

Timer1

Name	tmrHeli
Enabled	True
Interval	50

Timer2

Name	tmrMove
Enabled	True
Interval	50

- Images for the image list should be added in the order *Helicopter0.gif*,
  Helicopter1.gif then *Helicopter2.gif*. Always set the ImageSize property before
  adding images to the collection.

Write the code and add comments

- From the Project menu choose Add Existing Item. Add the module
  FormBackground.vb found in the *Modules* folder of the accompanying CD.

- There is only one small array to be declared at form level.

```
Dim objBit(1) As Bitmap ' an array of two bitmaps
```

- The array is populated (**instantiated**) with the images in the two picture boxes.

```
Private Sub Form1_Load(ByVal sender As Object, ByVal e As System.EventArgs) _
Handles MyBase.Load
    ' load images into the bitmap array
    objBit(0) = PictureBox2.Image
    objBit(1) = PictureBox2.Image
End Sub
```

- The procedure used to rotate the background is called on each tick of the timer.

```
Private Sub tmrMove_Tick(ByVal sender As System.Object, ByVal e As _
System.EventArgs) Handles tmrMove.Tick
    RotateBackground(Me, objBit, 2, WhichWay.Down) ' rotate backgroundimage
End Sub
```

- The helicopter has three bitmaps to produce its animation.

```
Private Sub tmrHeli_Tick(ByVal sender As System.Object, ByVal e As _
System.EventArgs) Handles tmrHeli.Tick
    Static Frame As Integer = 0
    Frame = (Frame + 1) Mod 3 ' advance to next frame
    picHeli.Image = imlHeli.Images.Item(Frame) ' load new image
End Sub
```

- The left and right cursor keys move the helicopter across the form.

```
Private Sub Form1_KeyDown(ByVal sender As Object, ByVal e As _
System.Windows.Forms.KeyEventArgs) Handles MyBase.KeyDown
    ' move the helicopter to the left or right
    If e.KeyCode = Keys.Left Then
        picHeli.Left -= 4
    ElseIf e.KeyCode = Keys.Right Then
        picHeli.Left += 4
    End If
End Sub
```

Try it out

Helicopter patrol – points to note

- The **bitmap** used for the background matches both top and bottom. For this type of image rotation an array of at least two bitmaps is needed.

- The size of the bitmap prevents its use in an image list. The maximum **ImageSize** for an image list is 256, 256. So the bitmap was put into a picture box with its Visible property set to *False*.

- Because the bitmap array has only two elements they can be assigned in two statements.

```
objBit(0) = PictureBox2.Image
objBit(1) = PictureBox2.Image
```

- The application of the RotateBackground procedure is a simple single line of code. The general concept of its inner workings should be understood. Each time the procedure is called a composite bitmap is created from the two current bitmaps in the rotation. Parts of each are sliced and joined to make up a single BackgroundImage for the form.

- The module FormBackground.vb has an enumeration and two procedures. All are declared **Public**. This means that when the module is added to a project the enumeration and the procedures are available to all procedures in all forms.

- One of the arguments of RotateBackground is an array of bitmaps. Just the name of the array is all that needs to be entered:

```
RotateBackground(Me, objBit, 2, WhichWay.Down)
```

- A picture box was used for the helicopter. The **transparent** background of its Image lets us look through to the image on the form.

- The cycling of images from an image list has become a standard method in producing **animation**:

```
Static Frame As Integer = 0
Frame = (Frame + 1) Mod 3 ' advance to next frame
```

- Likewise the keyboard control of an object on a form:

```
If e.KeyCode = Keys.Left Then
    picHeli.Left -= 4
ElseIf e.KeyCode = Keys.Right Then
    picHeli.Left += 4
End If
```

Because only two keys are being used **two way branching** was used instead of **multiple branching**.

Helicopter patrol – check what you have learnt

1   What must be true of images that are selected or created for a rotating background?

2   If there had been a larger number of images for the array, a For Each loop in Form Load is a better strategy. Write the code for this presuming the picture boxes were tagged 0,1, 2 etc.

3   Where possible, procedures should be kept as small as possible. What programming features have been used in this example to achieve this goal?

4   How would the call of the *ScrollBackground* procedure read if the background image is coming from *objBit*, each unit of movement is 4 pixels and the background is to move up.

5   Extend your answer to question 4 by writing the multiple branching required for a Form KeyDown procedure.

6   If a timer with an Interval of 100 has a background moving 4 pixels to the left with every tick, how many pixels/second and in which direction does a stationary object appear to be moving?

7   Show how the Static declared variable Frame gets its new value when its old value is 2.

8   Why are the contents of a module like *Formbackground.vb* declared Public?

9   Moving the background is not enough to give the impression of the object moving. What else should be put in place for the object?

10 Make a modification/extension of *Leap and land*. Instead of a moving character have the background move. Similarly have a random length platform cycle around the form at differing random speeds. The character could be rewarded for being able to successfully leap onto the moving platform (jewel graphics are provided). The whole time the character would be continuing to walk.

Program example: Endless road

Create a new Windows application with the name *Endless road*.

Create the interface

■ Add four picture boxes, six labels, two timers and an image list to the form.

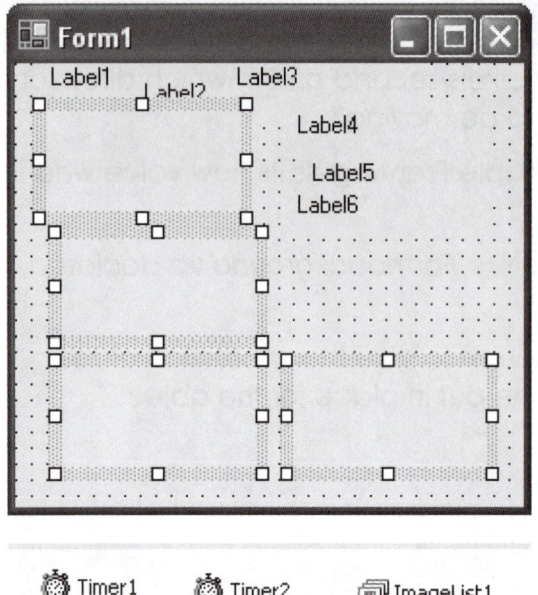

 Timer1   Timer2   ImageList1

- Set the following properties:

Form1

FormBorderStyle	FixedSingle
KeyPreview	True
MaximizeBox	False
Text	Endless road

PictureBox1

Name	picCar
BackColor	Transparent
Image	red rally car 8.gif
SizeMode	AutoSize

Label1

BackColor	Black
BorderStyle	Fixed3D
Font	MS Sans Serif Bold 8 points
ForeColor	White
Text	Time
TextAlign	MiddleCenter

Label2

BackColor	Black
BorderStyle	Fixed3D
Font	MS Sans Serif Bold 8 points
ForeColor	White
Text	Penalties
TextAlign	MiddleCenter

Label3

Name	lblMin
BackColor	Black
BorderStyle	Fixed3D
Font	MS Sans Serif Bold 12 points
ForeColor	White
Text	0
TextAlign	MiddleCenter

Label4

Name	lblSec
BackColor	Black
BorderStyle	Fixed3D
Font	MS Sans Serif Bold 12 points
ForeColor	White
Text	0
TextAlign	MiddleCenter

Label5

Name	lblTenths
BackColor	Black
BorderStyle	Fixed3D
Font	MS Sans Serif Bold 12 points
ForeColor	White
Text	0
TextAlign	MiddleCenter

Label6

Name	lblPenalty
BackColor	Black
BorderStyle	Fixed3D
Font	MS Sans Serif Bold 12 points
ForeColor	White
Text	0
TextAlign	MiddleCenter

PictureBox2

Image	roadseq0.bmp
Visible	False

PictureBox3

Image	roadseq1.bmp
Visible	False

PictureBox4

Image	roadseq2.bmp
Visible	False

ImageList1

Name	imlCars
Images	(see below)
ImageSize	96, 96

Timer1

Name	tmrRotate
Enabled	True
Interval	100

Timer2

Name	tmrStopwatch
Enabled	True
Interval	100

- Images for the image list should be added in the order *red rally car 0.gif*, *red rally car 1.gif, red rally car 2.gif … red rally car 16.gif*. The images represent the car pointing in different directions. Each successive image has a rotational difference of 11.25°. Thank you to Reiner Prokein for all the digital artwork.

Write the code and add comments

- From the Project menu choose Add Existing Item. Add the module *FormBackground.vb* found in the *Modules* folder of the accompanying CD. This module contains the procedure *RotateBackground* and the **enumeration** *WhichWay*.

- The car will be rotating through various angles so trigonometry functions are needed. These are contained in the imported namespace *System.Math*. *System.Math* has a wide variety of Mathematical functions as well as the constants PI and e.

```
Imports System.Math
```

- Declare the following **form level** variables

```
Dim objBack(2) As Bitmap ' array of 3 bitmaps for the background
Dim WhichCar As Integer = 8 ' current car image
Dim X0, Y0 As Integer ' coordinates of the centre of the car picture box
Dim L As Integer ' centre of car to front bumper
Const PIXELMOVE As Integer = 4 ' number of pixels to rotate each tick
```

- There are only three elements in the Bitmap array so it is easy to load them with assignment statements. This procedure also calculates the Y coordinate of the center of the car and L the distance of the center to the front bumper.

```
Private Sub Form1_Load(ByVal sender As Object, ByVal e As System.EventArgs) _
Handles MyBase.Load
    objBack(0) = PictureBox1.Image
    objBack(1) = PictureBox2.Image
    objBack(2) = PictureBox3.Image
    Y0 = picCar.Top + picCar.Height / 2
    L = picCar.Height / 2 - 10
End Sub
```

- This procedure rotates the three bitmaps that make up the form's background, calculates the position of the centre of the front bumper to check if it is off the road. The calculation depends on the functions Sin and Cos and the constant PI of *System.Math*.

```
Private Sub tmrRotate_Tick(ByVal sender As System.Object, ByVal e As _
System.EventArgs) Handles tmrRotate.Tick
    Dim X1, Y1 As Integer ' coordinates of the centre of the front bumper
    RotateBackground(Me, objBack, PIXELMOVE, WhichWay.Down)
    Dim bm As Bitmap = Me.BackgroundImage ' the image was changed on the last line
    picCar.Left += PIXELMOVE * Cos(11.25 * WhichCar * PI / 180)
    X0 = picCar.Left + picCar.Width / 2 ' X coord. of centre of car
    ' X coord. of centre of front bumper
    X1 = X0 + L * Cos(11.25 * WhichCar * PI / 180)
    ' Y coord. of centre of front bumper
    Y1 = Y0 - L * Sin(11.25 * WhichCar * PI / 180)
    ' check if car is off form or front bumper is in the rough
    If picCar.Left <= 0 Or picCar.Left + picCar.Width >= Me.Width Then ' off form
        lblPenalty.Text += 2 ' gain a double penalty
    ElseIf bm.GetPixel(X1, Y1).R = 186 And bm.GetPixel(X1, Y1).G = 186 And _
    bm.GetPixel(X1, Y1).B = 116 Then  ' in the rough
        lblPenalty.Text += 1 ' gain a single penalty
    End If
End Sub
```

- The cursor keys control the steering, acceleration and braking of the car. For the steering we must make certain that WhichCar stays in the 0 to 16 range. When accelerating there would be a problem if the Interval of the timer became too small. So the limit was set at 10.

```
Private Sub Form1_KeyDown(ByVal sender As Object, ByVal e As _
System.Windows.Forms.KeyEventArgs) Handles MyBase.KeyDown
    Select Case e.KeyCode
        Case Keys.Right ' turn right
            If WhichCar > 0 Then
                WhichCar -= 1
                picCar.Image = imlCars.Images.Item(WhichCar)
            End If
        Case Keys.Left ' turn left
            If WhichCar < 16 Then
                WhichCar += 1
                picCar.Image = imlCars.Images.Item(WhichCar)
            End If
        Case Keys.Up ' accelerate
            If tmrRotate.Interval > 10 Then
                tmrRotate.Interval -= 5
            End If
        Case Keys.Down ' brake
            tmrRotate.Interval += 5
    End Select
End Sub
```

- Each tick of this timer is one tenth of a second.

```
Private Sub tmrStopwatch_Tick(ByVal sender As System.Object, ByVal e As _
System.EventArgs) Handles tmrStopwatch.Tick
    lblTenths.Text += 1
End Sub
```

- If ten tenths is reached the seconds advance by one. When that happens the tenths label is returned to 0.

```
Private Sub lblTenths_TextChanged(ByVal sender As Object, ByVal e As _
System.EventArgs) Handles lblTenths.TextChanged
    If lblTenths.Text = 10 Then ' 10 tenths, advance to next second
        lblSec.Text += 1
        lblTenths.Text = 0
    End If
End Sub
```

- If sixty seconds is reached the minutes advance by one. When the minutes increase by 1 the seconds label must return to 0.

```
Private Sub lblSec_TextChanged(ByVal sender As Object, _
ByVal e As System.EventArgs) Handles lblSec.TextChanged
    If lblSec.Text = 60 Then ' 60 seconds, advance to next minute
        lblMin.Text += 1
        lblSec.Text = 0
    End If
End Sub
```

Try it out

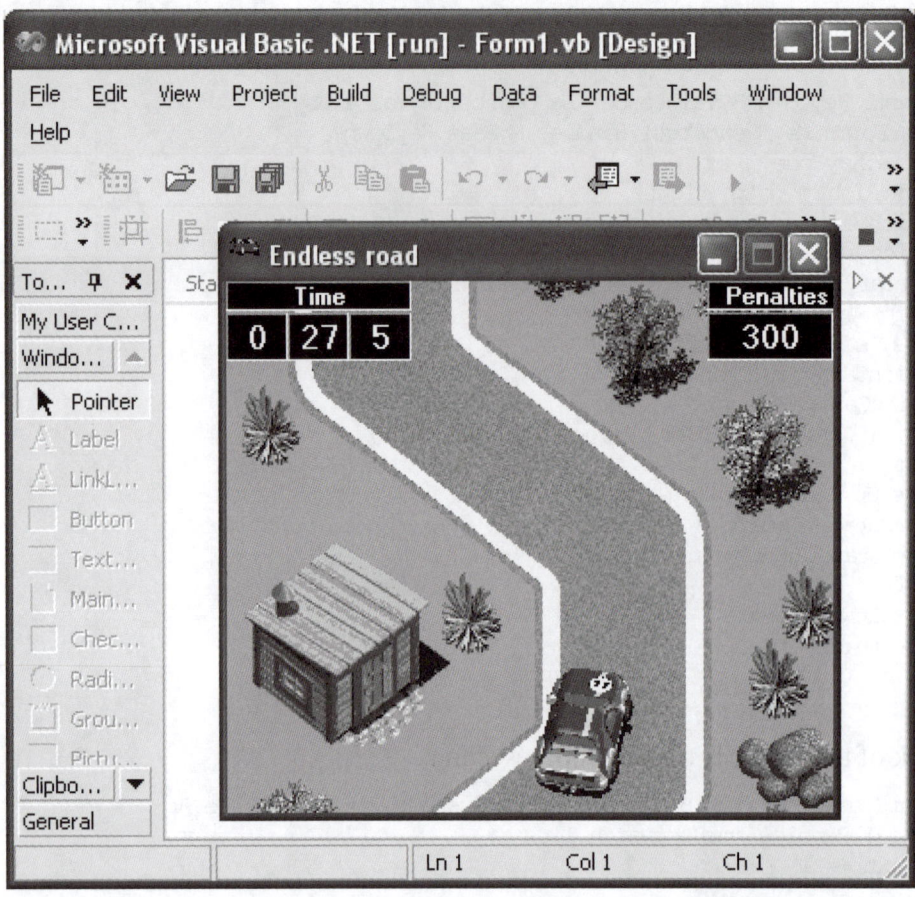

Endless road – points to note

- Like Helicopter patrol the bitmaps for the BackgroundImage are too large for an image list. They have been loaded into separate picture boxes that have their **Visible** property set to *False*.

- With only three bitmaps for the background it is still simpler to assign the elements of the array one by one instead of using a **For Each** loop in Form Load.

```
objBack(0) = New Bitmap(PictureBox1.Image)
objBack(1) = New Bitmap(PictureBox2.Image)
objBack(2) = New Bitmap(PictureBox3.Image)
```

- The use of the trigonometric functions **Sin** and **Cos** and the constant **PI** is the reason for the **Imports** statement at the top of the code.

```
Imports System.Math
```

System.Math also contains the functions **Abs, Log, Round, Sqrt, Tan** and many others.

- The car can be steered through a full 180°. The sixteen images of the car mean that there is an angle of 11.25° between each successive image. Multiples of this angle are used to calculate how far to the left or right the car should move with each tick of the timer:

```
picCar.Left += PIXELMOVE * Cos(11.25 * WhichCar * PI / 180)
```

  Note that the angle in degrees must be converted to **radians** for the Cos function, hence multiplying by Pi and dividing by 180.

- *tmrRotate_Tick* does have some code that needs to be studied closely. The inclusion of **comments** in the code always gives helpful assistance.

- Some **Trigonometry** is used to calculate the coordinates of the centre of the front bumper.

```
' X coord. of centre of front bumper
X1 = X0 + L * Cos(11.25 * WhichCar * PI / 180)
' Y coord. of centre of front bumper
Y1 = Y0 - L * Sin(11.25 * WhichCar * PI / 180)
```

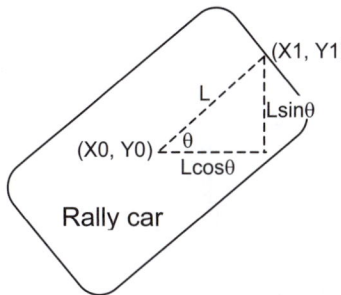

- The **GetPixel** method determines the colour of a pixel in a bitmap when the coordinates are given. It returns the **RGB** coding of the colour. In Endless road the 'rough' has the colour 186, 186, 116.

```
ElseIf bm.GetPixel(X1, Y1).R = 186 And bm.GetPixel(X1, Y1).G = 186 And _
bm.GetPixel(X1, Y1).B = 116 Then
```

- The Form **Keydown** event handler controls the steering, accelerating and braking. To increase the speed of the car the Interval of the timer must be decreased (but no less than 10):

```
If tmrRotate.Interval > 10 Then
    tmrRotate.Interval -= 5
End If
```

  To decrease the speed increase the Interval of the timer:

```
tmrRotate.Interval += 5
```

- The **TextChanged** event on the timing labels has each operating like a digital stopwatch.

```
If lblTenths.Text = 10 Then ' 10 tenths, advance to next second
    lblSec.Text += 1
    lblTenths.Text = 0
End If

If lblSec.Text = 60 Then ' 60 seconds, advance to next minute
    lblMin.Text += 1
    lblSec.Text = 0
End If
```

Endless road – check what you have learnt

1   What functions and constant from *System.Math* are used in this example?

2   Show how an angle of 36° can be converted into radians.

3   How was the rotational angle of 11.25° arrived at?

4   Which of the trigonometric functions is used for the calculation of the horizontal movement of the car?

5   Find out what each of the functions Abs, Log, Round, and Sqrt calculate.

6   From the image list, which of the images points

   a   left   b   right   c   straight up

7   The following is the code from a small application. The picture box has a colourful image of a tree. Explain what the application does.

```
Dim X, Y As Integer

Private Sub picTree_Click(ByVal sender As System.Object, ByVal e As _
System.EventArgs) Handles picTree.Click
    Dim bm As Bitmap = picTree.Image
    lblRed.Text = bm.GetPixel(X, Y).R
    lblGreen.Text = bm.GetPixel(X, Y).G
    lblBlue.Text = bm.GetPixel(X, Y).B
End Sub

Private Sub picTree_MouseMove(ByVal sender As Object, ByVal e As _
System.Windows.Forms.MouseEventArgs) Handles picTree.MouseMove
    X = e.X
    Y = e.Y
End Sub
```

8   What is this part of a condition checking?

```
picCar.Left + picCar.Width >= Me.Width
```

9   Each of the three backgrounds has a height of 384 pixels. How many laps have been completed when the background has moved 5,760 pixels?

10 To make the game a real test of skill there needs to be a start and a finish, a set number of laps. There will need to be a way of starting the time trial. At the finish the penalties could be converted into a time penalty.

Chapter 10

Telephones and tophats

Board games

Board games have three essential components:

- **Markers** – representing each of the players.
- **Board squares** – representing locations on which the players can land. It is on these squares that certain events of fortune or misfortune can occur.
- **Dice** – initiating the random moves of the players from one board square to another.

Markers

In a board game with four players it is possible to have a square occupied by any one of sixteen combinations, ranging from empty to having all four.

Each combination can be represented by a **binary number**. Here is a quick comparison of binary and decimal numbers:

Binary numbers	Decimal numbers
Use only digits 0 and 1	Use digits 0, 1, 2, 3, 4, 5, 6, 7, 8, 9
Place values are powers of 2	Place values are powers of 10
1, 2, 4, 8, 16, ...	1, 10, 100, 1000, 10000, ...
Are good for representing on-off, yes-no or true-false situations.	Are the most common way of counting in everyday situations.

For the markers the presence of a marker will be a 1 and its absence a 0. The place values we will use are: telephone 1, boot 2, tophat 4 and ocean liner 8. So the diagrams above can be represented by the binary numbers 0000, 0001, 0010, 0011, ... 1111 or in decimal, 0, 1, 2, 3, ... 15.

For example, adding the tophat to a square would mean adding 4, removing a tophat from a square would mean subtracting 4.

$$2 + 4 = 6$$
$$0010 + 0100 = 0110$$

$$13 - 4 = 9$$
$$1101 - 0100 = 1001$$

Should there be only three markers there would only be eight (2^3) combinations. With five markers there would be thirty-two (2^5) combinations.

With four markers the sixteen images (0000 to 1111) can be loaded into an image list control. The indexes of the images are 0 to 15.

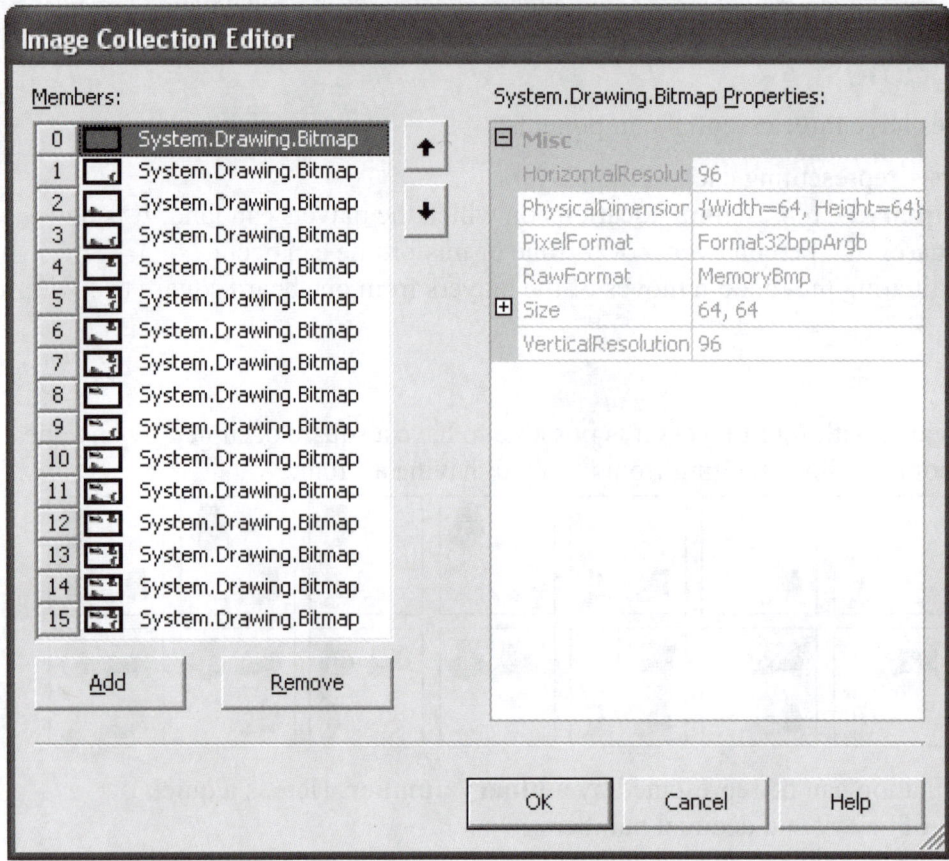

Board squares

The BoardSquare class

BoardSquare is a **subclass** of PictureBox that has been created for the applications of this book (see Appendix 2). It has three additional properties:

- **SquareIndex** – an Integer to identify each control when being placed into an array.
- **GotoSquare** – an Integer to identify a square number a player should move on to.
- **Markers** – an Integer to indicate which players have markers on this square.

Dice and other random number generators

Throughout history man has used devices like coins, dice and playing cards to generate randomness in games. In Egypt dice have been uncovered in archaeological excavations that date back to 6000 BC. Four-suited decks of cards evolved in the Muslim world and were imported into Europe in the fourteenth century.

In Visual Basic the **Rnd** function returns a value less than 1, but greater than or equal to 0. This can be represented by a number line graph:

To generate whole numbers for coins, dice or cards the following general formula can be used:

```
Int(Rnd() * (upper - lower + 1))  + lower
```

Examples:

To generate random numbers from 1 to 6, upper = 6, lower = 1, use the formula

```
Int(Rnd() * 6)  + 1
```

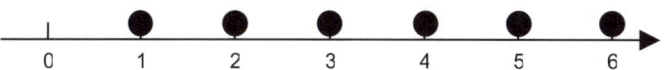

To generate random numbers from 0 to 51, upper = 51, lower = 0, use the formula

```
Int(Rnd() * 52)
```

Simulating dice

To simulate the rolling of a dice we not only need a method to generate random numbers, but also images of the die faces.

These images can be loaded into an image list control giving them indexes 0 to 5:

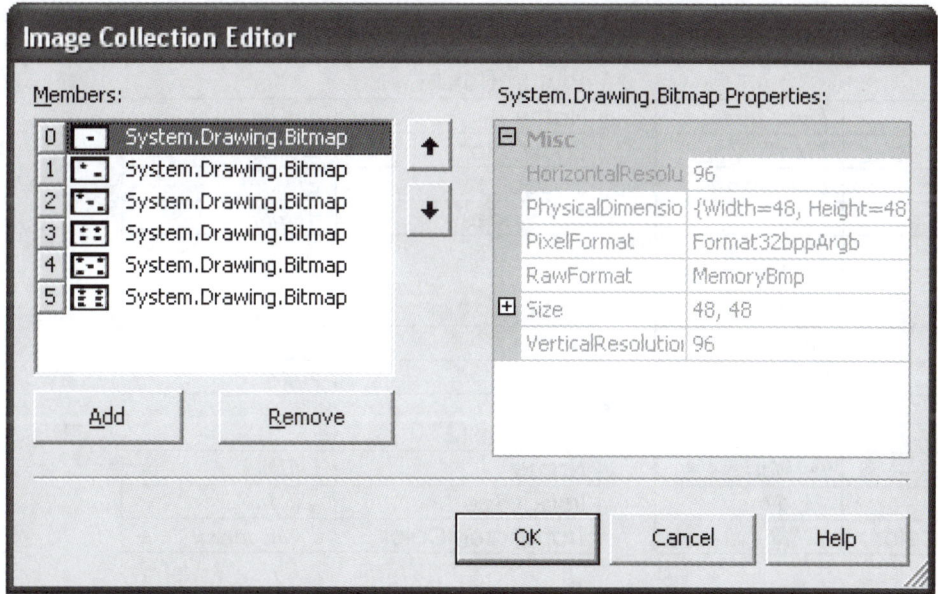

Dice that roll

Static images of dice do not give the impression of a 'roll'. Nor do they project a sense of randomness. Allowing a dice to progress through a small random sequence while rotating is a more impressive simulation.

The programming example that follows uses:

- An **image list** to hold the dice images
- A **timer** to progress through a sequence of images
- A **module** containing a **function** to rotate an image
- A **module** containing a **procedure** to keep an image centred

Program example: Power of 2

Create a new Windows application with the name *Power of 2*.

Create the interface

- Add thirteen board squares, a picture box, a button, two timers and two image lists to the form.

- Immediately rename BoardSquare13 to BoardSquare0. This will make the other board square property settings a little easier to follow.

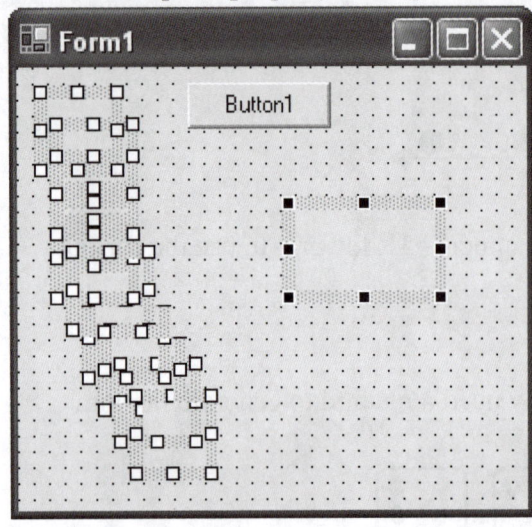

🕐 Timer1   🕐 Timer2   🖼 ImageList1   🖼 ImageList2

- Set the following properties:

Form1

BackColor	LightGreen
FormBorderStyle	FixedSingle
Icon	(you choose)
MaximizeBox	False
Text	The power of 2

PictureBox1

Name	picDie
BackColor	Transparent
Image	Five.gif
SizeMode	AutoSize

Timer1

Name	tmrRoll
Interval	100

Timer2

Name	tmrMove
Interval	400

ImageList1

Name	imlMarkers
ImageSize	64, 64
TransparentColor	128, 64, 0

ImageList2

Name	imlDice
ImageSize	48, 48
TransparentColor	Transparent

Button1

Name	btnRoll
BackColor	DarkGray
ForeColor	White
Text	

BoardSquare0

Size	64, 64
SquareIndex	0

BoardSquare1

BackgroundImage	Square1.bmp
Size	64, 64
SquareIndex	1

- BoardSquare2 to BoardSquare12 are to have property settings corresponding to those for BoardSquare1.

- The image list *imlMarkers* is to have the bitmaps *Objects 0000.bmp* to *Objects 1111.bmp* loaded into its Images collection.

- The image list *imlDice* is to have the bitmaps *One.gif* to *Six.gif* loaded into its Images collection.

Write the code and add comments

- Add the modules *Positioning.vb* and *RotateImage.vb* to the project.

- The following Imports statement must be entered at the top of the code window.

```
Imports BoardSquares
```

- Make the following **form level** declarations of variables and constants:

```
Dim DieCentre As Point ' centre of the die picture box
Const LASTSQUARE As Integer = 12 ' number of squares on the board
Dim Square(LASTSQUARE) As BoardSquare ' array of BoardSquares
Dim Player() As String = {"", "Telephone", "Boot", "Tophat", "Liner"}
Dim Position() As Integer = {0, 0, 0, 0, 0} ' all players start at 0
Dim RollCount, StopAt, WhoseTurn As Integer
```

- During the form load the centre of the die is calculated, the boardsquare array is **instantiated** and a random first player is selected.

```
Private Sub Form1_Load(ByVal sender As Object, ByVal e As System.EventArgs) _
Handles MyBase.Load
    Dim obj As Object, I As Integer
    ' calculate the centre of the die picture box
    DieCentre = New Point(picDie.Left + picDie.Width / 2, picDie.Top + _
    picDie.Height / 2)
    ' populate the BoardSquare array
    For Each Obj In Me.Controls
        If TypeOf Obj Is BoardSquare Then
            I = Obj.SquareIndex
            Square(I) = Obj ' add object to array
        End If
    Next obj
    Square(0).Markers = 8 + 4 + 2 + 1 ' all markers start on zero square
    Square(0).Image = imlMarkers.Images.Item(8 + 4 + 2 + 1)
    Randomize()
    WhoseTurn = Int(Rnd() * 4) + 1 ' random starting player, 1-4
    btnRoll.Text = Player(WhoseTurn) + "'s roll"
End Sub
```

- Each tick of this timer 'rolls' the dice through a certain angle.

```
Private Sub tmrRoll_Tick(ByVal sender As System.Object, ByVal e As _
System.EventArgs) Handles tmrRoll.Tick
    Const ANGLE As Integer = 53, LASTROLL As Integer = 10
    Randomize()
    Dim DieNum As Integer = Int(Rnd() * 6) + 1 ' the die number for this roll (1-6)
    ' load and rotate image from image list
    picDie.Image = Rotate(imlDice.Images.Item(DieNum - 1), ANGLE * RollCount)
    CentreOn(DieCentre, picDie) ' keep the rotating die centred
    RollCount += 1 ' keep count of no. of rolls
    If RollCount = LASTROLL Then ' die to stop rolling
        tmrRoll.Stop() ' stop the die rolling
        ' find where the marker should stop
        StopAt = Position(WhoseTurn) + DieNum
        If StopAt > LASTSQUARE Then
            StopAt -= LASTSQUARE
        End If
        tmrMove.Start() ' start moving the marker
    End If
End Sub
```

- A click of this button starts the die rolling.

```
Private Sub btnRoll_Click(ByVal sender As System.Object, ByVal e As _
System.EventArgs) Handles btnRoll.Click
    RollCount = 0
    btnRoll.Enabled = False ' can't click another roll
    tmrRoll.Start() ' start the die rolling
End Sub
```

- This **general** procedure contains the set of steps to progress to the next player. This procedure is called in other event procedures.

```
Private Sub Next_Player()
    WhoseTurn += 1 ' advance to next player
    If WhoseTurn > 4 Then
        WhoseTurn = 1 ' go back to first player
    End If
    tmrMove.Stop() ' stop moving the marker
    btnRoll.Enabled = True ' ready for next player's roll
    btnRoll.Text = Player(WhoseTurn) + "'s roll"
End Sub
```

- Each tick of the move timer moves a marker on to the next square. Each square associated with each move must have both its Markers and Image properties changed. This has to occur when a square is entered and when it is exited.

```
Private Sub tmrMove_Tick(ByVal sender As System.Object, ByVal e As _
System.EventArgs) Handles tmrMove.Tick
    Dim CurrentPos As Integer = Position(WhoseTurn)
    ' change contents of starting square
    Square(CurrentPos).Markers -= 2 ^ (WhoseTurn - 1)
    Square(CurrentPos).Image = imlMarkers.Images.Item(Square(CurrentPos).Markers)
    ' advance to next square
    CurrentPos += 1
    If CurrentPos > LASTSQUARE Then
        CurrentPos = 1 ' start back at 1
    End If
    ' change contents of next square
    Position(WhoseTurn) = CurrentPos
    Square(CurrentPos).Markers += 2 ^ (WhoseTurn - 1)
    Square(CurrentPos).Image = imlMarkers.Images.Item(Square(CurrentPos).Markers)
    ' check if player has reached the 'stopat' square
    If CurrentPos = StopAt Then ' reached final square
        Next_Player
    End If
End Sub
```

Try it out

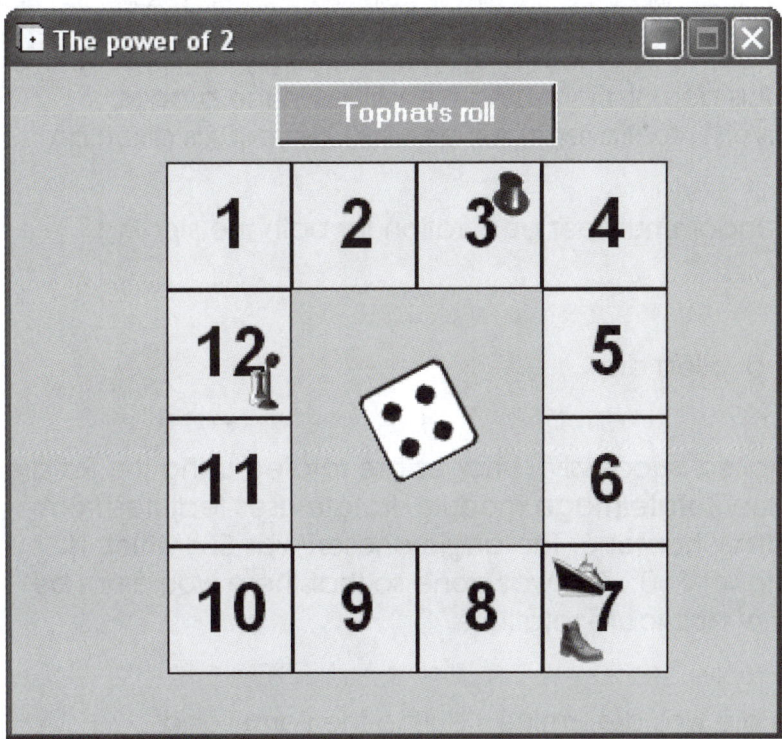

The power of two – points to note

- The **BoardSquare** class is a **subclass** of PictureBox that has three additional properties specifically for board games: **SquareIndex** to assist in array creation, **GotoSquare** to assist in the granting of fortune or misfortune, and **Markers** to indicate which players are on the square.

- The value of the **Markers** property corresponds to the **Index** of an image in an ImageList. In this example the Indexes range from 0 (no markers present) to 15 (all markers present) with each marker having the value of a power of 2 (1, 2, 4 0r 8).

  The starting BoardSquare, Square(0), has a Markers value of 15 as this is where all the players begin the game:

  ```
  Square(0).Markers = 8 + 4 + 2 + 1 ' all markers start on zero square
  Square(0).Image = imlMarkers.Images.Item(8 + 4 + 2 + 1)
  ```

  The following lines of code subtract and add the value of a marker to a square respectively:

  ```
  Square(CurrentPos).Markers -= 2 ^ (WhoseTurn - 1)
  Square(CurrentPos).Markers -= 2 ^ (WhoseTurn - 1)
  ```

  For example, if WhoseTurn has a value of 4 (the liner) then 2^3 (8) would be the value that is either subtracted or added.

- The **TransparentColor** property of an ImageList specifies the colour that will appear transparent when an image is displayed. The colour may be expressed by name eg Gray, or numerically as RGB eg 128, 64, 0.

- The variable Player is declared as an **array of String**:

```
Dim Player() As String = {"", "Telephone", "Boot", "Tophat", "Liner"}
```

The values of the elements of the array, from Player(0) to Player(4), are also assigned in this declaration using the values in the braces. Because only Player(1) to Player(4) will be used Player(0) is given an 'empty' value.

- Note the use of **random number** generation for both the starting player

```
WhoseTurn = Int(Rnd() * 4) + 1 ' random starting player, 1-4
```

and the value of a rolled die

```
Dim DieNum As Integer = Int(Rnd() * 6) + 1 'the die number for this roll(1-6)
```

- When the die is 'rolled' successive images are rotated using the **Rotate** procedure from the **RotateImage** module. Rotate uses features from GDI+ mentioned in Chapter 6. The angle chosen was 53° which is clearly not a factor of 360°. This was done so that there would not be the appearance of duplicate rotations.

```
picDie.Image = Rotate(imlDice.Images.Item(DieNum - 1), ANGLE * RollCount)
```

The centre of the die was determined during the Form Load

```
DieCentre = New Point(picDie.Left + picDie.Width / 2, picDie.Top + _
picDie.Height / 2)
```

This location is maintained when the die is rotated:

```
CentreOn(DieCentre, picDie) ' keep the rotating die centred
```

The power of two – check what you have learnt

1   How many images of markers would be necessary for a board game with six different markers?

2   A square has two markers present and its Markers property has a value of 9. Show how you can calculate this value using powers of 2.

3   RGB colours can be specified from 0, 0, 0 to 255, 255, 255. How many possible colours do these combinations make possible?

4   In this application two arrays were declared and their elements given values at the same time (instantiated). The dimension of the array is determined by the number of values in the braces. Make a declaration of a String array that will contain the names of the colours of a rainbow.

5   What Rnd expression would be used to generate a random number from each of the following sets?

   a   0, 1, 2, 3, 4, 5   b   1, 2, 3, 4, 5, 6   c   2, 3, 4, ... 12

6   Point is a class that only has three properties. Two of them are named simply X and Y, representing the x and y coordinates of the point. Make a declaration for a point named MyLoc then initialise it with a the location that is the exact centre of the form.

7   In the case of the 'rolling' die, what would be some unsuitable values to use for ANGLE?

8   The following loop is used in the Form Load procedure:

```
For Each Obj In Me.Controls
    If TypeOf Obj Is BoardSquare Then
        I = Obj.SquareIndex
        Square(I) = Obj ' add object to array
    End If
Next Obj
```

Why would you *not* populate the array in the following way?

```
Dim I As Integer = 0
For Each Obj In Me.Controls
    If TypeOf Obj Is BoardSquare Then
        Square(I) = Obj ' add object to array
        I += 1
    End If
Next Obj
```

9   The Rotate function that was used in this example produces a new rotated image from a given image. Write a line of code that will rotate the image in a picture box *picCard* through an angle of 15°.

10 Clearly this programming example is only a shell of a board game that requires some interesting ideas to turn it into a game. You could 'pay' each player money as they complete a circuit; some squares could be 'lose a turn' squares; some squares could be 'goto' or 'jump ahead' squares; you could allow players to buy an extra roll …

Program example: Snakes and ladders

Create a new Windows application with the name *Snakes and ladders.*

Create the interface

■   Add eleven board squares (eventually a hundred and one will be needed), a picture box, a button, two timers and two image lists to the form.

■   After adding the board squares immediately rename the eleventh to *BoardSquare0*. This will save a lot of confusion when there are a hundred and one board squares on the form.

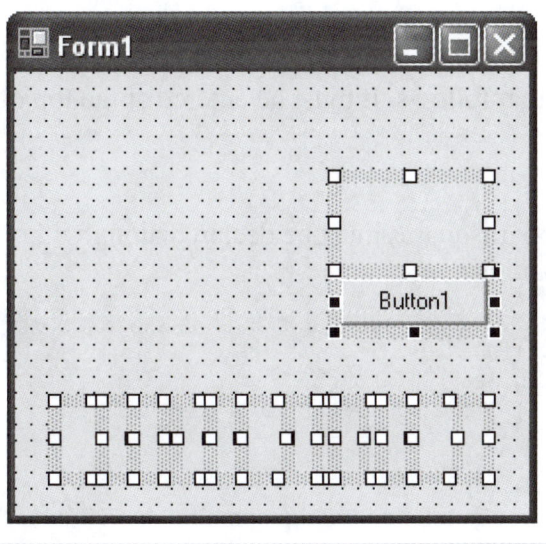

- Set the following properties:

Form1

BackColor	LightGreen
MaximizeBox	False
Text	Snakes and ladders

PictureBox1

Name	picDie
Image	Six.gif
SizeMode	AutoSize

Button1

Name	btnRoll
Text	

Timer1

Name	tmrMove
Interval	500

Timer2

Name	tmrRoll
Interval	100

ImageList1

Name	imlDice
ImageSize	48, 48

ImageList2

Name	imlMarkers
ImageSize	32, 32

BoardSquare0

Image	Colours 1111.gif
Size	32, 32
SquareIndex	0

BoardSquare1

BackgroundImage	SL01.bmp
Size	32, 32
GotoSquare	38
SquareIndex	1

BoardSquare2

BackgroundImage	SL02.bmp
Size	32, 32
GotoSquare	0
SquareIndex	2

- The remaining board squares up to BoardSquare100 have corresponding property settings. However because of the locations of the snakes and the ladders certain squares have particular GotoSquare settings. For example BoardSquare1 has a GotoSquare setting of 38 as it has a ladder to take the player to that square. The other squares that require settings will be obvious when the whole board is assembled.

- The image list *imlMarkers* is to have the bitmaps *Colours 0000.bmp* to *Colours 1111.bmp* loaded into its Images collection.

- The image list *imlDice* is to have the bitmaps *One.gif* to *Six.gif* loaded into its Images collection.

Write the code and add comments

- Add the modules *Positioning.vb* and *RotateImage.vb* to the project. A procedure and a function are needed from each.

- The following Imports statement makes the contents of the **namespace** *BoardSquares* available to the code that follows. It must be entered at the top of the code window.

```
Imports BoardSquares
```

- A large array of a hundred and one boardsquares must be declared along with arrays for the players' names and positions.

```
Dim Square(100) As BoardSquare
Dim DieCentre As Point ' centre of the rolling die
Dim Player() As String = {"", "Green", "Magenta", "Yellow", "Red"}
Dim Position() As Integer = {0, 0, 0, 0, 0} ' the square number a player is on
Dim WhoseTurn As Integer ' 1, 2, 3 or 4
Dim StopAt As Integer ' square number a marker stops at
```

- During the form load the center of the die is calculated, the BoardSquare array is **instantiated** according to the value set for each of the SquareIndex properties. A random first player is also selected.

```
Private Sub Form1_Load(ByVal sender As System.Object, ByVal e As _
System.EventArgs) Handles MyBase.Load
    Dim Obj As Object, I As Integer
    For Each Obj In Me.Controls
        If TypeOf Obj Is BoardSquare Then
            I = Obj.SquareIndex
            Square(I) = Obj ' add to array
        End If
    Next Obj
    DieCentre = New Point(picDie.Left + picDie.Width / 2, picDie.Top _
    + picDie.Height / 2)
    Square(0).Markers = 8 + 4 + 2 + 1 ' all markers start on zero square
    Square(0).Image = imlMarkers.Images.Item(8 + 4 + 2 + 1)
    Randomize()
    WhoseTurn = Int(Rnd() * 4) + 1 ' random starting player, 1-4
    ' player's name concatenated to a literal
    btnRoll.Text = Player(WhoseTurn) + "'s roll"
End Sub
```

- A click of this button starts the die rolling.

```
Private Sub btnRoll_Click(ByVal sender As System.Object, ByVal e As _
System.EventArgs) Handles btnRoll.Click
    btnRoll.Enabled = False
    tmrRoll.Start()
End Sub
```

- This **general procedure** contains the set of steps to progress to the next player. Note the way in which the Text property of the button is set with a **concatenation**.

```
Private Sub Next_Player()
    WhoseTurn += 1 ' advance to next player
    If WhoseTurn > 4 Then
        WhoseTurn = 1 ' back to first player
    End If
    ' player's name concatenated to a literal
    btnRoll.Text = Player(WhoseTurn) + "'s roll"
    btnRoll.Enabled = True
End Sub
```

- This Winner procedure announces the winner and moves the markers back ready to start a new game. This **general procedure** is used in other event procedures.

```
Private Sub Winner()
    Dim I As Integer
    MessageBox.Show(Player(WhoseTurn) + " wins!", "Snakes & Ladders", _
    MessageBoxButtons.OK, MessageBoxIcon.Exclamation)
    For I = 1 To 4 ' vacate all current positions
        Square(Position(I)).Image = imlMarkers.Images.Item(0)
        Square(Position(I)).Markers = 0
        Position(I) = 0 ' all four back to start
    Next I
    Square(0).Image = imlMarkers.Images.Item(8 + 4 + 2 + 1)
    Square(0).Markers = 8 + 4 + 2 + 1
End Sub
```

- Each tick of the move timer moves a marker on to the next square. Each square associated with each move must have both its Markers and Image properties changed. This has to occur when a square is entered and when it is exited.

```
Private Sub tmrMove_Tick(ByVal sender As Object, ByVal e As System.EventArgs) _
Handles tmrMove.Tick
    Dim CurrentPos As Integer = Position(WhoseTurn)
    ' change contents of starting square
    Square(CurrentPos).Markers -= 2 ^ (WhoseTurn - 1) ' remove this marker
    Square(CurrentPos).Image = imlMarkers.Images.Item(Square(CurrentPos).Markers)
    ' advance to next square
    CurrentPos += 1
    ' change contents of next square
    Position(WhoseTurn) = CurrentPos
    Square(CurrentPos).Markers += 2 ^ (WhoseTurn - 1) ' add this marker
    Square(CurrentPos).Image = imlMarkers.Images.Item(Square(CurrentPos).Markers)
    If CurrentPos = StopAt Then   ' arrived at stopping square
        tmrMove.Stop()
        If Square(StopAt).GoToSquare > 0 Then   ' either a snake or a ladder
            ' remove marker from this stopat position
            Square(CurrentPos).Markers -= 2 ^ (WhoseTurn - 1)
            Square(CurrentPos).Image = _
            imlMarkers.Images.Item(Square(CurrentPos).Markers)
            ' move marker to the goto square
            CurrentPos = Square(CurrentPos).GoToSquare
            Square(CurrentPos).Markers += 2 ^ (WhoseTurn - 1)
            Square(CurrentPos).Image = _
            imlMarkers.Images.Item(Square(CurrentPos).Markers)
            Position(WhoseTurn) = CurrentPos
            If CurrentPos = 100 Then ' arrived at last square
                Winner()
            End If
        ElseIf StopAt = 100 Then ' arrived at last square
            Winner()
        End If
        Next_Player()
    End If
End Sub
```

- Each tick of this timer 'rolls' the dice through a certain angle. The last value of the die, before it stops rolling, is the value used for the move.

```
Private Sub tmrRoll_Tick(ByVal sender As System.Object, ByVal e As _
System.EventArgs) Handles tmrRoll.Tick
    Const ANGLE As Integer = 53, LASTROLL As Integer = 10
    Dim Roll As Integer
    Static RollCount As Integer = 0
    Randomize()
    Roll = Int(Rnd() * 6) ' random number 0-5
    picDie.Image = Rotate(imlDice.Images.Item(Roll), ANGLE * RollCount)
    CentreOn(DieCentre, picDie)
    RollCount += 1
    If RollCount = LASTROLL Then
        StopAt = Position(WhoseTurn) + Roll + 1
        RollCount = 0
        tmrRoll.Stop()
        If StopAt <= 100 Then
            tmrMove.Start()
        Else ' a stopat square greater than 100
            Next_Player()
        End If
    End If
End Sub
```

Try it out

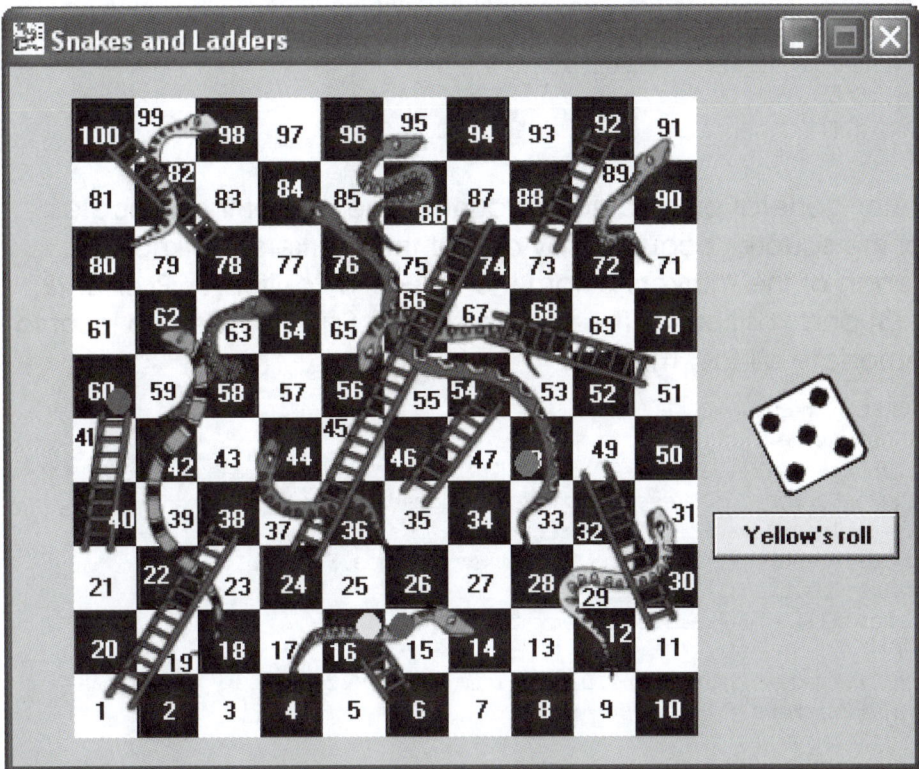

Snakes and ladders – points to note

- The GotoSquare property of a BoardSquare provides a means of delivering good fortune or misfortune to a player landing on that square.

- The **Interval** property of tmrMove was set to 500 (½ second). This was made slow enough to make the moves appear deliberate.

- It is customary to write the names of **constants** in upper case:

  ```
  Const ANGLE As Integer = 53, LASTROLL As Integer = 10
  ```

- The following line of code sets the Markers property of Square(0) to 15:

  ```
  Square(0).Markers = 8 + 4 + 2 + 1 ' all markers start on zero square
  ```

  It is expressed this way to emphasise the way in which it was calculated.

- **Concatenation** of Strings is used effectively. When WhoseTurn has a value of 1

  ```
  Player(WhoseTurn) + "'s roll"
  ```

  Has the value "Green's roll".

  When WhoseTurn has a value of 2

  ```
  Player(WhoseTurn) + "'s roll"
  ```

  Has the value "Magenta's roll" etc.

- As soon as the button is clicked it disables itself to prevent a player clicking more than once. When the move is finished it is enabled.

```
Private Sub btnRoll_Click(ByVal sender As System.Object, ByVal e As _
System.EventArgs) Handles btnRoll.Click
    btnRoll.Enabled = False
    tmrRoll.Start()
End Sub
```

- The Winner **general procedure** announces the winner then vacates each of the squares occupied by one of the markers. It is known where each of the markers is from the values in Position(1), Position(2), Position(3) and Position(4). The starting square Square(0) is also reset to accommodate all four markers.

```
Private Sub Winner()
    Dim I As Integer
    MessageBox.Show(Player(WhoseTurn) + " wins!", "Snakes & Ladders", _
    MessageBoxButtons.OK, MessageBoxIcon.Exclamation)
    For I = 1 To 4 ' vacate all current positions
        Square(Position(I)).Image = imlMarkers.Images.Item(0)
        Square(Position(I)).Markers = 0
        Position(I) = 0 ' all four back to start
    Next I
    Square(0).Image = imlMarkers.Images.Item(8 + 4 + 2 + 1)
    Square(0).Markers = 8 + 4 + 2 + 1
End Sub
```

- **Conatenation** takes place each time it is a new player's turn and when a winner is announced. In each case a variable's value is concatenated with a **literal**.

```
Player(WhoseTurn) + " wins!"
```

Snakes and ladders – check what you have learnt

1   Overall, on this snakes and ladders board, is there more good fortune or more misfortune?

2   In what way does a computerised game of snakes and ladders completely remove any elements of error or bias?

3   What two properties of an ImageList must be set before any bitmaps are loaded into the Images collection?

4   Under what circumstances would you leave the TransparentColor property of an ImageList with its default value of Transparent?

5   What is the purpose of the Randomize statement when generating random numbers?

6   General procedures are not absolutely necessary. In this example two were used: Winner and Next_Player. Why do you suppose the decision was made to use these two general procedures?

7   Examine the code in RotateImage.vb (Appendix 1). What is the advantage of having code modules like RotateImage made available?

8 Describe what is happening in this section of code:

```
If StopAt <= 100 Then
    tmrMove.Start()
Else ' a stopat square greater than 100
    Next_Player()
End If
```

9 Suggest which traditional board games could be suitably adapted to computerised versions.

10 Beyond clicking the button the user has no input to influence the game. Give the players the feeling of having some control by being able to regulate how hard they roll the die. A **trackbar** was used on the form shown below.

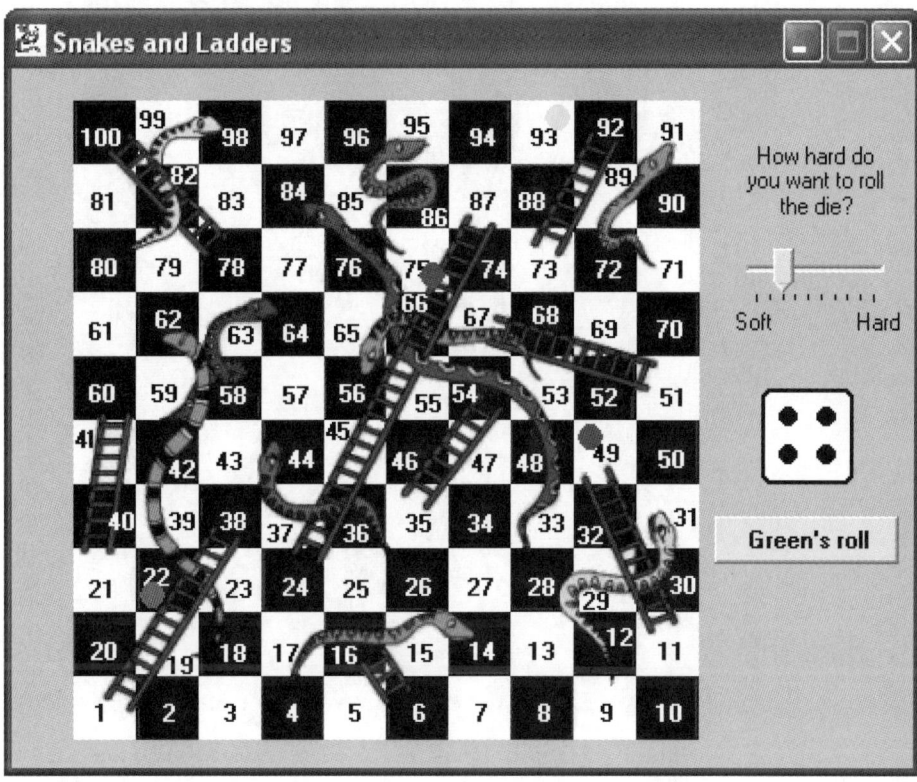

Chapter 11

Blocks and dots

Mazes

The history of mazes goes back over three and a half thousand years in many countries around the world. They have been a part of myths and legends, ceremonies, games and art. Famous hedge mazes like Hampton Court Palace still attract thousands of visitors each year.

The computer games *Pac Man* and *Dung Beetles* (also known as *Mega-Bug*) were popular maze-based games created in the early 1980s.

The mazes in the applications to follow have square components, each with sixteen possible combinations of open and closed sides. The first program example uses the images shown below:

This simple 4×3 maze was made from a selection of the above blocks.

The MazeBlock class

MazeBlock is a subclass of PictureBox (see Appendix 2) that has been created for the following program examples. It has six additional properties:

- **GridX** and **GridY** – Integers to identify the grid position of the block.
- **OpenEast, OpenWest, OpenNorth** and **OpenSouth** – Boolean values indicating if the block is open in a particular direction.

Program example: Mouse maze

Create a new Windows application with the name *Mouse maze.*

Create the interface

- The MazeBlock control must first be added to the toolbox.
- From the Tools menu choose Add/Remove Toolbox Items.

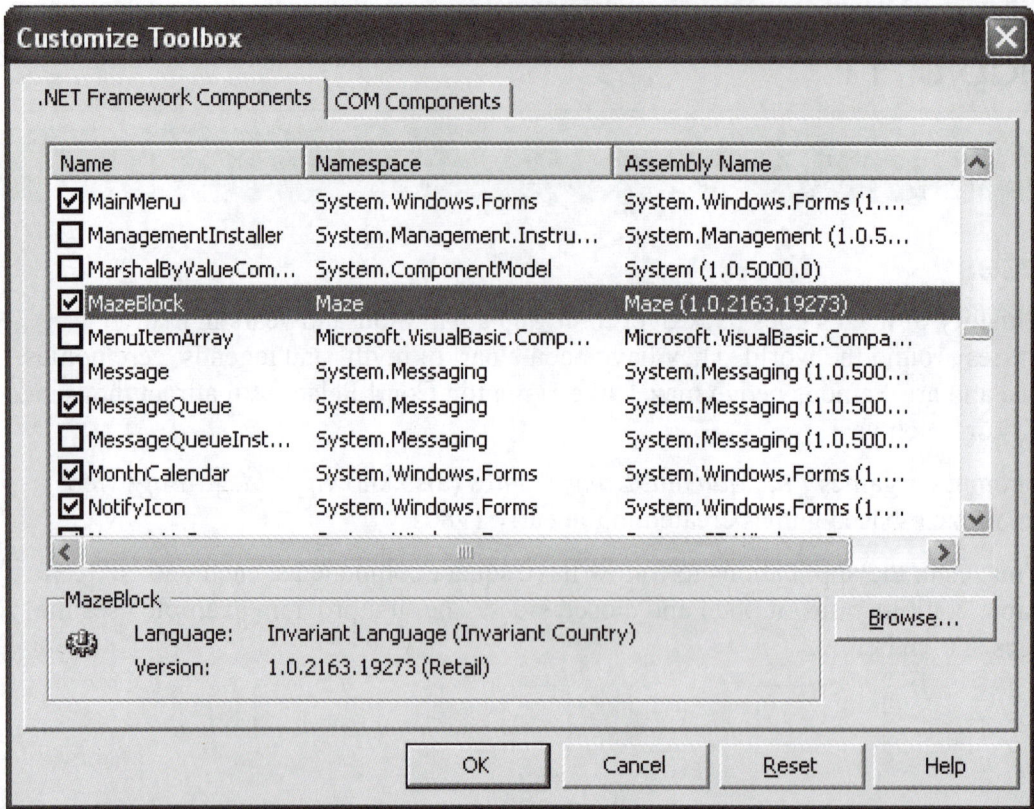

- Set the **GridSize** property of the form to *4, 4*. The maze blocks will need to be moved four pixels at a time.
- Add twenty maze blocks, one picture box, four image lists and one timer to the form.

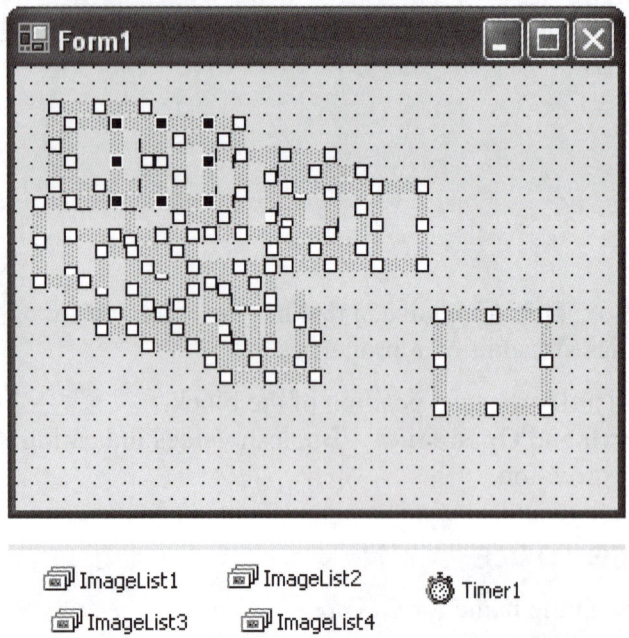

- It is advisable to insert a bitmap into the Image property of each maze block before arranging them into rows and columns. This will assist the correct positioning. It would be best to use the bitmap *plain block CCCC.gif* as it has a clear four sided border.

- Set the following properties:

Form1

GridSize	4, 4
Icon	(you choose)
MaximizeBox	False
Text	Mouse maze

PictureBox1

Name	picMouse
Image	Mouse walking east 0.gif
Location	18, 18
Size	64, 64

MazeBlock1

Image	Plain block CCCC.gif
Location	16, 16

Timer1

Name	tmrMove
Enabled	True
Interval	25

ImageList1

Name	imlMouseEast
ImageSize	64, 64

ImageList2

Name	imlMouseSouth
ImageSize	64, 64

ImageList3

Name	imlMouseWest
ImageSize	64, 64

ImageList4

Name	imlMouseNorth
ImageSize	64, 64

- The following are the GridX and GridY settings for the twenty maze blocks.

GridX = 0 GridY= 0	GridX = 1 GridY= 0	GridX = 2 GridY= 0	GridX = 3 GridY= 0	GridX = 4 GridY= 0
GridX = 0 GridY= 1	GridX = 1 GridY= 1	GridX = 2 GridY= 1	GridX = 3 GridY= 1	GridX = 4 GridY= 1
GridX = 0 GridY= 2	GridX = 1 GridY= 2	GridX = 2 GridY= 2	GridX = 3 GridY= 2	GridX = 4 GridY= 2
GridX = 0 GridY= 3	GridX = 1 GridY= 3	GridX = 2 GridY= 3	GridX = 3 GridY= 3	GridX = 4 GridY= 3

The images have been named in keeping with which sides are open and which are closed. For example the names of the first four below are *plain block CCCO.gif*, *plain block CCCC.gif*, *plain block CCOC.gif* and *plain block CCOO.gif*.

- The OpenEast, OpenSouth, OpenWest and OpenNorth properties of each maze block has to be set according to the maze arrangement you have selected. Make sure that adjoining blocks have property settings that agree. For example if a block has its OpenEast property set to *True* then the block to its right has to have its OpenWest property *True*.

- Each image list has a set of nine bitmaps for its Images collection. The image list *imlMouseEast* has the bitmaps *Mouse walking east 0.gif* to *Mouse walking east 8.gif*. Thank you to Reiner Prokein for the mouse bitmaps.

Write the code and add comments

■ The imports statement must be entered at the top of the code window. Importing this **namespace** ensures all of its contents will be recognized in the code to follow.

```
Imports Maze ' namespace containing MazeBlock class
```

■ **Enumerations** are sets of integers with more user-friendly names. This enumeration provides a clear way of expressing directions.

```
Private Enum Direction
    East = 0
    South = 1
    West = 2
    North = 3
End Enum
```

■ One array of maze blocks must be declared at form level.

```
Dim Block(4, 3) As MazeBlock ' 5 blocks wide, 4 blocks high
Dim X As Integer = 0, Y As Integer = 0 ' X and Y coordinates on the maze
Dim Whichway As Direction = Direction.East ' current moving direction
Dim WalkCount As Integer = 0 ' counts pixels up to 68 (width of a block)
```

■ The form load procedure is used to populate the array. It is a two-dimensional array so it has two indexes, one for the columns, one for the rows.

```
Private Sub Form1_Load(ByVal sender As Object, ByVal e As System.EventArgs) _
Handles MyBase.Load
    Dim obj As Object, I, J As Integer
    For Each obj In Me.Controls
        If TypeOf obj Is MazeBlock Then
            I = obj.GridX
            J = obj.GridY
            Block(I, J) = obj
        End If
    Next obj
End Sub
```

■ On each tick of the timer the mouse 'walks' until it is in the centre of a maze block (WalkCount = 0). A random direction is then selected until one is found that is possible to use.

```
Private Sub tmrMove_Tick(ByVal sender As System.Object, ByVal e As _
System.EventArgs) Handles tmrMove.Tick
    Static WhichImage As Integer = 0
    Dim I, J As Integer
    Randomize()
    WhichImage = (WhichImage + 1) Mod 9 ' 0-8 range of values
    I = X \ 68 ' calculates which block the mouse is on
    J = Y \ 68
    If WalkCount = 0 Then ' at a new block, get a new direction to move
        Do
            Whichway = Int(Rnd() * 4) ' select random direction 0-3
        Loop Until Whichway = Direction.East And Block(I, J).OpenEast Or _
                Whichway = Direction.North And Block(I, J).OpenNorth Or _
                Whichway = Direction.South And Block(I, J).OpenSouth Or _
                Whichway = Direction.West And Block(I, J).OpenWest
        WalkCount = 2 ' on next tick mouse will move
    Else ' Walkcount > 0, move the mouse
        Select Case Whichway ' move according to chosen direction
            Case Direction.East
                picMouse.Image = imlMouseEast.Images.Item(WhichImage)
                picMouse.Left += 2
                X += 2
```

```
      Case Direction.North
         picMouse.Image = imlMouseNorth.Images.Item(WhichImage)
         picMouse.Top -= 2
         Y -= 2
      Case Direction.South
         picMouse.Image = imlMouseSouth.Images.Item(WhichImage)
         picMouse.Top += 2
         Y += 2
      Case Direction.West
         picMouse.Image = imlMouseWest.Images.Item(WhichImage)
         picMouse.Left -= 2
         X -= 2
   End Select
   WalkCount += 2 ' 2 pixels
   If WalkCount > 68 Then ' reached the next block
      WalkCount = 0 ' on the next tick choose a new direction
   End If
  End If
End Sub
```

Try it out

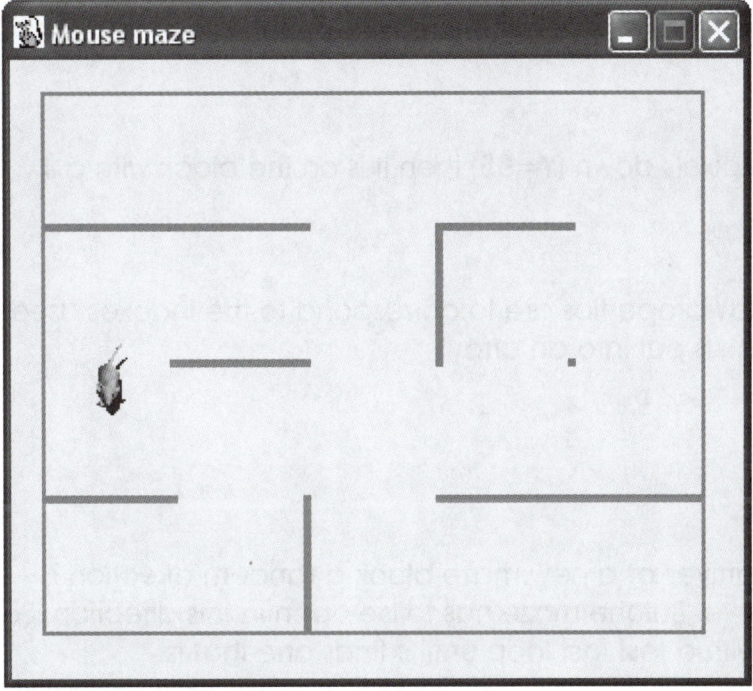

Mouse maze – points to note

- The MazeBlock control is a **subclass** of PictureBox created especially for these applications. It inherits all the properties of a PictureBox and has six additional properties suited to its special purpose.

- The default **GridSize** property of a form is 8, 8. Controls will snap to the coordinates of this grid. It was set to 4, 4 for this application as finer adjustments were needed.

- When it is decided which sides of a particular maze block are to be open, the Image property and the OpenEast, OpenNorth, OpenSouth and OpenWest properties should agree.

- The **enumeration** Direction is really just four Integers. However the names of the members of the enumeration add clarity to the code.

```
Private Enum Direction
    East = 0
    South = 1
    West = 2
    North = 3
End Enum
```

  The user decides on the name of the enumeration and the names of each of the values within it.

- Block is declared as a form level variable:

```
Dim Block(4, 3) As MazeBlock ' 5 blocks wide, 4 blocks high
```

  Because the array has two indexes it is referred to as a **two dimensional array**.

- **Integer division** (no remainder) is used to calculate which block the mouse is on at every tick of the timer. For example if the mouse has moved 142 pixels to the right (X=142) then it is on the block with an I index of 2.

```
I = X \ 68
```

  If it has moved 85 pixels down (Y=85) then it is on the block with a J index of 1.

```
J = Y \ 68
```

- The **GridX** and **GridY** properties are to correspond to the indexes used when a maze block is put into an array:

```
If TypeOf obj Is MazeBlock Then
    I = obj.GridX
    J = obj.GridY
    Block(I, J) = obj
End If
```

- When the mouse arrives at a new maze block a random direction is chosen for it to move. But the maze has to be open in this direction. So it will keep trying with a **test last loop** until it finds one that is.

```
Do
    Whichway = Int(Rnd() * 4) ' select random direction 0-3
Loop Until Whichway = Direction.East And Block(I, J).OpenEast Or _
Whichway = Direction.North And Block(I, J).OpenNorth Or _
Whichway = Direction.South And Block(I, J).OpenSouth Or _
Whichway = Direction.West And Block(I, J).OpenWest
```

- When the mouse has moved 68 pixels in a particular direction (counted with WalkCount) then it has arrived at a new block:

```
If WalkCount > 68 Then ' reached the next block
    WalkCount = 0 ' on the next tick choose a new direction
End If
```

- Once a direction has been decided on for the mouse to move **multiple branching** is used to carry out the action:

```
Select Case Whichway ' move according to chosen direction
   Case Direction.East
      picMouse.Image = imlMouseEast.Images.Item(WhichImage)
      picMouse.Left += 2
      X += 2
```

Mouse maze – check what you have learnt

1 Why was a special subclass created for this application?

2 a What are the two possible values for the properties OpenEast, OpenNorth, OpenSouth and OpenWest?

  b How many different combinations of the above properties are there?

3 Enumerations are broadly used in Visual Basic. They are really just sets of Integers. What is the advantage in using enumerations?

4 Arrays can have more than one dimension as was the case in this program example. How many elements are there in an array that is declared:

```
Dim Booking(6, 3, 5) As String
```

5 There are three types of division in Visual Basic (Real, Integer and Remainder). Integer division divides then discards the remainder. Calculate the following:

  a 10 \ 6   b 16 \ 5   c 20 \ 4

6 A **test last loop** is a looping structure that repeats certain action(s) until a certain condition is met. How could one get into the undesirable situation of being 'stuck' in an endless loop?

7 Which line of code advances mouse image to be used by 1?

8 At what rate is the mouse moving through the maze (pixels per second)?

9 In the Mouse maze folder there is another set of mouse bitmaps. They are animation sequences of the mouse standing up on its hind legs.

Extend the program example to have the mouse pause, in the occasional square, to raise itself up on its hind legs.

10 In this example you compose your own maze at design time. Write a program to create a random maze.

Start by having all the maze squares closed on all four sides. Commence creating a maze at a randomly chosen square. Randomly choose a wall to open, then move through that opening to the new square. Continue doing this until you have visited a certain number of new squares.

The form shown below has a random maze that stops after seventeen of the twenty squares has been visited. Please note that this is a very difficult task!

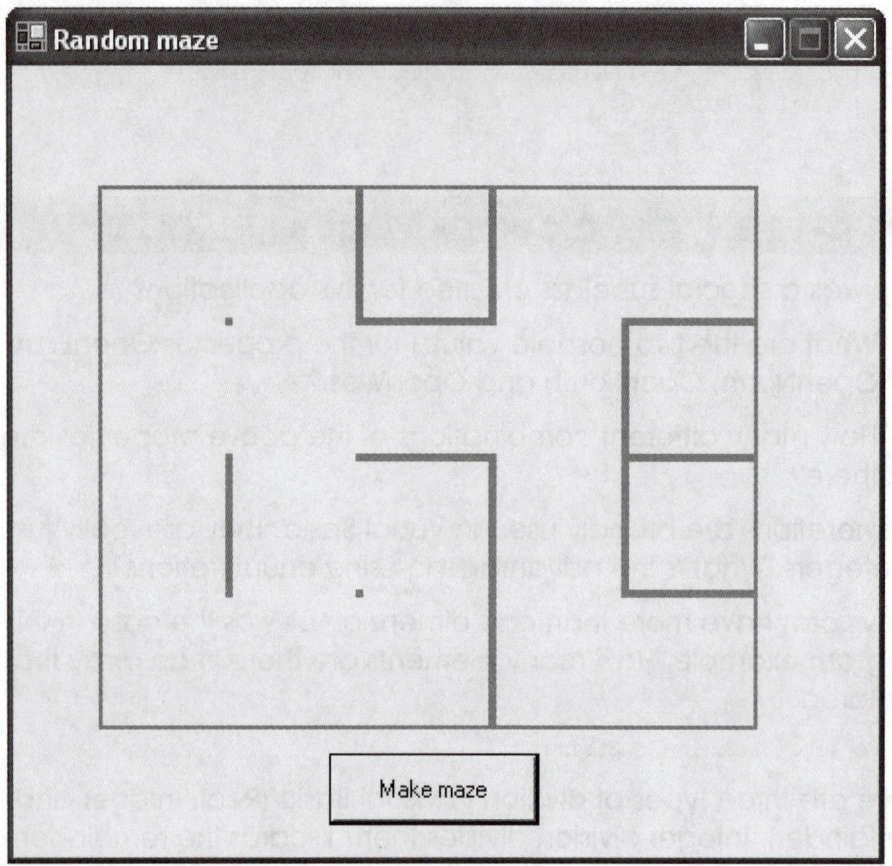

Program example: Dot eater

Create a new Windows application with the name *Dot eater*.

Create the interface

- The MazeBlock control should have already been added to the toolbox in the previous example.

- Add two picture boxes, twenty maze blocks, twenty dots, four labels, two image lists, three timers and one main menu.

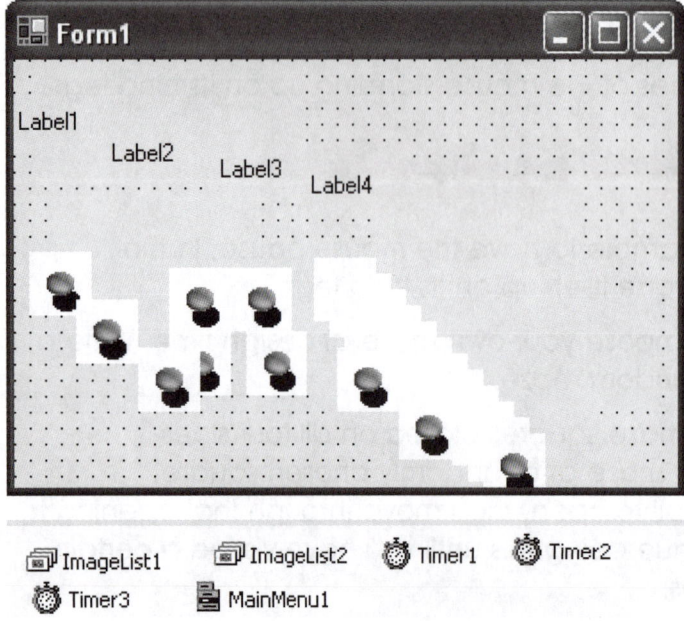

■ Set the properties as shown:

Form1

KeyPreview	True
MaximizeBox	False
Text	Dot eater

PictureBox1

Name	picEater
Image	blinking blue east 0.bmp
SizeMode	AutoSize

Label1

Font	MS Sans Serif
	8 points
	Bold
Text	Score
TextAlign	MiddleCenter

Label2

Font	MS Sans Serif
	8 points
	Bold
Text	Lives
TextAlign	MiddleCenter

Label3

Name	lblScore
BackColor	255, 255, 192
BorderStyle	Fixed3D
Font	MS Sans Serif
	14 points
	Bold
ForeColor	Magenta
Text	0
TextAlign	MiddleCenter

Label4

Name	lblLives
BackColor	255, 255, 192
BorderStyle	Fixed3D
Font	MS Sans Serif
	14 points
	Bold
ForeColor	Magenta
Text	10
TextAlign	MiddleCenter

MazeBlock1

Image	blue bricks BBBB.bmp
GridX	0
GridY	0
Location	16, 16
OpenEast	False
OpenNorth	False
OpenSouth	False
OpenWest	False
SizeMode	AutoSize

Dot1

GridX	0
GridY	0
Location	32, 32

PictureBox2

Name	picGhost
Image	red ghost 0.bmp
SizeMode	AutoSize

ImageList1

Name	imlEater
ImageSize	32, 32

ImageList2

Name	imlGhost
ImageSize	32, 32

Timer1

Name	tmrEater
Enabled	True
Interval	200

Timer2

Name	tmrGhost
Enabled	True
Interval	500

Timer1

Name	tmrGhostMove
Enabled	False
Interval	500

■ Apply the GridX and GridY settings to the maze blocks in the same way described in *Mouse maze*. Use the same grid settings for the dots.

■ For the image list *imlEater*, load the images *blinking blue east 0.bmp* to *blinking blue east 0.bmp*, then the south, west and north images in that order.

■ Load the images *red ghost 0.bmp* to *red ghost 15.bmp* into *imlGhost*.

- Make these Text settings in the main menu:

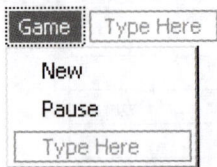

- Now make the following settings for these menu items:

Name	ShortCut	Text
mnuNew	*CtrlN*	*New*
mnuPause	*CtrlP*	*Pause*

Write the code and add comments

- This line of code should be entered at the top of the code window. Importing this namespace ensures all of its contents will be recognized in the code that follows.

```
Imports Maze ' namespace containing MazeBlock and Dot classes
```

- This enumeration provides a clear way of expressing directions.

```
Private Enum Direction
    East = 0
    South = 1
    West = 2
    North = 3
End Enum
```

- There are a number of form level variables to be declared as described below:

```
Dim EaterDir As Direction = Direction.East ' current direction of the eater
Dim EaterX As Integer = 0, EaterY As Integer = 0 ' eater coordinates
Dim GhostX As Integer = 4, GhostY As Integer = 3 ' ghost coordinates
Dim Square(4, 3) As MazeBlock ' 5 blocks wide, 4 blocks high
Dim Food(4, 3) As Dot
Dim GameOver As Boolean = True
```

- The Food and Square arrays are populated when the form is loaded.

```
Private Sub Form1_Load(ByVal sender As Object, ByVal e As System.EventArgs) _
Handles MyBase.Load
    Dim obj As Object, X, Y As Integer
    For Each obj In Me.Controls
        If TypeOf obj Is Dot Then
            X = obj.GridX ' GridX and GridY properties give position
            Y = obj.GridY
            Food(X, Y) = obj ' add to food array
        ElseIf TypeOf obj Is MazeBlock Then
            X = obj.GridX
            Y = obj.GridY
            Square(X, Y) = obj ' add to square array
        End If
    Next obj
End Sub
```

- The following procedure produces an animation of the eater, cycling through sixteen images.

```
Private Sub tmrEater_Tick(ByVal sender As System.Object, ByVal e As _
System.EventArgs) Handles tmrEater.Tick
    Static Frame As Integer = 0
    Frame = (Frame + 1) Mod 16 ' frames from 0 to 15
    picEater.Image = imlEater.Images.Item(EaterDir * 16 + Frame)
End Sub
```

- The cursor keys control the movement of the doteater. Movement will only be permitted if the square is open in the direction chosen. Multiple branching is the ideal structure for a KeyDown event procedure.

```
Private Sub Form1_KeyDown(ByVal sender As Object, ByVal e As _
System.Windows.Forms.KeyEventArgs) Handles MyBase.KeyDown
    Select Case e.KeyCode
        Case Keys.Right
            If Square(EaterX, EaterY).OpenEast Then
                EaterDir = Direction.East ' selects a set of eater images
                picEater.Left += 64 ' move one square left
                EaterX += 1 ' adjust eater's X coordinate
                CheckFood()
            End If
        Case Keys.Left
            If Square(EaterX, EaterY).OpenWest Then
                EaterDir = Direction.West ' selects a set of eater images
                picEater.Left -= 64 ' move one square right
                EaterX -= 1 ' adjust eater's X coordinate
                CheckFood()
            End If
        Case Keys.Up
            If Square(EaterX, EaterY).OpenNorth Then
                EaterDir = Direction.North ' selects a set of eater images
                picEater.Top -= 64 ' move one square up
                EaterY -= 1 ' adjust eater's Y coordinate
                CheckFood()
            End If
        Case Keys.Down
            If Square(EaterX, EaterY).OpenSouth Then
                EaterDir = Direction.South ' selects a set of eater images
                picEater.Top += 64 ' move one square down
                EaterY += 1 ' adjust eater's Y coordinate
                CheckFood()
            End If
    End Select
End Sub
```

- This general procedure checks if the doteater is allowed to eat food. If there is food where the doteater lands it disappears and the doteater gets a point. Note however that the doteater cannot eat if the game has been declared over or if it is being paused. Make sure you have copied *Bleep.wav* into the Bin folder of this application.

```
Private Sub CheckFood()
    If Food(EaterX, EaterY).Visible And Not GameOver And Not mnuPause.Checked Then
        PlayWaveFile("Bleep.wav") ' an eating sound
        Food(EaterX, EaterY).Visible = False ' dot disappears
        lblScore.Text += 1 ' eater gets a point
    End If
End Sub
```

- The following procedure produces an animation of the ghost, cycling through sixteen images.

```
Private Sub tmrGhost_Tick(ByVal sender As System.Object, _
ByVal e As System.EventArgs) Handles tmrGhost.Tick
    Static Frame As Integer = 0
    Frame = (Frame + 1) Mod 16 ' frames from 0 to 15
    picGhost.Image = imlGhost.Images.Item(Frame)
End Sub
```

- The ghost has some 'intelligence'. If the eater is to the north the ghost will attempt to move north etc. If none of these are possible it will randomly choose a direction in which it is able to move.

```
Private Sub tmrGhostMove_Tick(ByVal sender As System.Object, _
ByVal e As System.EventArgs) Handles tmrGhostMove.Tick
    Randomize()
    Dim PickDir As Direction
    ' Get the ghost to seek out the eater by trying
    ' to head in the direction of the eater
    If EaterY < GhostY And Square(GhostX, GhostY).OpenNorth Then
        picGhost.Top -= 64 ' move one square up
        GhostY -= 1 ' adjust ghost's Y coordinate
    ElseIf EaterY > GhostY And Square(GhostX, GhostY).OpenSouth Then
        picGhost.Top += 64 ' move one square down
        GhostY += 1 ' adjust ghost's Y coordinate
    ElseIf EaterX < GhostX And Square(GhostX, GhostY).OpenWest Then
        picGhost.Left -= 64 ' move one square right
        GhostX -= 1 ' adjust ghost's X coordinate
    ElseIf EaterX > GhostX And Square(GhostX, GhostY).OpenEast Then
        picGhost.Left += 64 ' move one square left
        GhostX += 1 ' adjust ghost's X coordinate
    Else      ' check anywhere ghost can move
        Do
            PickDir = Int(Rnd() * 4) ' choose a random direction
        Loop Until PickDir = Direction.East And Square(GhostX, GhostY).OpenEast Or _
            PickDir = Direction.West And Square(GhostX, GhostY).OpenWest Or _
            PickDir = Direction.North And Square(GhostX, GhostY).OpenNorth Or _
            PickDir = Direction.South And Square(GhostX, GhostY).OpenSouth
        Select Case PickDir
            Case Direction.East
                picGhost.Left += 64 ' move one square east
                GhostX += 1 ' adjust ghost's X coordinate
            Case Direction.South
                picGhost.Top += 64 ' move one square south
                GhostY += 1 ' adjust ghost's Y coordinate
            Case Direction.West
                picGhost.Left -= 64 ' move one square west
                GhostX -= 1 ' adjust ghost's X coordinate
            Case Direction.North
                picGhost.Top -= 64 ' move one square north
                GhostY -= 1 ' adjust ghost's Y coordinate
        End Select
    End If
    ' If the ghost lands on the eater, the eater loses a life
    If picGhost.Location.Equals(picEater.Location) Then
        PlayWaveFile("Bonk.wav") ' the sound of a collision with eater
        lblLives.Text -= 1 ' lose a life
    End If
End Sub
```

- When a new game is selected all of the food is made visible, the points are reset and the ghost starts moving. Note the use of a **nested loop**.

```
Private Sub mnuNew_Click(ByVal sender As System.Object, _
ByVal e As System.EventArgs) Handles mnuNew.Click
    Dim I, J As Integer
    For I = 0 To XMax
        For J = 0 To YMax
            If Not (Food(I, J) Is Nothing) Then ' not all locations have food
                Food(I, J).Visible = True ' make food visible
            End If
        Next J
    Next I
    lblScore.Text = 0 ' reset score
    lblLives.Text = 10 ' reset lives
    GameOver = False
    tmrGhostMove.Start() ' start ghost moving
    mnuNew.Enabled = False ' can't start a new game
    mnuPause.Checked = False ' game is not paused
End Sub
```

- Pausing the game stops the ghost moving but does not allow the eater to eat any dots.

```
Private Sub mnuPause_Click(ByVal sender As Object, ByVal e As System.EventArgs) _
Handles mnuPause.Click
    mnuPause.Checked = Not mnuPause.Checked
    tmrGhostMove.Enabled = Not mnuPause.Checked
End Sub
```

- If twenty dots are eaten the game is over, the ghost stops moving and the player is able to start a new game.

```
Private Sub lblScore_TextChanged(ByVal sender As Object, _
ByVal e As System.EventArgs) Handles lblScore.TextChanged
    If lblScore.Text = 20 Then ' all dots eaten
        tmrGhostMove.Stop() ' stop ghost moving
        GameOver = True
        mnuNew.Enabled = True ' allow a new game
        MessageBox.Show("Congratulations, you've won!", "Dot Eater", _
        MessageBoxButtons.OK, MessageBoxIcon.Exclamation)
    End If
End Sub
```

- If all lives are lost the game is over, the ghost stops moving and the player is able to start a new game.

```
Private Sub lblLives_TextChanged(ByVal sender As Object, _
ByVal e As System.EventArgs) Handles lblLives.TextChanged
    If lblLives.Text = 0 Then ' all lives lost
        tmrGhostMove.Stop() ' stop ghost moving
        GameOver = True
        mnuNew.Enabled = True ' allow a new game
        MessageBox.Show("Game Over! You've lost all your lives.", "Dot Eater", _
        MessageBoxButtons.OK, MessageBoxIcon.Stop)
    End If
End Sub
```

Try it out

Dot eater – points to note

- **Menu items** are a space saving alternative to **buttons**.

- Menu items often have **ShortCut** keys so they can be activated with the keyboard instead of the mouse.

- **Boolean** variables have one of the values *True* or *False*. They are used as **flags** to indicate whether something has happened.

  ```
  Dim GameOver As Boolean = True
  ```

- Rather than having a separate image list for each of the four directions of the doteater, all sixty four images are in the one image list. The sets of images are in the order East, South, West and North. This is the same sequence as the **enumeration**. In this way the required image can be easily selected:

  ```
  picEater.Image = imlEater.Images.Item(EaterDir * 16 + Frame)
  ```

  If the eater direction is East EaterDir will have a value of 0, so the images will be taken from the first sixteen. If the eater direction is South EaterDir will have a value of 1, so the images will be taken from the second sixteen etc.

- Unless a path has been specified *PlayWaveFile* will expect to find the wave file in the same folder as the EXE file (Bin).

  ```
  PlayWaveFile("Bleep.wav")
  ```

- The code of the key that has been pressed is passed into the **KeyDown** procedure through the **e** argument. That makes it a simple process to take the appropriate action with a Select Case statement:

```
Select Case e.KeyCode
    Case Keys.Right
        If Square(EaterX, EaterY).OpenEast Then
            EaterDir = Direction.East ' selects a set of eater images
            picEater.Left += 64 ' move one square left
            EaterX += 1 ' adjust eater's X coordinate
```

- With a good selection of variable names and appropriate expressions, some code can almost read like natural language:

```
If Food(EaterX,EaterY).Visible And Not GameOver And Not mnuPause.Checked Then
```

- Starting and stopping a timer can be done using methods:

```
tmrGhostMove.Start()
tmrGhostMove.Stop()
```

Alternatively it can be done by setting the Enabled property:

```
tmrGhostMove.Enabled = True
tmrGhostMove.Enabled = False
```

- If all elements of a two dimensional array need to be accessed a **nested loop** may be necessary. Nested loops have an inner and an outer loop.

```
For I = 0 To XMax
    For J = 0 To YMax
        If Not (Food(I, J) Is Nothing) Then ' not all locations have food
            Food(I, J).Visible = True ' make food visible
        End If
    Next J
Next I
```

For each single increment of the outer loop the inner loop must go through a full cycle. When the outer loop is completed all elements of the array have been accessed.

- Strangely Points and Locations cannot be compared with =. So the following code is illegal:

```
If picGhost.Location = picEater.Location Then
```

Rather, it must be expressed

```
If picGhost.Location.Equals(picEater.Location) Then
```

- Properties that have **Boolean** values can easily be toggled using the **Not** operator: *True* goes to *False*, *False* goes to *True*.

```
mnuPause.Checked = Not mnuPause.Checked
```

Dot eater – check what you have learnt

1   Why are shortcut keys especially important while playing a key controlled game?

2   a   What is a flag?

    b   What variable is used as a flag in this example?

    c   Where does this flag has its value set and where is it used?

3   Good use is made of the enumeration Direction in this example. Message boxes use enumerations to specify buttons and icons. Detail these two enumerations.

4   Keys is also an enumeration. Some of its members are Keys.Left, Keys.Right etc. Find the enumeration member for

    a   the spacebar   b   the Esc key   c   the Ctrl key

5   Where should wave file sound effects be placed?

6   Write the following line of code in ordinary English:

```
If Food(EaterX,EaterY).Visible And Not GameOver And Not mnuPause.Checked Then
```

7   All elements of a Boolean array declared

```
Dim Occupied(4, 7) As Boolean
```

are to be assigned *False*. Write the nested loop to perform this task.

8   Write another nested loop for the array in question 6. However, instead of assigning all the elements to *False*, toggle the values to their opposite value.

9   In what way does the ghost have some 'intelligence'?

10🖳 There is a need to give the game increasing difficulty as the eater accumulates points (food that is not static, a faster ghost, more than one ghost…). Similarly the rewards could become greater (special bonus food, the ability to jump some walls…). Implement some of these ideas.

Chapter 12

How to be sharp

Managing fifty two images

A regular deck of playing cards consists of four suits with thirteen cards in each suit. So, in constructing a card game application, there has to be a logical way of storing and accessing these fifty-two images. An image list control is the best way of managing this.

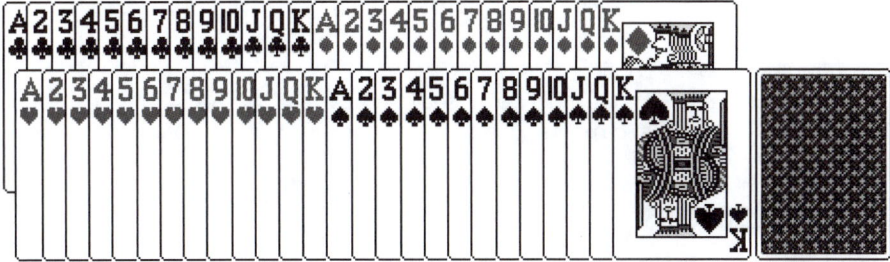

After adding the images, from Ace to King for each suit, the cards will have indexes from 0-12, 13-25, 26-38 and 39-51. The image with index 52 is a 'cover' card.

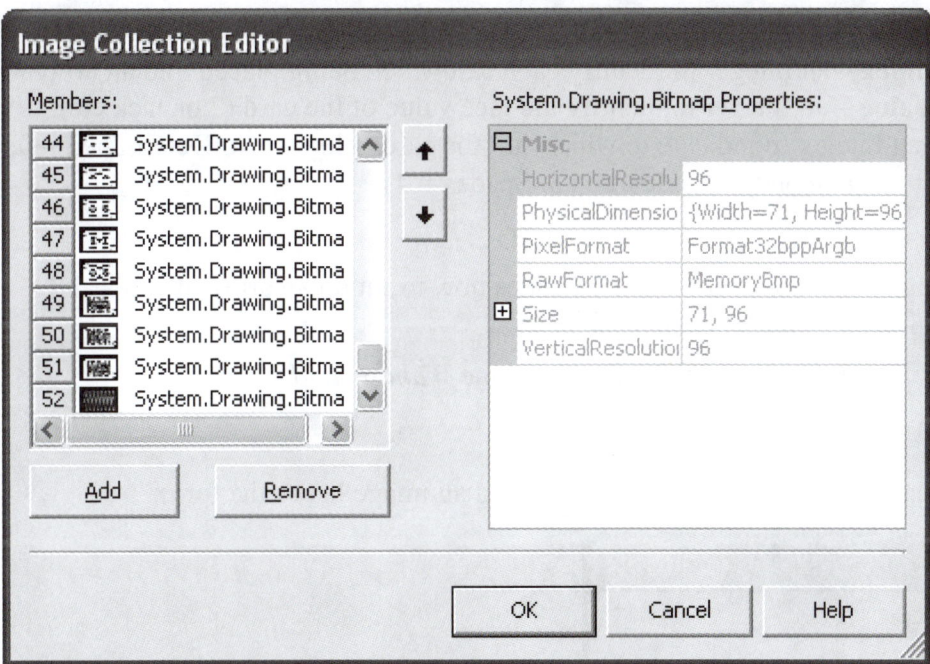

Selecting random cards

The **Rnd** function can be used to select a random card from a deck of fifty-two:

```
WhichCard = Int(Rnd() * 52) ' random number 0-51
```

After selecting a random card, the value and suit of the card can be calculated with **Remainder Division** (Mod) and **Integer division (\\)**:

```
CardValue = WhichCard Mod 13 + 1 ' evaluates from 1 to 13
Suit = WhichCard \ 13 + 1 ' evaluates from 1 to 4
```

Avoiding repeat cards

To correctly simulate dealing cards from a well-shuffled deck, we must avoid selecting the same card more than once. To do this a Boolean array is declared to parallel the cards in the image list:

```
Dim Dealt(51) As Boolean
```

By default all elements of this array have a value of *False*. Each time a card is dealt the corresponding element in the array is assigned a *True* value. For example:

```
Dealt(12) = True
```

marks the King of Clubs as having been dealt. So each time we are about to deal a card we must first check that it hasn't been dealt. If it has then we must try again. The following portion of code, involving a **test last loop**, shows this process:

```
Do
    WhichCard = Int(Rnd() * 52) ' random number 0-51
Loop Until Not Dealt(WhichCard) ' must not be a dealt card
Dealt(WhichCard) = True ' now this card is dealt
```

Another useful subclass

A picture box would do to hold the image of a card, but in a card game there are additional properties that would need to be accessed. **PlayingCard** is a **subclass** of PictureBox (see Appendix 2) that has been created for the program examples that follow. It has three additional properties:

- **CardIndex** – an Integer to identify each card when being placed into an array.
- **CardValue** – an Integer to identify the face value of the card (7 or Jack etc).
- **Suit** – an Integer to indicate to which suit the card belongs (NotDetermined = 0, Clubs = 1, Diamonds = 2, Hearts = 3, Spades = 4).

Program example: Want a hand?

The following simple application demonstrates how to set up an array of cards and deal random hands until the whole deck is used.

Create a new Windows application with the name *Want a hand*.

Create the interface

- Add a playing card, two buttons, a label and an image list to the form.

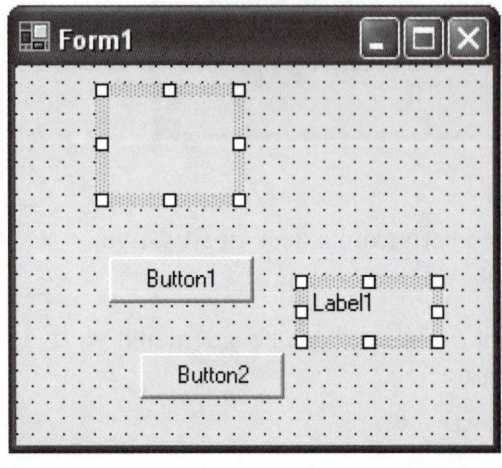

ImageList1

■ Set the following properties:

Form1

BackColor	255, 224, 192
Icon	(you choose)
MaximizeBox	False
Text	Want a hand?

PlayingCard1

CardIndex	0
Image	Cover1.gif
SizeMode	AutoSize

Button1

Name	btnDeal
Text	Deal a hand

Button2

Name	btnShuffle
Text	Shuffle deck

Label1

Name	lblHands
BorderStyle	Fixed3D
Font	MS Sans Serif 10 points Bold
Text	0
TextAlign	MiddleCenter

ImageList1

Name	imlCards
ImageSize	71, 96
TransparentColor	Transparent

■ Copy and paste PlayingCard1 until there are five cards. The CardIndexes should be 0, 1, 2, 3 and 4.

■ Add all the card images to *imlCards*. Start with the Ace, 2 to 10, Jack, Queen and King. Add the suits in the order Clubs, Diamonds, Hearts and Spades.

Write the code and add comments

■ Importing this namespace makes all its contents available to this application.

```
Imports PlayingCards
```

■ Two arrays will be needed at form level.

```
Dim Card(4) As PlayingCard ' an array of 5 cards
Dim Dealt(51) As Boolean ' indicates which cards have been dealt
```

■ The PlayingCard array is instantiated during form load.

```
Private Sub Form1_Load(ByVal sender As Object, ByVal e As System.EventArgs) _
Handles MyBase.Load
    Dim Obj As Object, I As Integer
    For Each Obj In Me.Controls ' check all controls on the form
        If TypeOf Obj Is PlayingCard Then
            I = Obj.CardIndex
            Card(I) = Obj ' add PlayingCard to the array
        End If
    Next Obj
End Sub
```

■ 'Shuffling' in this procedure actually means to assign the whole deck as being not dealt. For this a **For Next** loop is used.

```
Private Sub btnShuffle_Click(ByVal sender As System.Object, ByVal e As _
System.EventArgs) Handles btnShuffle.Click
    Dim I As Integer
    For I = 0 To 51
        Dealt(I) = False ' set all cards not dealt
    Next I
    For I = 0 To 4 ' cover all 5 cards
        Card(I).Image = imlCards.Images.Item(52) ' get cover image from imagelist
    Next I
    lblHands.Text = 0
    btnDeal.Enabled = True ' can now deal a hand
End Sub
```

■ This is the procedure that selects random cards checking that the one chosen has not already been dealt.

```
Private Sub btnDeal_Click(ByVal sender As System.Object, ByVal e As _
System.EventArgs) Handles btnDeal.Click
    Dim I, WhichCard As Integer
    Randomize()
    For I = 0 To 4 ' deal 5 cards
        Do
            WhichCard = Int(Rnd() * 52) ' random number 0-51
        Loop Until Not Dealt(WhichCard) ' must not be a dealt card
        Dealt(WhichCard) = True ' now this card is dealt
        Card(I).Image = imlCards.Images.Item(WhichCard) ' get image from imagelist
    Next I
    lblHands.Text += 1 ' one more hand
End Sub
```

■ Once ten hands have been dealt there are only two cards that haven't been used. So it is time to 'shuffle'.

```
Private Sub lblHands_TextChanged(ByVal sender As Object, ByVal e As _
System.EventArgs) Handles lblHands.TextChanged
    If lblHands.Text = 10 Then ' 50 cards have been dealt
        btnDeal.Enabled = False ' unable to deal
    End If
End Sub
```

Try it out

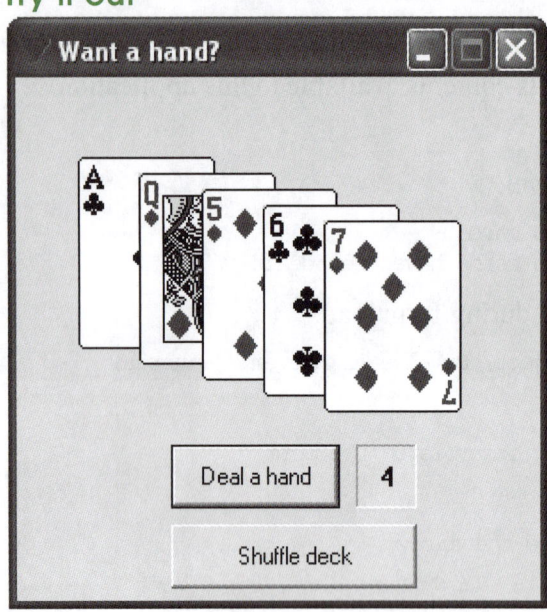

Want a hand – points to note

■ The five playing cards are assigned to an array. To be certain of a particular card being assigned to a particular element the **CardIndex** property is given the required Index value.

```
I = Obj.CardIndex
Card(I) = Obj ' add PlayingCard to the array
```

■ A **Boolean** array with fifty-two elements has been used to mark which cards have been dealt:

```
Dim Dealt(51) As Boolean ' indicates which cards have been dealt
```

Once all cards have been dealt, a newly shuffled deck can be simulated by assigning all elements to *False* with a **For Next** loop:

```
For I = 0 To 51 ' all cards not dealt
    Dealt(I) = False
Next I
```

■ To turn over or cover the five cards, change its image to the cover graphic:

```
For I = 0 To 4 ' cover all 5 cards
    Card(I).Image = imlCards.Images.Item(52) ' get cover image from imagelist
Next I
```

■ A **Do Loop Until** loop keeps trying until it finds a card that has not been dealt. Once found it must be immediately marked as dealt.

```
Do
    WhichCard = Int(Rnd() * 52) ' random number 0-51
Loop Until Not Dealt(WhichCard) ' must not be a dealt card
Dealt(WhichCard) = True ' now this card is dealt
```

■ The **TextChanged** event is raised each time an assignment is made to the Text property of a control.

■ Assigning *False* to the **Enabled** property of a button effectively prevents a user from clicking it.

Want a hand – check what you have learnt

1   There are three division operations in Visual Basic. Which two give an Integer result?

2   Which card (value and suit) in the image list has an index of

   a 11   **b** 15   **c** 46

3   A small theatre has 200 seats (numbered 1 to 200). In a program a Boolean array named *Reserved* keeps track of which seats are reserved. Write a For Next loop to set all the elements in the array *False*.

4   The following line of code selects a random card from the deck:

```
WhichCard = Int(Rnd() * 52)
```

   Write a line of code that selects a random Heart from the deck.

5   Which property setting effectively prevents a user from clicking a button?

6   Examine this code from the *lblHands_TextChanged* procedure

```
If lblHands.Text = 10 Then ' 50 cards have been dealt
    btnDeal.Enabled = False ' unable to deal
End If
```

   How many cards have not been dealt when the condition is *True*?

7   Some looping structures are called test first loops. Why do you think Do Loop Until is called a test last loop?

8   When an Integer variable is declared, by default its value is 0. What is the default value of a Boolean variable?

9   Write the declaration for an array of four text boxes named *Player*.

10   Extend *Want a hand* so that it counts how many cards of each suit are dealt with each hand. An array of labels is recommended as well as taking note of how to determine suit as described early in this chapter.

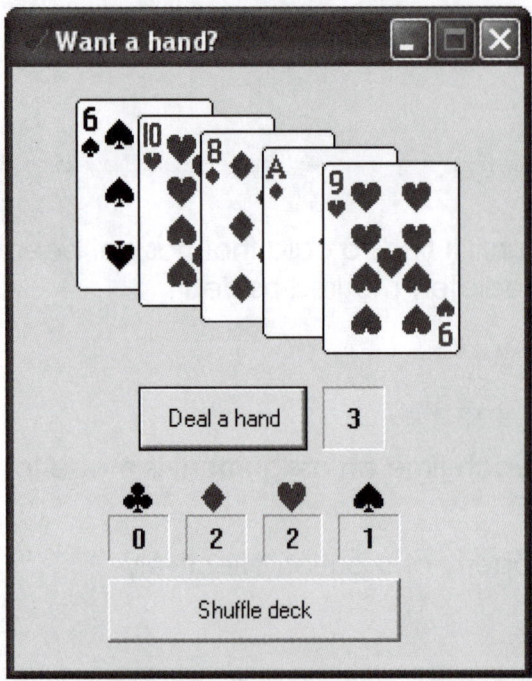

Program example: Pontoon

Create a new Windows application with the name *Pontoon*. The rules of Pontoon are relatively simple compared to other card games. Even so there is considerable complexity in this application.

Create the interface

■   Add a playing card, three labels, five buttons, a combo box, a status bar, an image list, a timer and a main menu to the form.

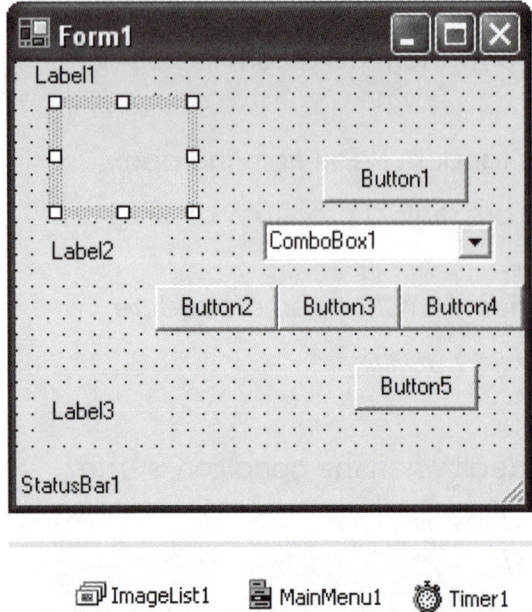

■ Set the following properties:

Form1

BackColor	Green
Icon	(you choose)
MaximizeBox	False
Text	Pontoon

PlayingCard1

CardIndex	0
Image	Cover1.gif
SizeMode	AutoSize

Button1

Name	btnDealFirst
Font	MS Sans Serif 10 points Regular
Text	Deal first card

Button2

Name	btnBuy
Enabled	False
Font	MS Sans Serif 10 points Regular
Text	Buy

Button3

Name	btnTwist
Enabled	False
Font	MS Sans Serif 10 points Regular
Text	Twist

Button4

Name	btnSit
Enabled	False
Font	MS Sans Serif 10 points Regular
Text	Sit

Button5

Name	btnPlayAgain
Enabled	False
Font	MS Sans Serif 10 points Regular
Text	Play again

ComboBox1

Name	cmbStartBet
Enabled	False
Font	MS Sans Serif 10 points Regular
Text	Starting stake

Label1

Font	MS Sans Serif 9 points Bold
ForeColor	White
Text	BANKER

Label2

Font	MS Sans Serif 9 points Bold
ForeColor	White
Text	PLAYER

Label3

Font	MS Sans Serif 9 points Bold
ForeColor	White
Text	Click an Ace to adjust total

ImageList1

Name	imlCards
ImageSize	71, 96
TransparentColor	Transparent

StatusBar1

ShowPanels	True

■ Copy and paste PlayingCard1 until there are ten cards: five for the banker, five for the player.

■ The CardIndexes for the banker are 0 to 4; for the player they are 5 to 9. Group five cards together for the banker and five cards for the player.

■ Add all the card images to *imlCards*. Start with the Ace, 2 to 10, Jack, Queen and King. Add the suits in the order Clubs, Diamonds, Hearts and Spades.

- Add the following to the **Items collection** of *cmbStartBet*:

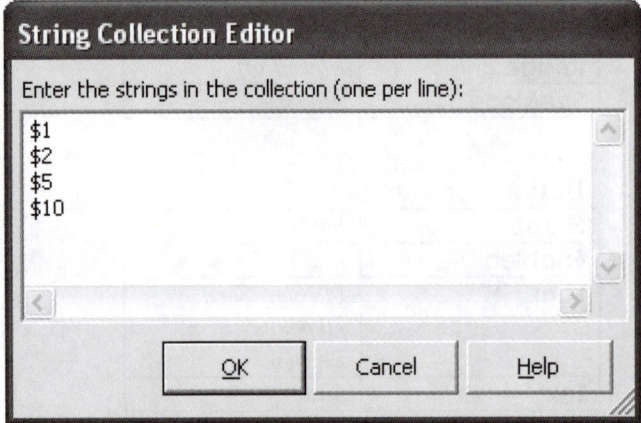

- Add these members to the **Panels collection** of the status bar:

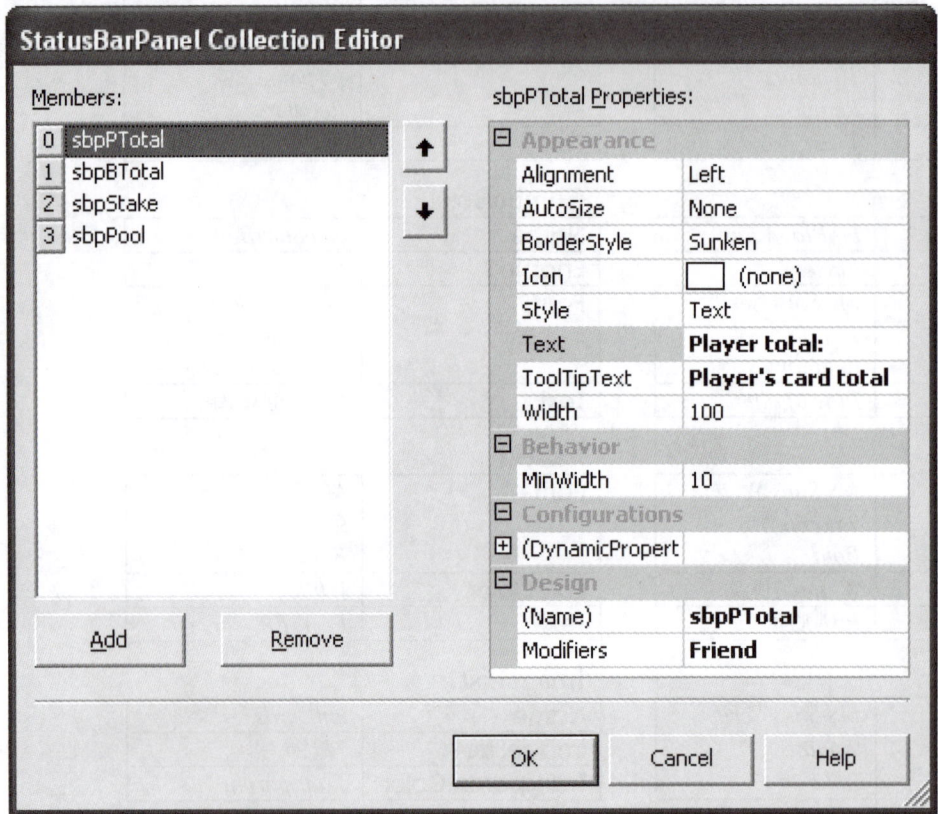

- Set the following properties of the Panels collection members:

Name	sbpPTotal		Name	sbpBTotal
Text	Player total:		Text	Banker total:
TooltipText	Player's card total		TooltipText	Banker's card total
Width	100		Width	100

Name	sbpStake		Name	sbpPool
Text	Stake:		Text	Pool: $100
TooltipText	Amount player has spent buying cards		TooltipText	Amount left in Player's pool of money
Width	80		Width	80

- Enter the following into the main menu.

MenuItem2

Name	*mnuRules*
Shortcut	*CtrlR*
Text	*Rules of Pontoon*

- From the Project menu choose Add Windows Form.
- Add a rich text box to the new form.

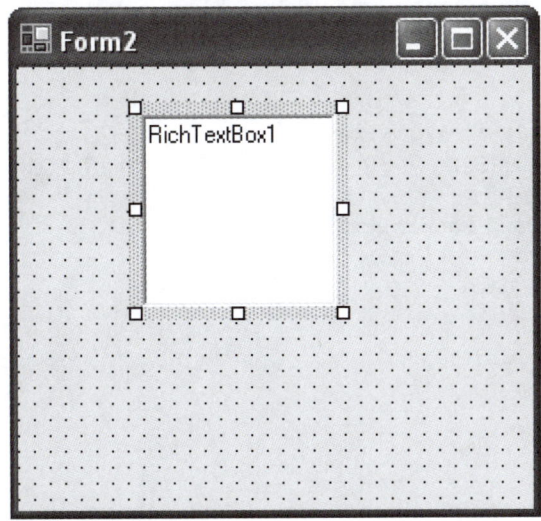

- Set the following properties:

Form2

Icon	*(you choose)*
Text	*The rules of Pontoon*

RichTextbox1

Name	*rtbRules*
BackColor	*255, 255, 192*
Dock	*Fill*
ReadOnly	*True*

- The rich text file *Rules of Pontoon.rtf* must be copied to the Bin folder.

Write the code and add comments

- This **Imports** statement makes all the resources of this namespace available to the application.

```
Imports PlayingCards
```

- **Enumerations** assist in having code that is easy to follow.

```
Private Enum HandResult ' enumeration to describe possible hands
    Bust = 0
    TotalOnly = 1
    FiveCardTrick = 2
    Pontoon = 3
End Enum
```

■ These are the variables required at **form level**. It is important that the names chosen are descriptive of their function.

```
Dim Card(9) As PlayingCard ' 10 possible cards
Dim Dealt(51) As Boolean ' indicates which cards are dealt
Dim PlayerCardCount, BankerCardCount As Integer ' no. of cards dealt
Dim PlayerTotal, BankerTotal As Integer ' total face value of each hand
Dim PlayerResult, BankerResult As HandResult ' description of each hand
Dim Stake As Integer, Pool As Integer = 100 ' amount bet and ammount left
Dim ExtraTen, PlayerAce, BankerAce As Boolean ' variables to indicate Aces
```

■ All these objects have to be initialised at the start of each hand. This is a **general procedure** that is called in three other procedures.

```
Private Sub Initialise()
    Dim I As Integer
    For I = 0 To 51 ' all cards not dealt
        Dealt(I) = False
    Next I
    For I = 0 To 1
        Card(I).Image = imlCards.Images.Item(52) ' card cover
        Card(I + 5).Image = imlCards.Images.Item(52)
    Next I
    For I = 2 To 4 ' last 3 cards for player and banker not visible
        Card(I).Visible = False ' banker's card
        Card(I + 5).Visible = False ' player's card
    Next I
    ExtraTen = False
    BankerAce = False
    PlayerAce = False
    ' all buttons and combo box disabled
    ' except for first card button
    btnDealFirst.Enabled = True
    cmbStartBet.Enabled = False
    cmbStartBet.Text = "Starting stake"
    btnBuy.Enabled = False
    btnTwist.Enabled = False
    btnSit.Enabled = False
    btnPlayAgain.Enabled = False
    PlayerCardCount = 0
    BankerCardCount = 0
    Stake = 0
    ' reset text of status bar panels
    sbpPTotal.Text = "Player total:"
    sbpBTotal.Text = "Banker total:"
    sbpStake.Text = "Stake:"
End Sub
```

■ The array of playing cards has to be populated at form load. When a PlayingCard is found it is put into the array.

```
Private Sub Form1_Load(ByVal sender As Object, ByVal e As System.EventArgs) _
Handles MyBase.Load
    Dim Obj As Object, I As Integer
    For Each Obj In Me.Controls
        If TypeOf Obj Is PlayingCard Then
            I = Obj.CardIndex
            Card(I) = Obj ' add playingcard to Card array
        End If
    Next Obj
    Initialise() ' starting values of properties and variables
End Sub
```

- This general procedure deals cards to both the player and the banker, depending on the value of the **argument** CardIndex that passes a value into it.

```
Private Sub DealCard(ByVal CardIndex As Integer)
    Dim WhichCard As Integer
    Randomize()
    ' must not get an already dealt card
    Do
        WhichCard = Int(Rnd() * 52) ' select random number 0-51
    Loop Until Not Dealt(WhichCard)
    Dealt(WhichCard) = True
    ' get image from imagelist
    Card(CardIndex).Image = imlCards.Images.Item(WhichCard)
    Card(CardIndex).Visible = True
    Card(CardIndex).BringToFront() ' give a layered look to cards
    Card(CardIndex).CardValue = (WhichCard Mod 13) + 1 ' face value of card
    If Card(CardIndex).CardValue = PlayingCard.PlayingCardValue.Ace Then
        If CardIndex <= 4 Then ' banker has Ace
            BankerAce = True
        Else ' player has Ace
            PlayerAce = True
        End If
    End If
End Sub
```

- The click of this button deals the first card to the player. When this card is dealt the player can then place a bet. The button then has to be disabled so the player cannot deal another first card.

```
Private Sub btnDealFirst_Click(ByVal sender As System.Object, _
ByVal e As System.EventArgs) Handles btnDealFirst.Click
    DealCard(5) ' deal first card to player (Index=5)
    PlayerCardCount += 1
    cmbStartBet.Enabled = True
    btnDealFirst.Enabled = False
End Sub
```

- This function simply adds up the value of the cards. It is a **user-defined function**. The arguments that are passed in tell the function the Index of the starting card and how many cards are being added into the total. Note the way in which it counts a 10 or a picture card as 10. The function **returns** a value to the procedure that called it.

```
Private Function CalculateTotal(ByVal StartCard As Integer, _
ByVal NoOfCards As Integer) As Integer
    Dim I As Integer, Tot As Integer = 0
    For I = StartCard To StartCard + NoOfCards - 1
        If Card(I).CardValue >= PlayingCard.PlayingCardValue.Ten Then
            Tot += 10 ' 10 or picture card
        Else
            Tot += Card(I).CardValue ' add face value
        End If
    Next I
    If StartCard > 4 And ExtraTen Then ' player chooses 11 for Ace
        Tot += 10
    End If
    Return Tot
End Function
```

- When the starting bet is selected the second card is dealt to the player. Take particular note of how another event procedure can be raised. In this procedure the *btnSit_Click* procedure is raised without the user clicking the button. It is done for the user automatically.

```
Private Sub cmbStartBet_SelectedValueChanged(ByVal sender As Object, _
ByVal e As System.EventArgs) Handles cmbStartBet.SelectedValueChanged
    Stake = cmbStartBet.Text
    sbpStake.Text = "Stake: $" & Stake
    Pool -= Stake ' reduce pool by stake
    sbpPool.Text = "Pool: $" & Pool
    DealCard(6) ' deal player's 2nd card
    PlayerCardCount += 1
    cmbStartBet.Enabled = False
    btnBuy.Enabled = True ' can now buy
    btnTwist.Enabled = True ' can now twist
    btnSit.Enabled = True ' can now sit
    PlayerTotal = CalculateTotal(5, PlayerCardCount)
    If PlayerAce And PlayerTotal = 11 Then ' player has pontoon
        ExtraTen = True
        PlayerTotal = 21
        sbpPTotal.Text = "Player total: " & PlayerTotal
        btnBuy.Enabled = False ' cannot buy
        btnTwist.Enabled = False ' cannot twist
        btnSit.Enabled = False
        btnSit_Click(Me, Nothing) ' automatically sit with pontoon
    End If
    sbpPTotal.Text = "Player total: " & PlayerTotal
End Sub
```

- Event procedures can handle more than one event as is the case in this procedure. The clicking of any of the player's cards will trigger this procedure. Note the multiple **Handles**. It simply toggles the value of an Ace between one and eleven.

```
Private Sub PlayingCard6_Click(ByVal sender As System.Object, _
ByVal e As System.EventArgs) Handles PlayingCard6.Click, PlayingCard7.Click, _
PlayingCard8.Click, PlayingCard9.Click
    ' only responds to clicking an Ace dealt to Player
    If sender.CardValue = PlayingCard.PlayingCardValue.Ace Then
        ExtraTen = Not ExtraTen ' toggle ExtraTen
        ' recalculate after changing Ace
        PlayerTotal = CalculateTotal(5, PlayerCardCount)
        sbpPTotal.Text = "Player total: " & PlayerTotal
    End If
End Sub
```

- This general procedure deals another card to the player checking to see if it's OK for another to be dealt. Note again the automatic clicking of *btnSit*.

```
Private Sub AnotherPlayerCard()
    DealCard(PlayerCardCount + 5) ' deal one card to player
    PlayerCardCount += 1
    PlayerTotal = CalculateTotal(5, PlayerCardCount)
    sbpPTotal.Text = "Player total: " & PlayerTotal
    If PlayerCardCount = 5 Or PlayerTotal > 21 Or Pool <= 0 Then
        ' 5 cards, bust or no money - must finish
        btnBuy.Enabled = False
        btnTwist.Enabled = False
        btnSit.Enabled = False
        btnSit_Click(Me, Nothing)
    End If
End Sub
```

- Buying a card involves adjusting the pool.

```
Private Sub btnBuy_Click(ByVal sender As System.Object, _
ByVal e As System.EventArgs) Handles btnBuy.Click
    Stake += cmbStartBet.Text ' increase stake
    sbpStake.Text = "Stake: $" & Stake
    Pool -= cmbStartBet.Text ' reduce pool
    sbpPool.Text = "Pool: $" & Pool
    AnotherPlayerCard()
End Sub
```

- A twist deals a card for free. But when you get a card for free you can't buy another card.

```
Private Sub btnTwist_Click(ByVal sender As System.Object, _
ByVal e As System.EventArgs) Handles btnTwist.Click
    btnBuy.Enabled = False ' cannot buy after twist
    AnotherPlayerCard()
End Sub
```

- This procedure simply announces that the player has won then calculates the winnings.

```
Private Sub PlayerWins(ByVal Multiple As Integer)
    Dim Message As String = "Player wins. You get your stake back plus "
    If Multiple = 2 Then
        Message += "double "
    End If
    Message += "your stake."  ' building Message with concatenation
    MessageBox.Show(Message, "Pontoon", MessageBoxButtons.OK, _
    MessageBoxIcon.Information)
    ' if player wins single, banker pays stake and player also gets stake back
    ' if player wins double, banker pays twice stake and player also gets stake back
    Pool += Stake * (1 + Multiple)
    sbpStake.Text = "Stake:"
    sbpPool.Text = "Pool: $" & Pool  ' concatenation of a String with a number
    btnPlayAgain.Enabled = True
End Sub
```

- This procedure makes the announcement that the banker has won then takes the appropriate amount from the player's pool. The banker can take the amount bet by the player or twice the amount bet by the player. This is determined by the value of the argument Multiple.

```
Private Sub BankerWins(ByVal Multiple As Integer)
    Dim Message As String = "Banker wins. You lose "
    If Multiple = 2 Then
        Message += "double "
    End If
    Message += "your stake."
    MessageBox.Show(Message, "Pontoon", MessageBoxButtons.OK, _
    MessageBoxIcon.Information)
    ' if banker wins double, player pays from bet and pool
    ' if banker wins single, player pays from bet only
        Pool -= Stake * (Multiple - 1)
    sbpStake.Text = "Stake:"
    sbpPool.Text = "Pool: $" & Pool
    btnPlayAgain.Enabled = True
End Sub
```

- Critical to the result of each game is determining the type of hand that has resulted. The enumeration created for this program provides a clear way of expressing this result. Here again we see a **user-defined function**.

```
Private Function CalculateResult(ByVal NoOfCards As Integer, _
ByVal CardTotal As Integer) As HandResult
    If CardTotal > 21 Then
        Return HandResult.Bust
    ElseIf NoOfCards = 5 Then
        Return HandResult.FiveCardTrick
    ElseIf CardTotal = 21 Then
        If NoOfCards = 2 Then
            Return HandResult.Pontoon
        Else
            Return HandResult.TotalOnly
        End If
    Else
        Return HandResult.TotalOnly
    End If
End Function
```

- The player decides what he/she wants to do. However when the player decides to sit it is the code in this procedure that will decide what is best for the banker. As you can see it is not an easy decision. The **enumeration** helps the readability of complex code.

```
Private Sub btnSit_Click(ByVal sender As System.Object, _
ByVal e As System.EventArgs) Handles btnSit.Click
    ' player is sitting, no more cards, calculate result
    btnBuy.Enabled = False
    btnTwist.Enabled = False
    btnSit.Enabled = False
    PlayerResult = CalculateResult(PlayerCardCount, PlayerTotal)
    ' deal first two cards to the banker
    DealCard(0)
    DealCard(1)
    BankerCardCount = 2
    BankerTotal = CalculateTotal(0, BankerCardCount)
    ' if banker has an ace, may advantage him to value it 11
    If BankerAce And (BankerTotal = 11 Or BankerTotal >= PlayerTotal - 10) Then
        BankerTotal += 10
    End If
    sbpBTotal.Text = "Banker total: " & BankerTotal
    ' calculate the banker's result with two cards
    BankerResult = CalculateResult(BankerCardCount, BankerTotal)
    ' check if there is a clear winner or banker needs more cards
    If PlayerResult = HandResult.Bust Then
        BankerWins(1) ' player is bust, banker must win
    ElseIf BankerResult = HandResult.Pontoon And PlayerResult < _
HandResult.Pontoon Then
        BankerWins(2) ' pontoon pays double
    ElseIf BankerResult = HandResult.Pontoon And PlayerResult = _
HandResult.Pontoon Then
        BankerWins(1) ' pontoon pays single when player also gets pontoon
    ElseIf BankerResult = HandResult.TotalOnly And PlayerResult = _
HandResult.TotalOnly And PlayerTotal <= BankerTotal Then
        BankerWins(1) ' banker has a better 2 card total than player
    ElseIf PlayerResult = HandResult.Pontoon And BankerResult < _
HandResult.Pontoon Then
        PlayerWins(2) ' player is paid double for pontoon
    ElseIf BankerResult < PlayerResult Or (BankerResult = PlayerResult And _
BankerTotal < PlayerTotal) Then
        tmrDealToBanker.Start() ' more cards for the banker
    End If
End Sub
```

- This timer procedure deals additional cards to the banker keeping watch on the consequences of each card.

```
Private Sub tmrDealToBanker_Tick(ByVal sender As System.Object, _
ByVal e As System.EventArgs) Handles tmrDealToBanker.Tick
    DealCard(BankerCardCount) ' deal a card to the banker
    BankerCardCount += 1
    BankerTotal = CalculateTotal(0, BankerCardCount)
    ' decide if Ace should be 11
    If BankerAce And BankerTotal + 10 >= PlayerTotal And BankerTotal <= 11 Then
        BankerTotal += 10
    End If
    sbpBTotal.Text = "Banker total: " & BankerTotal
    BankerResult = CalculateResult(BankerCardCount, BankerTotal)
    ' check if this card has resulted in a winner
    If BankerResult = HandResult.TotalOnly And PlayerResult = _
    HandResult.TotalOnly And PlayerTotal <= BankerTotal Then
        tmrDealToBanker.Stop() ' stop dealing cards to banker
        BankerWins(1)
    ElseIf BankerResult = HandResult.Bust Then
        tmrDealToBanker.Stop() ' stop dealing cards to banker
        If PlayerResult = HandResult.FiveCardTrick Then
            PlayerWins(2) ' banker pays double the stake
        Else
            PlayerWins(1) ' banker pays the stake
        End If
    ElseIf BankerResult = HandResult.FiveCardTrick Then
        tmrDealToBanker.Stop() ' stop dealing cards to banker
        If PlayerResult = HandResult.FiveCardTrick Then
            BankerWins(1) ' banker takes the stake
        Else
            BankerWins(2) ' banker takes double the stake
        End If
    End If
    ' if there is no winner the timer will not stop
    ' another card will be dealt to banker
End Sub
```

- To start another hand the player clicks this button.

```
Private Sub btnPlayAgain_Click(ByVal sender As System.Object, _
ByVal e As System.EventArgs) Handles btnPlayAgain.Click
    If Pool > 0 Then ' must have some money to play
        Initialise() ' starting values of properties and variables
    Else ' no more money to play
        MessageBox.Show("You have run out of money." + vbCr + _
        "Gambling with cards is a risky game" + vbCr + "Quit now!", "Pontoon", _
        MessageBoxButtons.OK, MessageBoxIcon.Warning)
    End If
End Sub
```

- When this menu item is clicked Form2 is displayed.

```
Private Sub mnuRules_Click(ByVal sender As System.Object, _
ByVal e As System.EventArgs) Handles mnuRules.Click
    Dim Form2 As New Form2
    Form2.ShowDialog() ' open instructions
End Sub
```

- The rich text box on Form2 contains the rules of Pontoon.

```
Private Sub Form2_Load(ByVal sender As Object, ByVal e As System.EventArgs) _
Handles MyBase.Load
    rtbRules.LoadFile("Rules of Pontoon.rtf")
End Sub
```

Try it out

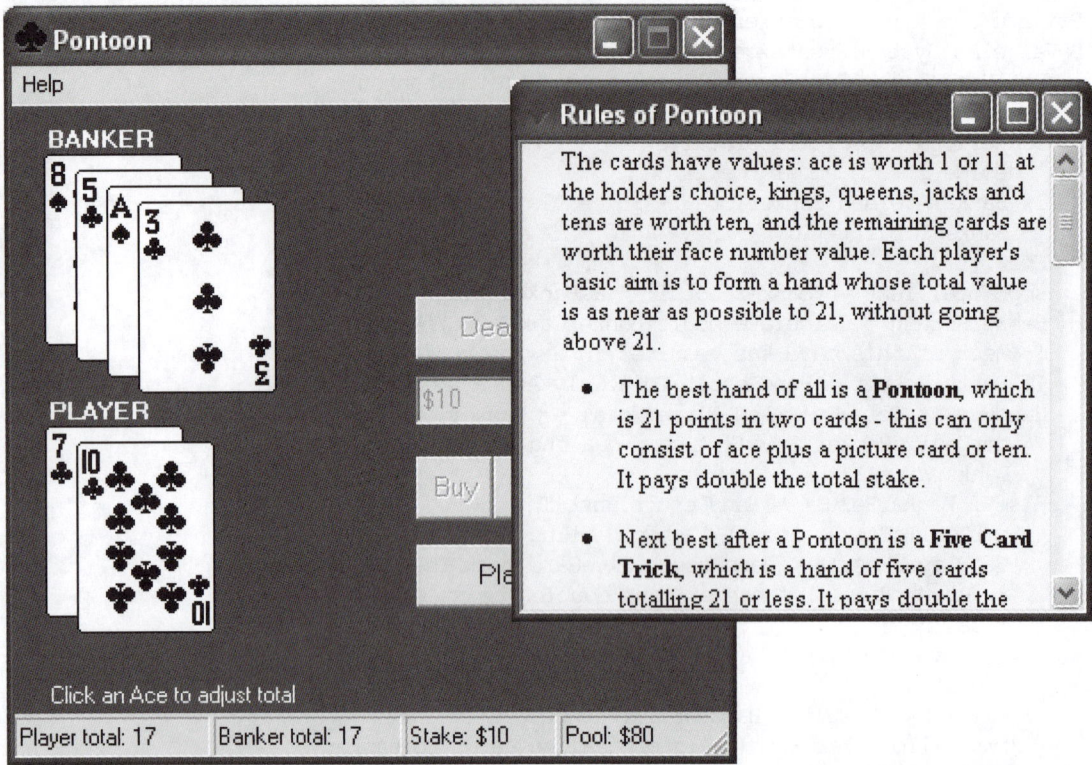

Pontoon – points to note

- A **combo box** has an **Items** collection. The items in this case are the betting options.

- A **status bar** has a **Panels** collection. The panels are used to communicate the state of the game. Each member of the Panels collection has its own set of properties.

- The Text property of each panel takes a **String** value. To join (**concatenate**) a number to a String the **ampersand (&)** character is used. When joining two Strings either the plus (+) or ampersand (&) will do.

```
sbpPTotal.Text = "Player total: " & PlayerTotal
```

- A **rich textbox** control was used on Form2. The rich textbox can hold formatted text. So it is possible to have different fonts, formatting options as well as graphics.

- The **Dock** property of the rich textbox has six different possible settings. These numeric settings are represented by an enumeration.

- An **enumeration** has been created for this program to describe the possible types of hands:

```
Private Enum HandResult ' enumeration to describe possible hands
    Bust = 0
    TotalOnly = 1
    FiveCardTrick = 2
    Pontoon = 3
End Enum
```

- An ace can have the value 1 or 11. For this reason several 'flag' variables were created.

  ```
  Dim ExtraTen, PlayerAce, BankerAce As Boolean ' variables to indicate Aces
  ```

- An Initialise procedure was created to make the large number of settings before the start of a new game. It is called in the *Form_Load* and the *btnPlayAgain_Click* procedures.

- There are a number of other **general procedures**: DealCard, AnotherPlayerCard, PlayerWins and BankerWins. The code has been packaged in these procedures because it is used more than once in other event procedures.

- There are also two **user-defined functions**: CalculateTotal and CalculateResult. Arguments feed values into the function and the function outputs a value of its own. The **Return** statement in the function sends out its value.

- In the card game Pontoon there is a relatively small number of comparisons to be made when deciding on a winner and the payout. Yet the code is still quite long and detailed in its examination of all possibilities.

- Note the way in which the second form is opened. The **ShowDialog** method ensures the form is **modal**. It has to be closed before you can return to Form1.

  ```
  Dim Form2 As New Form2
  Form2.ShowDialog() ' open instructions
  ```

Pontoon – check what you have learnt

1 Collections are widely used in Visual Basic.NET. What are the collections in this programming example?

2 What are the features of a rich text box that make it far superior to a regular text box?

3 The enumeration HandResult was declared. It holds the values 0, 1, 2 and 3. What is the advantage of an enumeration over simply declaring HandResult as an Integer?

4 the order of the members of HandResult significant?

5 The following three Boolean variables are declared at form level:

  ```
  Dim ExtraTen, PlayerAce, BankerAce As Boolean
  ```

  Each are used as 'flags' in the code. What does each variable flag?Is

6 In event handlers (or event procedures) what is the sender?

  ```
  Private Sub btnSit_Click(ByVal sender As System.Object, _
  ByVal e As System.EventArgs) Handles btnSit.Click
  ```

7 What are the only two possible values for the variable WhoseTurn?

  ```
  WhoseTurn = (WhoseTurn + 1) Mod 2
  ```

8 A decision is being made in the following code. Write it in ordinary English.

```
' decide if Ace should be 11
If BankerAce And BankerTotal + 10 >= PlayerTotal And BankerTotal <= 11 Then
    BankerTotal += 10
End If
```

9 If the banker gets a five card trick, and the player is sitting without a Pontoon hand, what are the only options?

```
ElseIf BankerResult = HandResult.FiveCardTrick Then
    tmrDealToBanker.Stop() ' stop dealing cards to banker
    If PlayerResult = HandResult.FiveCardTrick Then
        BankerWins(1) ' banker takes the stake
    Else
        BankerWins(2) ' banker takes double the stake
    End If
End If
```

10 Concentration is a well known card game for all ages. All fifty two cards are laid out face down. Each player has to turn over two cards at a time. If a pair is found they are removed, that player gets a point and another turn. If the player is unsuccessful then it's the other player's turn.

A procedure will need to be written to handle the Click event on all fifty two cards. To do this extend the **Handles** section of the code template:

```
Private Sub PlayingCard1_Click(ByVal sender As System.Object, _
ByVal e As System.EventArgs) Handles PlayingCard1.Click, _
PlayingCard10.Click, PlayingCard11.Click, PlayingCard12.Click, _
PlayingCard13.Click, PlayingCard14.Click, PlayingCard15.Click, _
```

and so on. To make reference to the particular object that was clicked use the **sender** argument. For example

```
I = (sender.Suit - 1) * 13 + (sender.CardValue - 1)
sender.Image = imlCards.Images.Item(I)
```

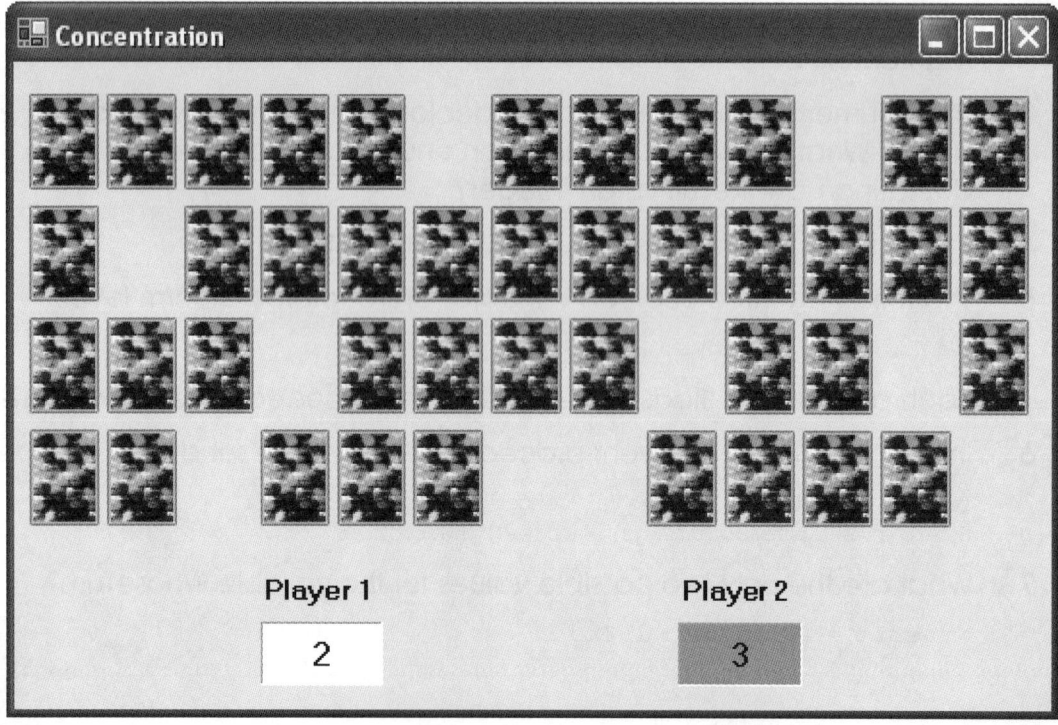

Chapter 13

Objects on the fly

The Controls Collection

Collections are widely used in Visual Basic.NET. A collection is a group of objects contained within another object. Regular use has already been made of the Images collection of an image list.

Another collection that has been used many times is the **Controls collection** of a form. During the form load this collection has been searched looking for particular objects:

```
Private Sub Form1_Load(ByVal sender As Object, ByVal e As System.EventArgs) _
Handles MyBase.Load
   Dim obj As Object, I As Integer = 0
   For Each obj In Me.Controls ' all controls on the form
      ' only those picture boxes tagged with "car"
      If TypeOf obj Is PictureBox AndAlso obj.Tag = "car" Then
         RallyCar(I) = obj ' assign this picturebox to an element of the array
         I += 1 ' increase I by 1 ready for the next assignment
      End If
   Next obj
End Sub
```

In the above procedure a **For Each** loop is used to look at all of the objects belonging to the Controls collection. In this case it was searching for picture boxes tagged "car".

Adding controls at run time

Typically when a form is being built for an application all the controls required are first placed on the form. But what if you are not sure how many controls are going to be required until the application is actually running? It may be necessary to add them as required.

The following two programming examples apply this concept. Controls are added and disposed of at run-time. Typically the process follows the following steps:
- A new control is created.
- The control is added to the parent's control collection (most often a form).
- Some starting properties are assigned.
- The control is used in the application.
- When no longer needed the control is disposed of.

Another useful subclass

Segment is a **subclass** of PictureBox that has been created for the following program example. It has one additional property:

- **SegmentIndex** – an Integer to identify each control when being placed into an array.

The full definition of the Segment class is included in Appendix 2.

Program example: Snake

Create a new Windows application with the name *Snake*.

Create the interface

- Add the Segment control to the toolbox. Browse to *SnakeParts.dll*.
- Add four labels, one picture box, twenty-one segments and three timers to the form.

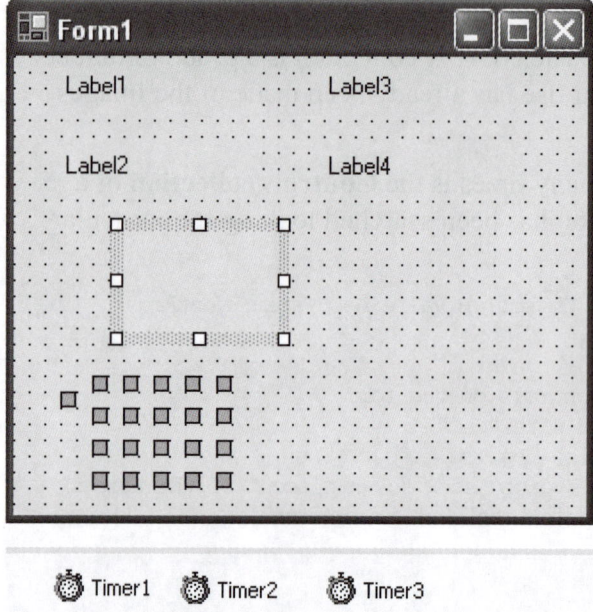

- Set the following properties:

Form1

BackColor	White
FormBorderStyle	FixedSingle
Icon	(you choose)
KeyPreview	True
MaximizeBox	False
Text	Feed the snake

PictureBox1

Name	picMouse
BackColor	Transparent
Image	Mouse.gif
Size	16, 16
SizeMode	StretchImage

Label1

Text	Time

Label3

Text	Score

Label2

Name	lblTime
BorderStyle	Fixed3D
Font	MS Sans Serif 12 points Bold
Text	100
TextAlign	MiddleCenter

Label4

Name	lblScore
BorderStyle	Fixed3D
Font	MS Sans Serif 12 points Bold
Text	0
TextAlign	MiddleCenter

Segment1

BackColor	DarkOliveGreen
SegmentIndex	0

Timer1

Name	tmrShowFood
Enabled	True
Interval	5000

Timer2

Name	tmrKeepTime
Enabled	True
Interval	1000

Timer3

Name	tmrMoveSnake
Enabled	True
Interval	100

- The other twenty segments (Segment2 to Segment 21) should be lined up in order beside the 'head' (Segment1). These segments should have their SegmentIndex properties set from 1 to 20.

Write the code and add comments

- From the Project menu choose Add Existing Item. Then add the code module *Collision.vb*. In the same way add the code module *PlayWave.vb*.

- Copy the wave file *gulp.wav* to the Bin folder. This is the eating sound effect.

- Declare this enumeration at form level. It allows for a simple means of specifying the direction of the moving snake.

```
Private Enum Direction
    East = 0
    South = 1
    West = 2
    North = 3
End Enum
```

- Declare the following variables at form level:

```
Dim Last As Integer = 20 ' the last index of the segment array
Dim SnakePart() As Segment ' the segments of the snake are an array
Dim WhichWay As Direction = Direction.West ' the direction the snake is moving
```

- The array of segments is created during the Form Load.

```
Private Sub Form1_Load(ByVal sender As System.Object, ByVal e _
As System.EventArgs)  Handles MyBase.Load
    ReDim SnakePart(Last)    ' array starts with 0 to 20
    Dim Ctl As Object, J As Integer
    For Each Ctl In Controls
        If TypeOf Ctl Is Segment Then
            J = Ctl.SegmentIndex
            SnakePart(J) = Ctl    ' add to SnakePart array
        End If
    Next Ctl
End Sub
```

- This procedure moves each segment of the snake, one after the other, starting with the tail then moving towards the head. A **For Next** loop is used.

```
Private Sub MoveAll()
    ' move each part to the location of the part before it
    Dim I As Integer
    For I = Last To 1 Step -1
        SnakePart(I).Location = SnakePart(I - 1).Location
    Next I
End Sub
```

- If the snake head collides with the mouse then he gets to eat it and subsequently grows by one additional segment.

```
Private Sub EatFood()
    ' check for a collision with the snake head and food
    If Collision(SnakePart(0), picMouse) Then
        lblScore.Text += 5  ' player gets 5 points
        PlayWaveFile("gulp.wav")
        picMouse.Visible = False
        GrowSnake()
    End If
End Sub
```

■   The snake grows by getting an extra segment added to its tail.

```
Private Sub GrowSnake()
    Dim Tail As New Segment        ' new tail to add to snake
    Me.Controls.Add(Tail)
    ' put it on the right side of the last snake part
    Tail.Top = SnakePart(Last).Top
    Tail.Left = SnakePart(Last).Left + 8
    Last += 1    ' now there is one more part
    ReDim Preserve SnakePart(Last)   ' increase elements in the array
    SnakePart(Last) = Tail   ' add Tail to the array
End Sub
```

■   Pressing the cursor keys changes the direction of the moving snake.

```
Private Sub Form1_KeyDown(ByVal sender As Object, ByVal e As _
System.Windows.Forms.KeyEventArgs) Handles MyBase.KeyDown
    Select Case e.KeyCode
        Case Keys.Up
            WhichWay = Direction.North
        Case Keys.Down
            WhichWay = Direction.South
        Case Keys.Left
            WhichWay = Direction.West
        Case Keys.Right
            WhichWay = Direction.East
    End Select
End Sub
```

■   This timer procedure moves the head of the snake. All the other parts follow each other.

```
Private Sub tmrMoveSnake_Tick(ByVal sender As System.Object, ByVal e As _
System.EventArgs) Handles tmrMoveSnake.Tick
    Dim I As Integer
    MoveAll()    ' all parts except the head follow each other
    Select Case WhichWay
        Case Direction.North
            SnakePart(0).Top -= 8    ' move head up
            If SnakePart(0).Top <= -8 Then ' past top of form
                SnakePart(0).Top = Me.Height + 8
            End If
        Case Direction.East
            SnakePart(0).Left += 8  ' move head to right
            If SnakePart(0).Left >= Me.Width Then ' past left of form
                SnakePart(0).Left = -8
            End If
        Case Direction.South
            SnakePart(0).Top += 8    ' move head down
            If SnakePart(0).Top >= Me.Height + 8 Then ' past bottom of form
                SnakePart(0).Top = -8
            End If
        Case Direction.West
            SnakePart(0).Left -= 8  ' move head to left
            If SnakePart(0).Left <= -8 Then ' past right of form
                SnakePart(0).Left = Me.Width
            End If
    End Select
    EatFood() ' check if this move eats food
    For I = 1 To Last    ' penalty for crossing over itself
        If Collision(SnakePart(0), SnakePart(I)) Then
            lblScore.Text -= 1 ' lose a point
        End If
    Next I
End Sub
```

- This timer procedure moves the mouse to a new random location on the form. Rather than separately adjust the Left and Top properties it is a single move to a new location.

```
Private Sub tmrShowFood_Tick(ByVal sender As System.Object, ByVal e As _
System.EventArgs) Handles tmrShowFood.Tick
    Dim X, Y As Integer
    Randomize()
    ' move mouse to a random location
    X = Int(Rnd() * (Me.DisplayRectangle.Width - picMouse.Width))
    Y = Int(Rnd() * (Me.DisplayRectangle.Height - picMouse.Height))
    picMouse.Location = New Point(X , Y)
    picMouse.Visible = True
End Sub
```

- Here each of the timers toggle between on and off.

```
Private Sub ToggleTimers()
    tmrKeepTime.Enabled = Not tmrKeepTime.Enabled
    tmrShowFood.Enabled = Not tmrShowFood.Enabled
    tmrMoveSnake.Enabled = Not tmrMoveSnake.Enabled
End Sub
```

- This procedure disposes of the segments added, restarts timers and resets labels ready for a new game.

```
Private Sub Restart()
    Dim I As Integer
    For I = 21 To Last  ' dispose of additional segemts
        SnakePart(I).Dispose()
    Next I
    Last = 20
    ReDim Preserve SnakePart(Last)  ' redimension the array
    lblTime.Text = 100
    lblScore.Text = 0
    ToggleTimers()  ' turn on all timers
    picMouse.Visible = True
End Sub
```

- This timer counts down the 100 seconds.

```
Private Sub tmrKeepTime_Tick(ByVal sender As System.Object, ByVal e As _
System.EventArgs) Handles tmrKeepTime.Tick
    lblTime.Text -= 1
End Sub
```

- If the time reaches 0 then the game is over. The player is given the option of playing again.

```
Private Sub lblTime_TextChanged(ByVal sender As Object, ByVal e As _
System.EventArgs) Handles lblTime.TextChanged
    If lblTime.Text = 0 Then   ' time's up
        ToggleTimers() ' turn off all timers
        picMouse.Visible = False
        If MessageBox.Show("Game over, play again?", "Feed the snake", _
        MessageBoxButtons.YesNo, MessageBoxIcon.Question) = DialogResult.Yes Then
            Restart()
        Else
            End
        End If
    End If
End Sub
```

Try it out

Snake – points to note

- Yet again this programming example has used a **subclass** designed to suit the requirements of this program.

- The declaration of the array of Segments is left open. The last index is not supplied. This is because it is not known how many there will be.

```
Dim SnakePart() As Segment ' the segments of the snake are an array
```

- The array is **redimensioned** in the Form_Load and subsequently each time the array has to grow. The use of the keyword **Preserve** ensures that all existing elements remain intact.

```
ReDim SnakePart(Last)    ' array starts with 0 to 20
```

and later

```
Last += 1    ' now there is one more part
ReDim Preserve SnakePart(Last)   ' increase elements in the array
```

- Custom made **functions** and **procedures** in the added code modules simplify the written code. Although Visual Basic.NET has a vast number of built-in functions and procedures, it has the facility for developers to create their own. The following code shows examples of this:

```
If Collision(SnakePart(0), picMouse) Then
    lblScore.Text += 5  ' player gets 5 points
    PlayWaveFile("gulp.wav")
    picMouse.Visible = False
    GrowSnake()
End If
```

- The GrowSnake procedure is an example of the technique outlined at the start of this chapter. A new control is created, added to the **Controls collection**, properties are set then it is added to the array.

- Note the way in which the mouse is moved to a new random location on the form.

```
X = Int(Rnd() * (Me.DisplayRectangle.Width - picMouse.Width))
Y = Int(Rnd() * (Me.DisplayRectangle.Height - picMouse.Height))
picMouse.Location = New Point(X , Y)
```

- The **Not** operator toggles a Boolean value. *True* goes to *False*, *False* goes to *True*.

```
tmrKeepTime.Enabled = Not tmrKeepTime.Enabled
```

- Finally when a new game starts all the created segments are disposed of using a **For Next** loop and the **Dispose** method.:

```
For I = 21 To Last  ' dispose of additional segemts
    SnakePart(I).Dispose()
Next I
```

Snake – check what you have learnt

1   Make a declaration for an array of String named Participant where it is unknown how many elements will be needed.

2   In this example controls are created at run time. Summarise the life of such a control.

3   The array SnakePart is dimensioned in three procedures. Write these three statements.

4   ReDim changes the size of an existing array. What keyword is used with ReDim to ensure all existing elements remain intact?

5   In which two procedures is the enumeration Direction used?

6   In an assignment statement, use the Location property to move a picture box *picTarget* to the location 200, 180.

7   Write the loop that disposes of the additional segments when a new game is to start.

8   A menu item *mnuSound* has a Boolean property Checked. Write the line of code that will toggle the value of this property.

9   When the segments of the snake are moved they are done from the largest index to the smallest. The **Step** keyword allows us to have the loop count backwards:

```
For I = Last To 1 Step -1
    SnakePart(I).Location = SnakePart(I - 1).Location
Next I
```

Why are they moved in this order and not from smallest index to largest?

10 Introduce another item of food for the snake, a rabbit. Have either the rabbit or the mouse appear randomly. The rabbit, being larger, is easier to catch, so it might return fewer points.

Program example: Tetraminos

Tetris is a popular game developed in 1985 by Alexey Pajitnov, Dmitry Pavlovsky, and Vadim Gerasimov. There have been many versions written for almost every computer platform. The following version is based on the Tetris concept, but the code is original. The coding of this application is not for the faint-hearted as it is long and, at times, quite complex.

Create a new Windows application with the name *Tetraminos*.

Create the interface

■ Add a panel, five labels, a list box, a timer and a main menu to the form.

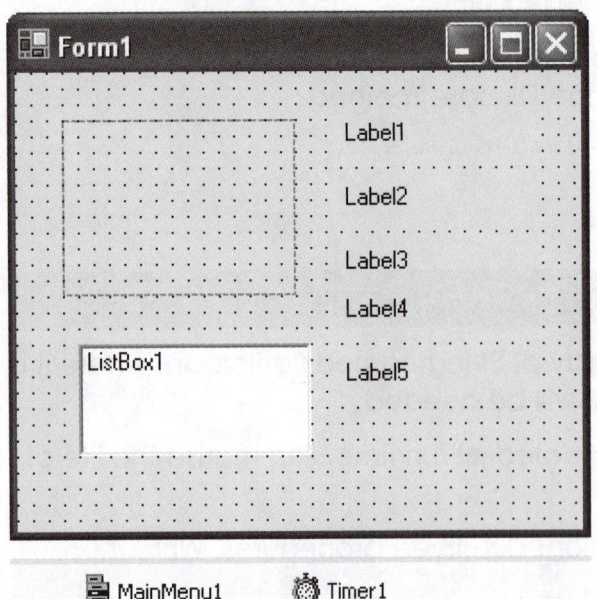

■ Set the following properties:

Form1

FormBorderstyle	FixedSingle
Icon	(you choose)
KeyPreview	True
MaximizeBox	False
Size	312, 264
StartPosition	CenterScreen
Text	Tetraminos

Panel1

Name	pnlBuild
BackColor	White
BorderStyle	FixedSingle
Location	8, 8
Size	180, 180

Label1

Text	Score

Label3

Text	Player

Label2

Name	lblScore
BorderStyle	Fixed3D
Text	0
TextAlign	MiddleCenter

Label4

Name	lblPlayer
BorderStyle	Fixed3D
Text	
TextAlign	MiddleCenter

Label5

Text	Use the cursor keys to move left right and rotate, spacebar to drop piece.

ListBox1

Name	lstHistory
BorderStyle	FixedSingle
Location	8, 8
Size	180, 184
Visible	False

Timer1

Name	tmrMovePiece
Interval	500

- Edit the text of the main menu so that the menus read as shown below. Use an ampersand character (&) immediately before the letter that is to be underlined. This sets the access key for the menu item:

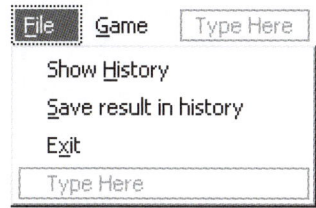 

- Set these properties of the menu items:

Name	Enabled	ShortCut	Text
mnuShowHistory	*True*	*CtrlH*	*Show &History*
mnuSave	*False*	*CtrlS*	*&Save result in history*
mnuExit	*True*		*E&xit*
mnuNew	*True*	*CtrlN*	*&New*
mnuPause	*False*	*CtrlP*	*&Pause*

Write the code and add comments

- From the Project menu add the existing item *PlayWave.vb*.

- Copy the files *pop.wav* and *hit.wav* to the Bin folder.

- Declare this enumeration at form level. It allows for a simple way of specifying the shape of a piece.

```
Private Enum ShapeType ' enumeration to name each shape
    Square = 0
    Straight = 1
    L = 2
    J = 3
    T = 4
    Z = 5
    S = 6
End Enum
```

- Declare these variables and constant at form level.

```
Dim NextPiece As ShapeType
Dim Square(,) As PictureBox ' coloured squares making each piece
Dim PCount As Integer = 0   ' count of pieces used
Dim Occupied(,) As String ' which grid positions are occupied and by what square
Dim MaxX, MaxY As Integer ' maximum X and Y grid positions
Const SIDE As Integer = 12 ' length of square side in pixels
Dim Player As String ' name of current player
Dim Speed As Integer = 500 ' slow speed
```

- This general procedure makes all the settings necessary for the beginning of a game.

```
Private Sub StartGame()
    ReDim Occupied(MaxX, MaxY) ' restart the occupied array
    ReDim Square(3, 0) ' restart the square array
    Dim I As Integer
    tmrMovePiece.Enabled = False ' stop pieces moving
    pnlBuild.Controls.Clear() ' clear all pieces from panel
    lblScore.Text = 0 ' score back to zero
    mnuSave.Enabled = False ' can't save until game is over
    mnuShowHistory.Checked = False ' if history is showing, hide it
    lstHistory.Visible = False
```

```
' get the name of the player - default at last player
Do
    Player = InputBox("Name of player?" + vbLf + vbLf + _
    "This is the name that will be" + vbLf + "recorded in the history file."_
    , "Tetraminos", Player)
Loop Until Player > "" ' must enter a name
lblPlayer.Text = Player ' put player's name in label
mnuShowHistory.Enabled = False ' don't allow show history while playing a game
mnuPause.Enabled = True ' can pause now game has started
mnuPause.Checked = False ' not checked indicates not paused
PCount = 0 ' restart count of pieces
For I = 0 To MaxX ' all X coordinates of last grid row
    Occupied(I, MaxY) = "999" ' occupied by dummy pieces
Next I
Randomize()
NextPiece = Int(Rnd() * 7) ' random shape type for first piece
MakePiece(NextPiece) ' make the chosen shape
tmrMovePiece.Enabled = True ' start moving the current piece
Speed = 500 ' start at slowest speed
tmrMovePiece.Interval = Speed ' timer set at this speed
End Sub
```

■   This procedure creates the four picture boxes that make up a single piece.

```
Private Sub MakePiece(ByVal Shape As ShapeType)
    Dim I As Integer, X As Integer = 96, Y As Integer = 0
    ' allocate colour according to chosen shape
    ' Square-red, Straight-blue, L-green, J-violet, T-black, Z-brown, S-lime
    Dim SquareColour() As Color = {Color.Red, Color.Blue, Color.Green, _
    Color.Violet, Color.Black, Color.Brown, Color.Lime}
    PCount += 1 ' another piece
    lblScore.Text += 1 ' get a point for each piece
    For I = 0 To 3
        Dim SquareTemp As New PictureBox ' create a new picturebox
        pnlBuild.Controls.Add(SquareTemp) ' add new picturebox to the panel
        SquareTemp.Size = New Size(SIDE, SIDE) ' set correct size
        SquareTemp.BackColor = SquareColour(Shape)
        ReDim Preserve Square(3, PCount) ' redimension array for one extra picturebox
        Square(I, PCount) = SquareTemp ' add new picturebox to array
    Next I
    ' organise squares to the chosen shape
    Select Case Shape
        Case ShapeType.Square
            Square(0, PCount).Location = New Point(X, Y)   ' pivot square
            Square(1, PCount).Location = New Point(X + SIDE, Y)
            Square(2, PCount).Location = New Point(X, Y + SIDE)
            Square(3, PCount).Location = New Point(X + SIDE, Y + SIDE)
        Case ShapeType.Straight
            Square(0, PCount).Location = New Point(X, Y)   ' pivot square
            Square(1, PCount).Location = New Point(X - SIDE, Y)
            Square(2, PCount).Location = New Point(X + SIDE, Y)
            Square(3, PCount).Location = New Point(X + SIDE * 2, Y)
        Case ShapeType.L
            Square(0, PCount).Location = New Point(X, Y + SIDE) ' pivot square
            Square(1, PCount).Location = New Point(X, Y + SIDE * 2)
            Square(2, PCount).Location = New Point(X, Y)
            Square(3, PCount).Location = New Point(X - SIDE, Y)
        Case ShapeType.J
            Square(0, PCount).Location = New Point(X, Y + SIDE) ' pivot square
            Square(1, PCount).Location = New Point(X, Y + SIDE * 2)
            Square(2, PCount).Location = New Point(X, Y)
            Square(3, PCount).Location = New Point(X + SIDE, Y)
```

```
     Case ShapeType.T
        Square(0, PCount).Location = New Point(X, Y)  ' pivot square
        Square(1, PCount).Location = New Point(X - SIDE, Y)
        Square(2, PCount).Location = New Point(X + SIDE, Y)
        Square(3, PCount).Location = New Point(X, Y + SIDE)
     Case ShapeType.Z
        Square(0, PCount).Location = New Point(X, Y)  ' pivot square
        Square(1, PCount).Location = New Point(X - SIDE, Y)
        Square(2, PCount).Location = New Point(X, Y + SIDE)
        Square(3, PCount).Location = New Point(X + SIDE, Y + SIDE)
     Case ShapeType.S
        Square(0, PCount).Location = New Point(X, Y) ' pivot square
        Square(1, PCount).Location = New Point(X + SIDE, Y)
        Square(2, PCount).Location = New Point(X, Y + SIDE)
        Square(3, PCount).Location = New Point(X - SIDE, Y + SIDE)
   End Select
End Sub
```

- The maximum X and Y grid positions are calculated.

```
Private Sub Form1_Load(ByVal sender As Object, ByVal e As System.EventArgs) _
Handles MyBase.Load
   ' calculate the maximum X and Y grid positions
   MaxX = pnlBuild.Width \ SIDE - 1
   MaxY = pnlBuild.Height \ SIDE
End Sub
```

- This timer procedure controls the progression of a piece down the screen.

```
Private Sub tmrMovePiece_Tick(ByVal sender As System.Object, ByVal e As _
System.EventArgs) Handles tmrMovePiece.Tick
   Dim I, X, Y As Integer
   Randomize()
   If OKtoMove(PCount, 0, SIDE) Then ' check piece can move
      For I = 0 To 3
         Square(I, PCount).Top += SIDE ' all 4 square move down
      Next I
   Else ' can't move so piece stops
      tmrMovePiece.Interval = Speed ' back to normal speed
      For I = 0 To 3
         ' calculate grid position of each square
         X = (Square(I, PCount).Left) \ SIDE
         Y = (Square(I, PCount).Top) \ SIDE
         ' set each grid position as occupied
         Occupied(X, Y) = CStr(I) + CStr(PCount)
      Next I
      CheckRow(PCount) ' check if rows occupied by this piece are full
      NextPiece = Int(Rnd() * 7) ' random shape type for next piece
      MakePiece(NextPiece) ' make the chosen shape
      If Not OKtoMove(PCount, 0, SIDE) Then
         ' if new piece can't move then game is over
         tmrMovePiece.Enabled = False ' stop the piece moving
         mnuPause.Enabled = False ' the game is over so no pausing
         mnuSave.Enabled = True ' enable ability to save result of this game
         MessageBox.Show("Game over!", "Tetraminos", MessageBoxButtons.OK, _
         MessageBoxIcon.Information)
      End If
   End If
End Sub
```

- This event handler controls the movement of the current piece to the left, right, clockwise and anticlockwise rotation.

```vb
Private Sub Form1_KeyDown(ByVal sender As Object, ByVal e As _
System.Windows.Forms.KeyEventArgs) Handles MyBase.KeyDown
    Dim I, L, T As Integer
    Select Case e.KeyCode
        Case Keys.Right ' move right
            ' check if all 4 squares can move right
            If OKtoMove(PCount, SIDE, 0) Then
                For I = 0 To 3
                    ' move each square
                    Square(I, PCount).Left += SIDE
                Next I
            End If
        Case Keys.Left ' move left
            ' check if all 4 squares can move left
            If OKtoMove(PCount, -SIDE, 0) Then
                For I = 0 To 3
                    ' move each square
                    Square(I, PCount).Left -= SIDE
                Next I
            End If
        Case Keys.Up ' rotate clockwise
            If OKtoRotate(PCount, "Clockwise") Then
                For I = 1 To 3
                    ' need to hold both Left and Top in variables as
                    ' both will be changed in terms of each other
                    L = Square(I, PCount).Left
                    T = Square(I, PCount).Top
                    ' rotate 3 squares clockwise around pivot square
                    Square(I, PCount).Left = Square(0, PCount).Left - _
                    (T - Square(0, PCount).Top)
                    Square(I, PCount).Top = Square(0, PCount).Top + _
                    (L - Square(0, PCount).Left)
                Next I
            End If
        Case Keys.Down ' rotate anticlockwise
            If OKtoRotate(PCount, "Anticlockwise") Then
                For I = 1 To 3
                    ' need to hold both Left and Top in variables as
                    ' both will be changed in terms of each other
                    L = Square(I, PCount).Left
                    T = Square(I, PCount).Top
                    ' rotate 3 squares anticlockwise around pivot square
                    Square(I, PCount).Left = Square(0, PCount).Left + _
                    (T - Square(0, PCount).Top)
                    Square(I, PCount).Top = Square(0, PCount).Top - _
                    (L - Square(0, PCount).Left)
                Next I
            End If
        Case Keys.Space ' slot it in
            PlayWaveFile("pop.wav") ' make a 'pop' sound
            tmrMovePiece.Interval = 10 ' speed up timer
    End Select
End Sub
```

- This general procedure checks the rows occupied by the last piece stopped. If any rows are full they drop down out of sight. It is by far the most complex procedure in the application, but also one of the most recognizable features of the game.

```
Private Sub CheckRow(ByVal PieceNo As Integer)
   Dim MinTop, MaxTop, I, J, R, X, Y As Integer
   Dim RowFull As Boolean
   ' find the row span of the piece just stopped
   MinTop = Square(0, PieceNo).Top
   MaxTop = Square(0, PieceNo).Top
   ' find the tops of the highest and lowest squares
   For I = 1 To 3 ' check other 3 squares
      If Square(I, PieceNo).Top < MinTop Then
         MinTop = Square(I, PieceNo).Top
      ElseIf Square(I, PieceNo).Top > MaxTop Then
         MaxTop = Square(I, PieceNo).Top
      End If
   Next I
   ' check all the rows spanned by the piece
   R = (MaxTop \ SIDE)
   Do
      RowFull = True ' presume row has been filled
      ' now check otherwise
      For I = 0 To MaxX
         If Occupied(I, R) = "" Then ' nothing in this grid position
            RowFull = False
         End If
      Next I
      If RowFull Then ' if the row is full
         PlayWaveFile("hit.wav") ' make a 'hit' sound
         lblScore.Text += 10 ' get 10 points for a full row
         For I = 0 To MaxX
            ' find grid position of each square
            X = CInt(Occupied(I, R).Substring(0, 1))
            Y = CInt(Occupied(I, R).Substring(1))
            Square(X, Y).Visible = False ' square no longer visible
            Square(X, Y).Dispose() ' release all resources
            Occupied(I, R) = "" ' space free to be occupied
         Next I
         ' move all pieces above this cleared row down one
         For J = R - 1 To 0 Step -1
            For I = 0 To MaxX
               If Occupied(I, J) > "" Then ' only move something if occupied
                  ' find grid position of each square
                  X = CInt(Occupied(I, J).Substring(0, 1))
                  Y = CInt(Occupied(I, J).Substring(1))
                  Square(X, Y).Top += SIDE ' move square down one
                  Occupied(I, J) = "" ' space free to be occupied
                  Occupied(I, J + 1) = CStr(X) + CStr(Y) ' space now occupied
               End If
            Next I
         Next J
      Else
         R = R - 1 ' row not full, check next row
      End If
   Loop Until R < MinTop \ SIDE
End Sub
```

- All left and right movements have to be checked first before they are allowed to go ahead. This is achieved by this **user-defined function**. It returns a value of True or False.

```
Private Function OKtoMove(ByVal PieceNo As Integer, ByVal dX As Integer, _
ByVal dY As Integer) As Boolean
    Dim I, X, Y As Integer
    Dim OK As Boolean = True
    For I = 0 To 3
        ' calculate where each square would move to
        X = (Square(I, PieceNo).Left + dX) \ SIDE
        Y = (Square(I, PieceNo).Top + dY) \ SIDE
        ' both X and Y must be in range
        If X < 0 Or X > MaxX Or Y < 0 Or Y = MaxY Then
            OK = False
        End If
        ' check if position is already occupied
        If OK Then ' in range, but already occupied?
            If Occupied(X, Y) > "" Then
                OK = False
            End If
        End If
    Next I
    Return OK
End Function
```

- All rotations have to be checked first before they are allowed to go ahead. This is achieved by this **user-defined function**. It returns a value of True or False.

```
Private Function OKtoRotate(ByVal PieceNo As Integer, ByVal Direction As String) _
As Boolean
    Dim I, L, T, X, Y As Integer
    Dim OK As Boolean = True
    For I = 1 To 3 ' Square(0, PieceNo) does not move, it is the pivot point
        L = Square(I, PieceNo).Left
        T = Square(I, PieceNo).Top
        If Direction = "Clockwise" Then
            ' calculate where each square would move to
            X = (Square(0, PieceNo).Left - (T - Square(0, PieceNo).Top)) \ SIDE
            Y = (Square(0, PieceNo).Top + (L - Square(0, PieceNo).Left)) \ SIDE
        ElseIf Direction = "Anticlockwise" Then
            ' calculate where each square would move to
            X = (Square(0, PieceNo).Left + (T - Square(0, PieceNo).Top)) \ SIDE
            Y = (Square(0, PieceNo).Top - (L - Square(0, PieceNo).Left)) \ SIDE
        End If
        ' both X and Y must be in range
        If X < 0 Or X > MaxX Or Y < 0 Or Y = MaxY Then
            OK = False
        End If
        ' check if position is already occupied
        If OK Then ' in range, but already occupied?
            If Occupied(X, Y) > "" Then
                OK = False
            End If
        End If
    Next I
    Return OK
End Function
```

- The Click of this menu item starts a game.

```
Private Sub mnuNew_Click(ByVal sender As Object, ByVal e As System.EventArgs) _
Handles mnuNew.Click
    StartGame()
End Sub
```

- A simple exit.

```
Private Sub mnuExit_Click(ByVal sender As Object, ByVal e As System.EventArgs) _
Handles mnuExit.Click
    End
End Sub
```

- This procedure toggles the pause check and the timer that moves the pieces.

```
Private Sub mnuPause_Click(ByVal sender As Object, ByVal e As System.EventArgs) _
Handles mnuPause.Click
    mnuPause.Checked = Not mnuPause.Checked
    tmrMovePiece.Enabled = Not tmrMovePiece.Enabled
End Sub
```

- This procedure adds the game result to the history file.

```
Private Sub mnuSave_Click(ByVal sender As Object, ByVal e As System.EventArgs) _
Handles mnuSave.Click
    Dim FileNum As Integer = FreeFile() ' get available file handle
    FileOpen(FileNum, "TetraminosHistory.txt", OpenMode.Append) ' open history file
    ' append this game result to the history file
    PrintLine(FileNum, lblPlayer.Text + ": " + lblScore.Text + "  " + _
    Format(Now, "dd/MM/yy"))
    FileClose(FileNum) ' close history file
    mnuSave.Enabled = False
End Sub
```

- This procedure reads the history text file and puts each line into a list box.

```
Private Sub mnuShowHistory_Click(ByVal sender As Object, ByVal e As _
System.EventArgs) Handles mnuShowHistory.Click
    mnuShowHistory.Checked = Not mnuShowHistory.Checked
    If mnuShowHistory.Checked Then
        Dim FileNum As Integer = FreeFile() ' get available file handle
        lstHistory.Items.Clear() ' clear all items from list box
        FileOpen(FileNum, "TetraminosHistory.txt", OpenMode.Input) 'open history file
            Do Until EOF(FileNum) ' keep going until end of file
                lstHistory.Items.Add(LineInput(FileNum)) ' add a line to the list box
            Loop
        FileClose(FileNum) ' close history file
        lstHistory.Visible = True ' show history list
    Else
        lstHistory.Visible = False ' hide history list
    End If
End Sub
```

Try it out

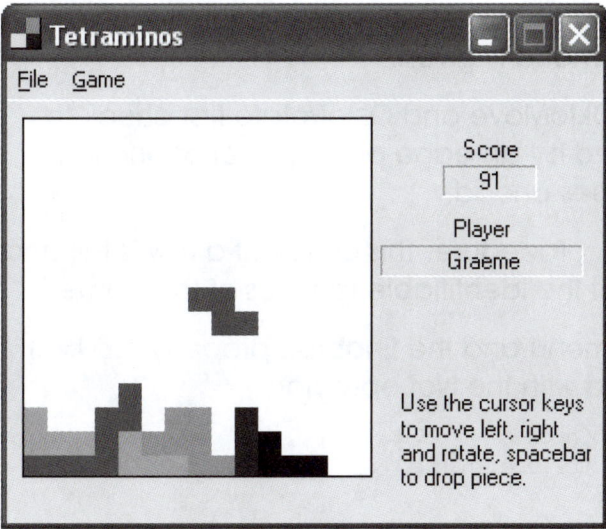

Tetraminos – points to note

- The game is played inside a **Panel** control. It is the **parent** of all the created shapes.

- Because Tetraminos is a keyboard controlled game most of the menu items have **shortcut** keys. **Access keys** are defined in the Text property by leading the key with **&** as shown on the menu items.

- The **enumeration** ShapeType names the seven possible coloured shapes.

- Like the Snake example there is an array that is unspecified in size. This array is two-dimensional:

```
Dim Square(,) As PictureBox ' coloured squares making each piece
```

- The whole area of the panel is divided into grid positions. The maximum coordinates is calculated in Form_Load:

```
' calculate the maximum X and Y grid positions
MaxX = pnlBuild.Width \ SIDE - 1
MaxY = pnlBuild.Height \ SIDE
```

- A player cannot commence a game without giving a name:

```
Do
    Player = InputBox("Name of player?" + vbLf + vbLf + _
    "This is the name that will be" + vbLf + "recorded in the history file."_
    , "Tetraminos", Player)
Loop Until Player > "" ' must enter a name
```

- Occupied is a **two-dimensional array** that indicates what parts of shapes are located in particular grid positions. This array determines when a piece has to stop and what pieces have to disappear from view.

- Each shape is 'built' from four picture boxes

```
Select Case Shape
    Case ShapeType.Square
        Square(0, PCount).Location = New Point(X, Y)   ' pivot square
        Square(1, PCount).Location = New Point(X + SIDE, Y)
        Square(2, PCount).Location = New Point(X, Y + SIDE)
        Square(3, PCount).Location = New Point(X + SIDE, Y + SIDE)
```

What is referred to as the pivot square is the square about which the shape rotates when this command is given.

- Two **user-defined functions** OktoMove and OktoRotate first check to see if either would be blocked by an edge of the panel or another shape. If the move is OK it goes ahead.

- CheckRow is a very complex procedure. This checks if a row is full and should slide away. It is one of the identifiable features of this game.

- The **Checked** property of a menu and the **Enabled** property are both **Boolean** and can be toggled with the **Not** operator.

```
mnuPause.Checked = Not mnuPause.Checked
tmrMovePiece.Enabled = Not tmrMovePiece.Enabled
```

- A text file is used to store the game history. Writing to a text file requires the statements **FileOpen**, **PrintLine** and **FileClose**. Reading from a text file requires **FileOpen**, **LineInput** and **FileClose**. Each of this is distinguished by the use of a file handle. This is to allow for the possibility of having more than one file open at a time.

- The last argument of FileOpen is filled with a member of an enumeration that specifies what operation is about to take place: **OpenMode.Input** – the file is to be read, **OpenMode.Output** – the file is to be written and **OpenMode.Append** – the file is to have additional lines written.

- When reading the contents of a text file, typically a **test-first loop** is used. In this case each line read is added to a list box.

```
Do Until EOF(FileNum) ' keep going until end of file
   lstHistory.Items.Add(LineInput(FileNum)) ' add a line to the list box
Loop
```

Tetraminos – check what you have learnt

1 a What is a shortcut key?

   b What is an access key?

2 The panel is 180 pixels square. How many grid positions are there given each picture box is 12 pixels square?

3 To what Controls collection, in the MakePiece procedure, are the newly created picture boxes added?

4 The following is alternative code to produce one of the shapes with a different pivot square. What shape is it?

```
Square(0, PCount).Location = New Point(X, Y)
Square(1, PCount).Location = New Point(X, Y + SIDE)
Square(2, PCount).Location = New Point(X, Y + SIDE * 2)
Square(3, PCount).Location = New Point(X + SIDE, Y + SIDE * 2)
```

5 During a rotation what is significant about the pivot square?

6 The following three lines of code produce one of the most identifiable features of this game. What are they doing?

```
Square(X, Y).Visible = False ' square no longer visible
Square(X, Y).Dispose() ' release all resources
Occupied(I, R) = "" ' space free to be occupied
```

7 An array SquareColor is declared and instantiated in the one line.

```
Dim SquareColour() As Color = {Color.Red, Color.Blue, Color.Green, _
Color.Violet, Color.Black, Color.Brown, Color.Lime}
```

Write the code for the alternative of declaring the array then assigning elements one by one.

8 Before a text file is opened a file handle is obtained. Why do the file operations require a file handle?

9 What are the three names of the OpenMode enumeration specifically for text files?

10 Enhance Tetraminos by adding two additional features:

- the option to preview the next piece (small preview pictures are provided on the accompanying CD)
- the option to turn on/off sound effects

Both these features should be controlled from the Game menu.

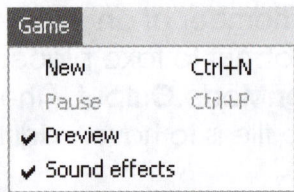

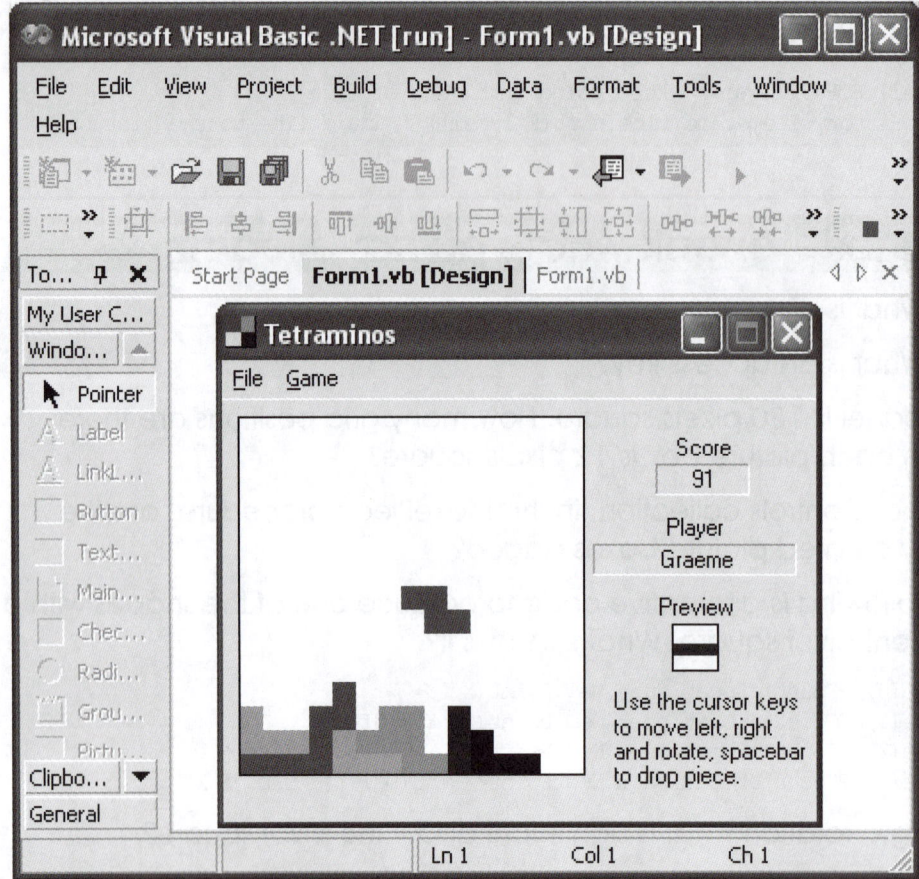

Chapter 14

Space hero

Space hero is an example application that embodies many of the techniques demonstrated in previous chapters. It has sound effects, animation, randomness, increasing difficulty, rewards and an opposition with some 'intelligence'.

Another useful subclass

Bullet is a **subclass** of PictureBox that has been created for *Space hero*. Of course it could be used with any application with similar requirements. It has three additional properties:

- **BulletIndex** – an Integer to identify each control when being placed into an array.
- **BulletType** – has the value Friendly or Enemy.
- **Moving** – a Boolean value to indicate whether the bullet should be moving.

The full definition of the Bullet class is included in Appendix 2.

Program example: Space hero

Create a new Windows application with the name *Space hero*.

Add the Bullet control to the toolbox:
- From the Tools menu choose 'Add/Remove Toolbox Items'.
- Browse to *Bullets.dll* on the accompanying CD.

Create the interface

- Add five labels, thirteen picture boxes, twenty bullets, seven timers and two image lists to the form.

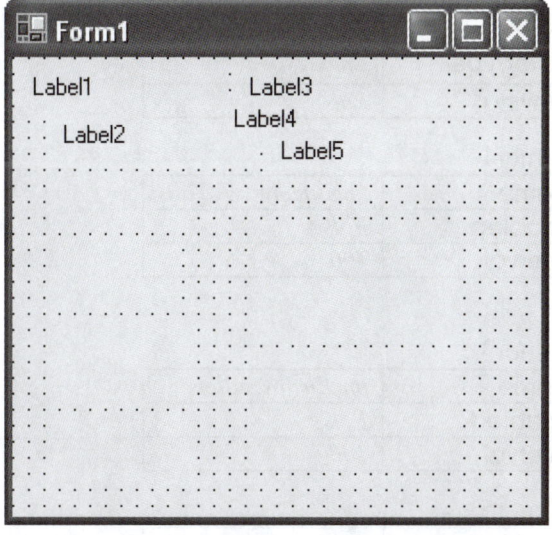

■ Set the following properties:

Form1

BackColor	Black
BackgroundImage	Stars.bmp
FormBorderStyle	Fixed Single
Icon	(you choose)
KeyPreview	True
MaximizeBox	False
Text	Space Hero

PictureBox11

Name	picExplosion
BackColor	Black
Image	Explosion 0.gif
SizeMode	AutoSize
Visible	False

Label1

BackColor	Black
Font	MS Sans Serif 9 Points Bold
ForeColor	White
Text	Lives
TextAlign	MiddleCenter

Label2

BackColor	Black
Font	MS Sans Serif 9 Points Bold
ForeColor	White
Text	Hits
TextAlign	MiddleCenter

Label3

Name	lblLives
BackColor	Black
BorderStyle	Fixed3D
Font	MS Sans Serif 9 Points Bold
ForeColor	White
Text	1

Label4

Name	lblHits
BackColor	Black
BorderStyle	Fixed3D
Font	MS Sans Serif 9 Points Bold
ForeColor	White
Text	0

PictureBox1 to PictureBox10

BackColor	Black
Image	Enemy.bmp
SizeMode	AutoSize
Tag	Enemy

PictureBox12

Name	picHero
BackColor	Black
Image	Hero.bmp
SizeMode	AutoSize

Bullet1 to Bullet10

BackColor	Black
BulletIndex	0 to 9
BulletType	Friendly
Moving	False

Bullet11 to Bullet20

BackColor	Black
BulletIndex	0 to 9
BulletType	Enemy
Moving	False

PictureBox13

Name	picBonus
BackColor	Black
Image	Bonus 0.bmp
SizeMode	AutoSize

Timer1

Name	tmrEnemy
Enabled	False
Interval	400

Timer2

Name	tmrEnemyCheck
Enabled	False
Interval	2000

Timer3

Name	tmrEnemyBullets
Enabled	False
Interval	100

Timer4

Name	tmrHeroBullets
Enabled	False
Interval	100

Timer5

Name	tmrExplosion
Enabled	False
Interval	100

Timer6

Name	tmrBonus
Enabled	False
Interval	100

Timer7

Name	tmrMoveBonus
Enabled	False
Interval	100

ImageList1

Name	imlBonus
ImageSize	14, 11

ImageList2

Name	imlExplosion
ImageSize	60, 50

■ Add the bitmaps *Bonus 0.bmp* to *Bonus 5.bmp* to the Images collection of *imlBonus*.

■ Add the bitmaps *Explosion 0.bmp* to *Explosion 10.bmp* to the Images collection of *imlExplosion*.

Write the code and add comments

■ From the Project menu choose 'Add Existing Item'. Add the code modules *Collision.vb*, *PlayWave.vb* and *Positioning.vb*.

■ Copy the wave files *destroy.wav, laser.wav* and *hit.wav* to the Bin folder.

■ Include the following Imports statements at the top of the code window.

```
Imports Bullets ' contains the Bullet class
```

■ The following constants and variables must be declared at form level for use in several procedures.

```
Const LASTENEMY As Integer = 9 ' the last enemy index
Const LASTBULLET As Integer = 9 ' the last bullet index
Dim HeroBullet(LASTBULLET), EnemyBullet(LASTBULLET) As Bullet ' arrays of bullets
Dim WhichHeroBullet, WhichEnemyBullet As Integer ' current bullet index being used
Dim Enemy(LASTENEMY) As PictureBox
```

■ This general procedure repositions all the enemy spaceships, stops and hides all bullets, resets the scoring labels and restarts all the timers.

```
Private Sub Initialise()
   Dim I As Integer
   For I = 0 To LASTENEMY  ' move enemy to top
      Enemy(I).Top = 24
   Next I
   For I = 0 To LASTBULLET ' stop and hide all bullets
      HeroBullet(I).Visible = False
      HeroBullet(I).Moving = False
      EnemyBullet(I).Visible = False
      EnemyBullet(I).Moving = False
   Next I
   lblLives.Text = 1    ' one life to start
   lblHits.Text = 0
   ' start with 1 less than first bullet
   WhichHeroBullet = -1
   WhichEnemyBullet = -1
   ' start all timers (except explosion)
   tmrEnemyBullets.Start()
   tmrHeroBullets.Start()
   tmrBonus.Start()
   tmrMoveBonus.Start()
   tmrEnemyCheck.Start()
   tmrEnemy.Start()
End Sub
```

- The right and left cursor keys control the movement of our hero while the spacebar fires a hero bullet.

```
Private Sub Form1_KeyDown(ByVal sender As Object, ByVal e As _
System.Windows.Forms.KeyEventArgs) Handles MyBase.KeyDown
    Select Case e.KeyCode
        Case Keys.Right
            picHero.Left += 4
        Case Keys.Left
            picHero.Left -= 4
        Case Keys.Space ' fire a hero bullet
            PlayWaveFile("laser.wav")
            WhichHeroBullet += 1      ' next bullet
            If WhichHeroBullet > LASTBULLET Then ' keep within range
                WhichHeroBullet = 0 ' back to first bullet
            End If
            CentreOn(picHero, HeroBullet(WhichHeroBullet))
            HeroBullet(WhichHeroBullet).Moving = True
            HeroBullet(WhichHeroBullet).Visible = True
    End Select
End Sub
```

- The bullet arrays and the enemy array are populated during the form load. The Initialise procedure is also called to make start of game settings.

```
Private Sub Form1_Load(ByVal sender As Object, ByVal e As System.EventArgs) _
Handles MyBase.Load
    Dim obj As Object, I As Integer, J As Integer = 0
    For Each obj In Me.Controls
        If TypeOf obj Is Bullet Then
            If obj.BulletType = Bullet.Classification.Friendly Then ' hero bullet
                I = obj.BulletIndex
                HeroBullet(I) = obj
            Else      ' enemy bullet
                I = obj.BulletIndex
                EnemyBullet(I) = obj
            End If
        ElseIf TypeOf obj Is PictureBox And obj.Tag = "Enemy" Then ' enemy spaceship
            Enemy(J) = obj
            J += 1
        End If
    Next obj
    Initialise()
End Sub
```

- This event handler scans each of the hero bullets to see if it is meant to be moving. If the Moving property is True then the bullet moves up the form.

```
Private Sub tmrHeroBullets_Tick(ByVal sender As System.Object, ByVal e As _
System.EventArgs) Handles tmrHeroBullets.Tick
    Dim I As Integer
    For I = 0 To LASTBULLET
        If HeroBullet(I).Moving Then ' check every bullet
            HeroBullet(I).Top -= 8 ' move bullet up the screen
        End If
    Next I
End Sub
```

- The rolling bonus graphic has six bitmaps that produce its animation.

```
Private Sub tmrBonus_Tick(ByVal sender As System.Object, ByVal e As _
System.EventArgs) Handles tmrBonus.Tick
    Static Frame As Integer = 0
    Frame = (Frame + 1) Mod 6 ' next frame, total of 6 frames
    picBonus.Image = imlBonus.Images.Item(Frame) ' load image from imagelist
End Sub
```

- A random member of the enemy array is chosen then moved down.

```
Private Sub tmrEnemy_Tick(ByVal sender As System.Object, ByVal e As _
System.EventArgs) Handles tmrEnemy.Tick
    Randomize()
    Dim I As Integer = Int(Rnd() * (LASTENEMY + 1)) ' choose a random enemy to move
    Enemy(I).Top += 16 ' move enemy spaceship down
End Sub
```

- This event handler scans each of the enemy bullets to see if it is meant to be moving. Only those with a Moving property True are moved down the screen.

```
Private Sub tmrEnemyBullets_Tick(ByVal sender As System.Object, ByVal e As _
System.EventArgs) Handles tmrEnemyBullets.Tick
    Dim I As Integer
    For I = 0 To LASTBULLET
        If EnemyBullet(I).Moving Then ' check every bullet
            EnemyBullet(I).Top += 8 ' move bullet down the screen
        End If
    Next I
End Sub
```

- In the following procedure all the enemy spacecraft are scanned to see if one of them has our hero in its sights. If it does it fires a bullet. Firing a bullet simply means setting the Moving property of the next available bullet to True and making it visible.

```
Private Sub tmrEnemyCheck_Tick(ByVal sender As System.Object, ByVal e As _
System.EventArgs) Handles tmrEnemyCheck.Tick
    Dim I As Integer = 0, EnemyFire As Boolean = False
    Do
        If InSightsVert(Enemy(I), picHero) Then ' enemy can fire at hero
            EnemyFire = True ' flags the enemy has fired a bullet
            WhichEnemyBullet += 1 ' next bullet
            If WhichEnemyBullet > LastBullet Then
                WhichEnemyBullet = 0 ' back to first bullet
            End If
            CentreOn(Enemy(I), EnemyBullet(WhichEnemyBullet)) ' centre bullet on enemy
            EnemyBullet(WhichEnemyBullet).Moving = True
            EnemyBullet(WhichEnemyBullet).Visible = True
        End If
        I += 1 ' next enemy
    Loop Until I > LASTENEMY Or EnemyFire
End Sub
```

- This procedure causes the eleven bitmaps of an explosion to produce this animation. When all bitmaps have been used the explosion is over.

```
Private Sub tmrExplosion_Tick(ByVal sender As System.Object, ByVal e As _
System.EventArgs) Handles tmrExplosion.Tick
    Static Frame As Integer = 0
    picExplosion.Image = imlExplosion.Images.Item(Frame) ' show this image
    Frame = (Frame + 1) Mod 11  ' next frame, total of 11 frames
    If Frame = 0 Then ' explosion is over
        picExplosion.Visible = False
        tmrExplosion.Stop()
    End If
End Sub
```

- The rolling bonus is moved down the screen with each tick of this timer.

```
Private Sub tmrMoveBonus_Tick(ByVal sender As System.Object, ByVal e As _
System.EventArgs) Handles tmrMoveBonus.Tick
    picBonus.Top += 8 ' move bonus picture box down
End Sub
```

- If our hero runs out of lives this game is over. All the timers are stopped. A message box offers the choice of playing again or ending the game.

```
Private Sub lblLives_TextChanged(ByVal sender As Object, ByVal e As _
System.EventArgs) Handles lblLives.TextChanged
    lblLives.Refresh()
    If lblLives.Text = 0 Then    ' out of lives, game over
        ' stop all timers
        tmrEnemyBullets.Stop()
        tmrHeroBullets.Stop()
        tmrBonus.Stop()
        tmrMoveBonus.Stop()
        tmrEnemyCheck.Stop()
        tmrEnemy.Stop()
        If MessageBox.Show("Game over, you have run out of lives!" & vbLf & _
        "Play again?", "Space Hero", MessageBoxButtons.YesNo, _
        MessageBoxIcon.Question) = vbYes Then
            Initialise() ' reset all positions and variables
        Else
            End
        End If
    End If
End Sub
```

- This procedure handles the location change of all ten picture boxes that make up the enemy array. If one happens to pass below the bottom of the form our hero loses a life. In this procedure the sender is the picture box that has had a location change.

```
Private Sub Enemy_LocationChanged(ByVal sender As Object, ByVal e As _
System.EventArgs) Handles PictureBox1.LocationChanged, _
PictureBox2.LocationChanged, PictureBox3.LocationChanged, _
PictureBox4.LocationChanged, PictureBox5.LocationChanged, _
PictureBox6.LocationChanged, PictureBox7.LocationChanged, _
PictureBox8.LocationChanged, PictureBox9.LocationChanged, _
PictureBox10.LocationChanged
    If sender.Top >= Me.Height Then    ' enemy gone below form
        lblLives.Text -= 1 ' lose a life
        sender.Top = -2 * sender.Height ' move enemy above top of form
    End If
End Sub
```

- This procedure handles the location change of all ten bullets that make up the enemy bullet array. If one collides with our hero then a life is lost. In this procedure the sender is the bullet that has had a location change.

```
Private Sub EnemyBullet_LocationChanged(ByVal sender As Object, ByVal e As _
System.EventArgs) Handles Bullet11.LocationChanged, Bullet12.LocationChanged, _
Bullet13.LocationChanged, Bullet14.LocationChanged, Bullet15.LocationChanged, _
Bullet16.LocationChanged, Bullet17.LocationChanged, Bullet18.LocationChanged, _
Bullet19.LocationChanged, Bullet20.LocationChanged
    If Collision(sender, picHero) Then ' enemy bullet hits hero
        sender.Visible = False
        lblLives.Text -= 1 ' lose a life
    ElseIf sender.Top >= Me.Height Then ' bullet off bottom of form
        sender.Moving = False
        sender.Visible = False
    End If
End Sub
```

- If a location change of the rolling bonus causes it to collide with our hero then a life is gained. If the bonus moves beyond the bottom of the form it restarts at a random location at the top of the form.

```
Private Sub picBonus_LocationChanged(ByVal sender As Object, ByVal e As _
System.EventArgs) Handles picBonus.LocationChanged
    If Collision(picHero, picBonus) Then ' hero scores a bonus
        PlayWaveFile("hit.wav")
        picBonus.Top = Me.Height  ' move to bottom of form
        lblLives.Text += 1 ' gain a life
    ElseIf picBonus.Top >= Me.Height Then ' bonus below bottom of form
        picBonus.Left = Rnd() * (Me.Width - picBonus.Width) ' random Left position
        picBonus.Top = -picBonus.Height ' above top of form
    End If
End Sub
```

- This procedure handles the location change of all ten bullets that make up the hero bullet array. If one collides with an enemy an explosion occurs and a point is gained. The sender is the bullet that has had a location change.

```
Private Sub HeroBullet_LocationChanged(ByVal sender As Object, ByVal e As _
System.EventArgs) Handles Bullet1.LocationChanged, Bullet2.LocationChanged, _
Bullet3.LocationChanged, Bullet4.LocationChanged, Bullet5.LocationChanged, _
Bullet6.LocationChanged, Bullet7.LocationChanged, Bullet8.LocationChanged, _
Bullet9.LocationChanged, Bullet10.LocationChanged
    Dim I As Integer = 0
    Do ' check all enemy spaceships
        If Collision(sender, Enemy(I)) Then ' bullet hits enemy
            PlayWaveFile("destroy.wav")
            Enemy(I).Visible = False
            tmrEnemy.Interval -= 1 ' enemy moves a little faster
            sender.Moving = False ' stop bullet moving
            sender.Visible = False ' bullet disappears, replaced by explosion
            picExplosion.Location = Enemy(I).Location    ' move explosion to enemy
            Enemy(I).Top = -2 * Enemy(I).Height ' move enemy above top of form
            Enemy(I).Visible = True ' enemy visible again
            lblHits.Text += 1 ' extra hits point
            ' start explosion
            picExplosion.Visible = True
            tmrExplosion.Start() ' start the explosion sequence
        End If
        I += 1
    Loop Until I > LASTENEMY or picExplosion.Visible
    If sender.Top <= 0 Then  ' bullet off top of form
        sender.Moving = False ' stop bullet moving
        sender.Visible = False ' make bullet not visible
    End If
End Sub
```

Try it out

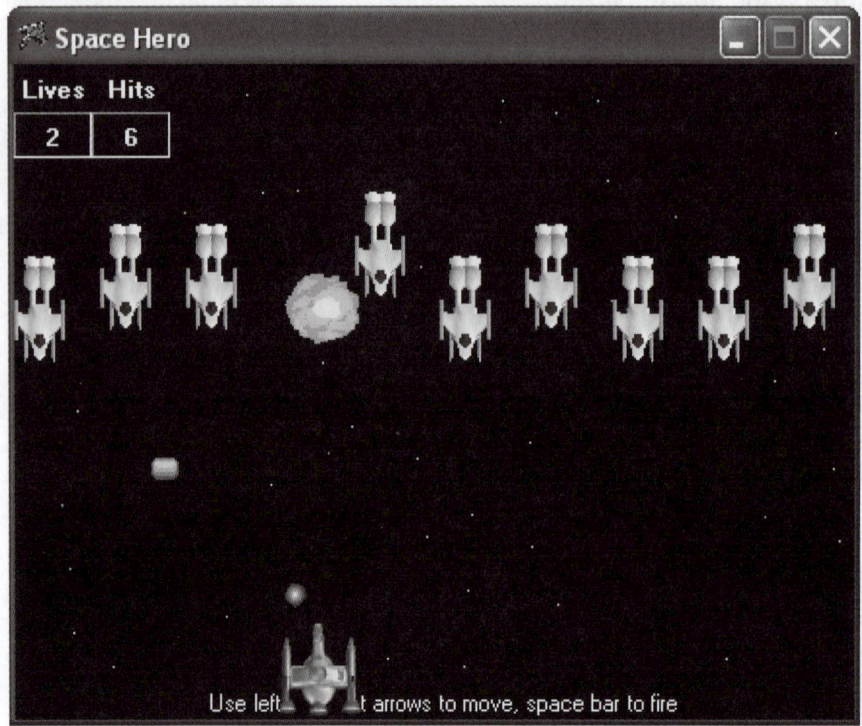

Space hero – points to note

- Useful functions and procedures, contained in the **code modules** *Collision.vb*, *PlayWave.vb* and *Positioning.vb*, have been written specifically for game development (see Appendix 1).

- Timers are important controls in this application as they largely dictate the pace of action. You may want to make your own adjustments to the Interval property of each.

- A **subclass Bullet** was developed specifically for this application. It has three additional properties to those of the PictureBox class: BulletIndex, BulletType and Moving.

- **General procedures** like Initialise are common to many games. Variables and property values need to be set at the start of a game. The procedure is called in two other procedures.

- **Constants** like LASTENEMY and LASTBULLET are used for two reasons. The names are more descriptive in the code than a number. If you wanted to alter the number of enemy or bullets you would only have to change the code in one place.

```
Const LASTENEMY As Integer = 9 ' the last enemy index
Const LASTBULLET As Integer = 9 ' the last bullet index
```

- There are only ten bullets each for the hero and the enemy. They are reused over and over again:

```
WhichHeroBullet += 1     ' next bullet
If WhichHeroBullet > LASTBULLET Then ' keep within range
   WhichHeroBullet = 0 ' back to first bullet
End If
```

- The timers controlling the bullets are constantly checking them all to see if they should be moving:

```
For I = 0 To LASTBULLET
    If HeroBullet(I).Moving Then ' check every bullet
        HeroBullet(I).Top -= 8 ' move bullet up the screen
    End If
Next I
```

- Every two seconds the timer *tmrEnemyCheck* scans the enemy craft to see if one of them has the hero in its sights. If so it fires a bullet. Firing a bullet is a matter of centring the bullet on the craft then setting its Moving and Visible properties:

```
CentreOn(Enemy(I), EnemyBullet(WhichEnemyBullet)) ' centre bullet on enemy
EnemyBullet(WhichEnemyBullet).Moving = True
EnemyBullet(WhichEnemyBullet).Visible = True
```

- Our hero can lose lives in two ways. He loses a life if he collides with an enemy bullet or if an enemy craft makes it pass him. Lives can be gained by colliding with the rolling bonus.

```
If Collision(picHero, picBonus) Then ' hero scores a bonus
    PlayWaveFile("hit.wav")
    picBonus.Top = Me.Height  ' move to bottom of form
    lblLives.Text += 1 ' gain a life
```

- Each time the bonus returns to the top it is placed in a random position for the next descent.

```
picBonus.Left = Rnd() * (Me.Width - picBonus.Width) ' random Left position
```

- Three of the **event handlers** (event procedures) respond to the events of multiple objects. For example the following procedure handles the LocationChanged event for all ten hero bullets.

```
Private Sub HeroBullet_LocationChanged(ByVal sender As Object, ByVal e As _
System.EventArgs) Handles Bullet1.LocationChanged, Bullet2.LocationChanged, _
Bullet3.LocationChanged, Bullet4.LocationChanged, Bullet5.LocationChanged, _
Bullet6.LocationChanged, Bullet7.LocationChanged, Bullet8.LocationChanged, _
Bullet9.LocationChanged, Bullet10.LocationChanged
```

- In any event handler the **sender** is the object that raised the event. In the above example it could be any one of the ten bullets.

```
If Collision(sender, Enemy(I)) Then ' bullet hits enemy
```

Space hero – check what you have learnt

1   What procedure and what function was used from the Positioning module?

2   Find instances in the code where each of the Bullet properties, BulletIndex, BulletType and Moving are used.

3   In which two places is the Initialise procedure called?

4   Why do you suppose that the names of constants are written in upper case letters?

5   Modifications to this game may require more bullets. As well as adding additional Bullet controls, what change would need to be made to the code?

6   What line of code determines that an enemy craft has safely got by our hero?

7   How does the explosion animation turn itself off?

8   Why *not* randomly locate the rolling bonus with the following line?

```
picBonus.Left = Rnd() * Me.Width
```

9   Why do we rarely make use of the sender argument?

10 I'm sure you could think of many ways of improving Space hero. You are encouraged to do so. Here are some thoughts to consider:

- a key for the hero so that he can simultaneously move and fire
- when the enemy fires the enemy on the left and right also fire
- a small explosion when the enemy bullet hits our hero
- a form containing clear play instructions
- a history file recording players scores and dates

Chapter 15

Deployment benefits

The bad old days

In the early days of MS-DOS installing an application was often as simple as copying an EXE file, and perhaps a handful of other files, from a floppy disk. But the application development process was long and tedious. All aspects of the functionality of the application had to be programmed from scratch.

The arrival of Windows helped simplify the application development process by providing many **common services** like the user interface, printing and clipboard functions. However the downside was the necessity for complex setup programs that installed all the necessary **DLL**s (Dynamic Link Libraries) and made entries into the Windows registry. There have been many difficulties associated with these installations. The complications that have arisen from hundreds of DLLs have been referred to as 'DLL hell'.

.NET deployment

The **.NET framework** has addressed these shortcomings by largely relying on **class libraries** for the functionality of .NET applications. These class libraries are all a part of the .NET framework that is installed with the operating system. So a developer still has all the common services of the Windows environment but has a greatly simplified **deployment package**. Visual Studio .NET applications are compiled as **assemblies**. Assemblies are so self-contained that they can be installed by copying to a computer that has the .NET framework installed. In the commercial environment, however, it is still preferable to have an installation program with a clearly presented graphical user interface (**GUI**).

A deployment example: SnakeSetup

There are a vast number of options within the process of creating a deployment package. The example that follows uses a typical set of circumstances. The *Snake* game will be used, however any of the preceding games would be suitable.

■   Open the *Snake* solution. As with all the other applications to this point, there is only one project shown in the solution explorer.

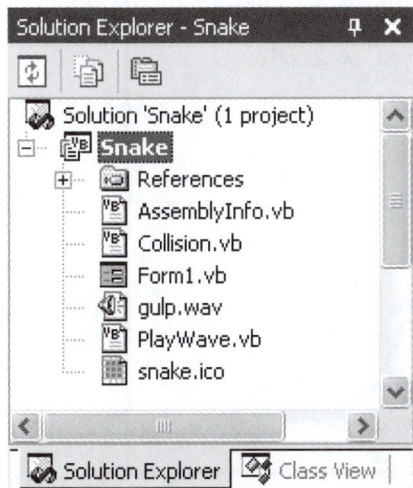

- From the File menu choose to add a new project.
- Select 'Setup and Deployment Projects' as the project type, then choose Setup Wizard as the template.

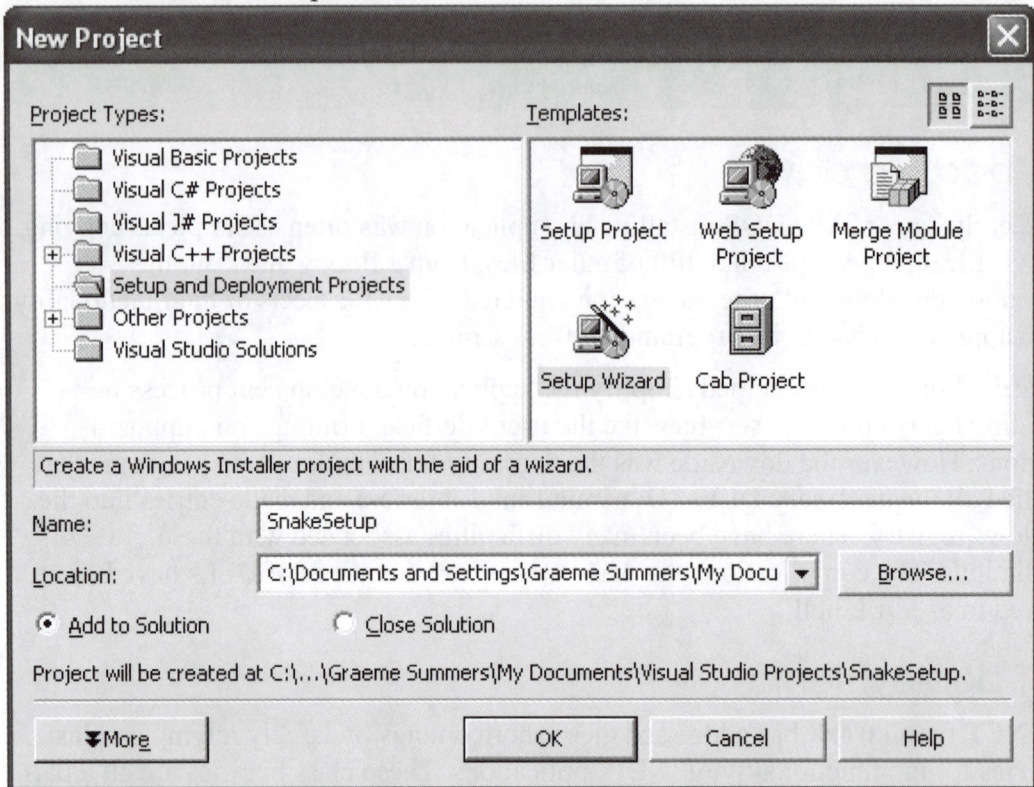

- Give the project a name, for this example *SnakeSetup* seems logical.
- It is most important that 'Add to Solution' option is chosen before proceeding.

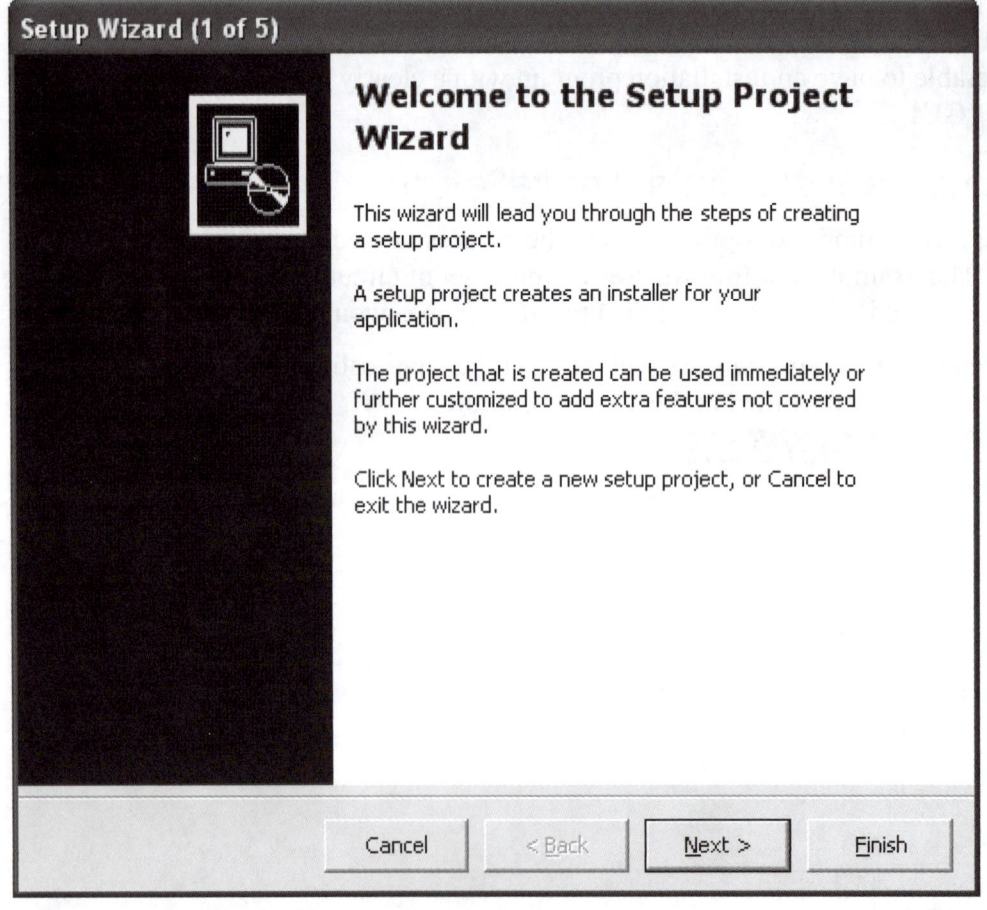

■ We will be creating a setup program to install a Windows application.

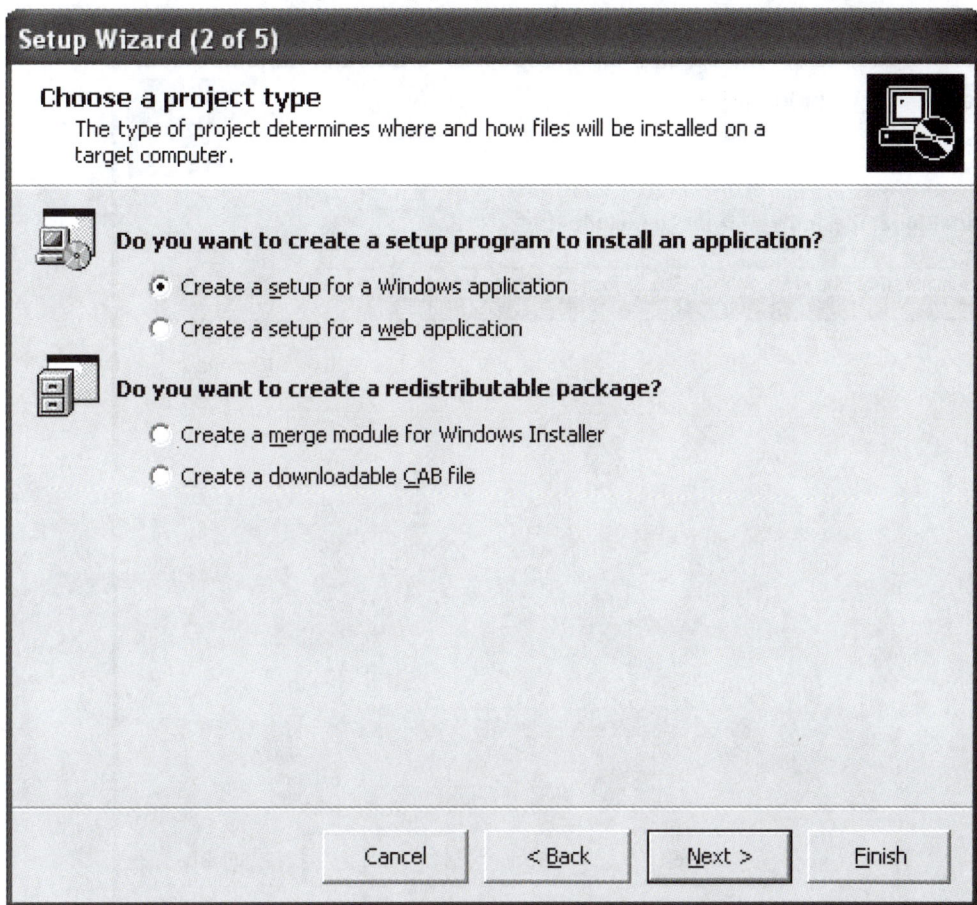

■ The EXE file of the application (primary output) is all that is required.

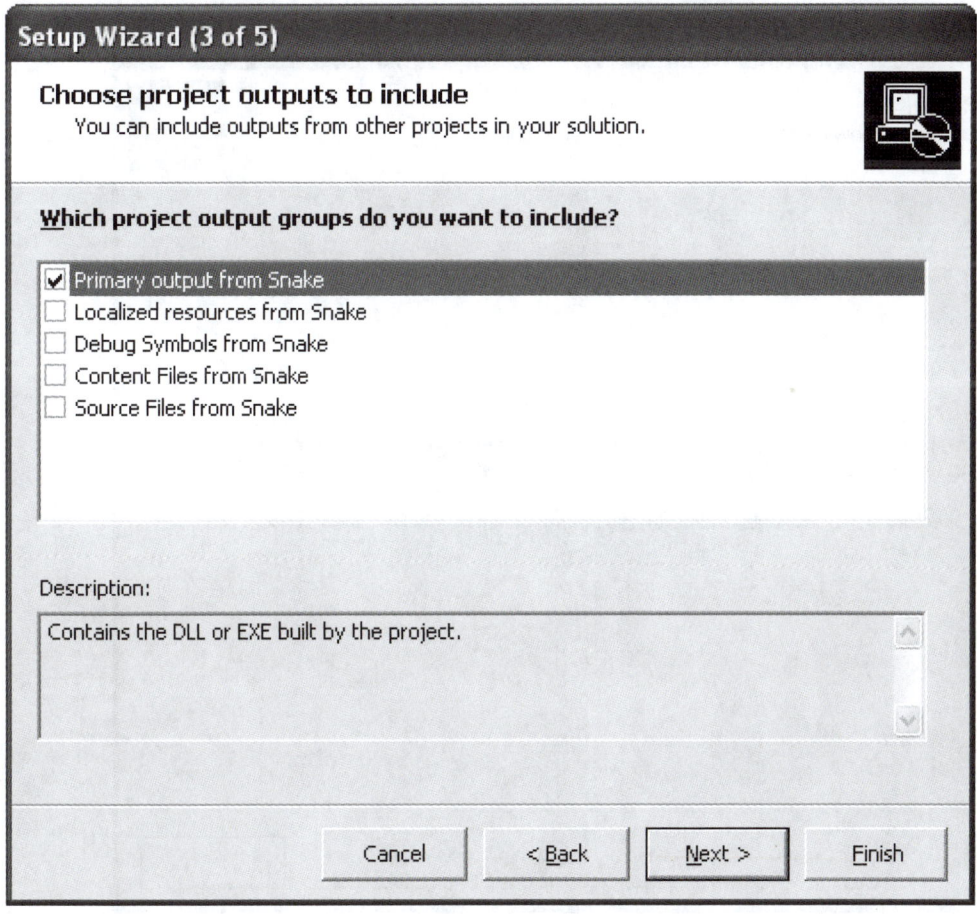

- Browse to *ReadMe.txt* and *gulp.wav*. Both these files will be added.

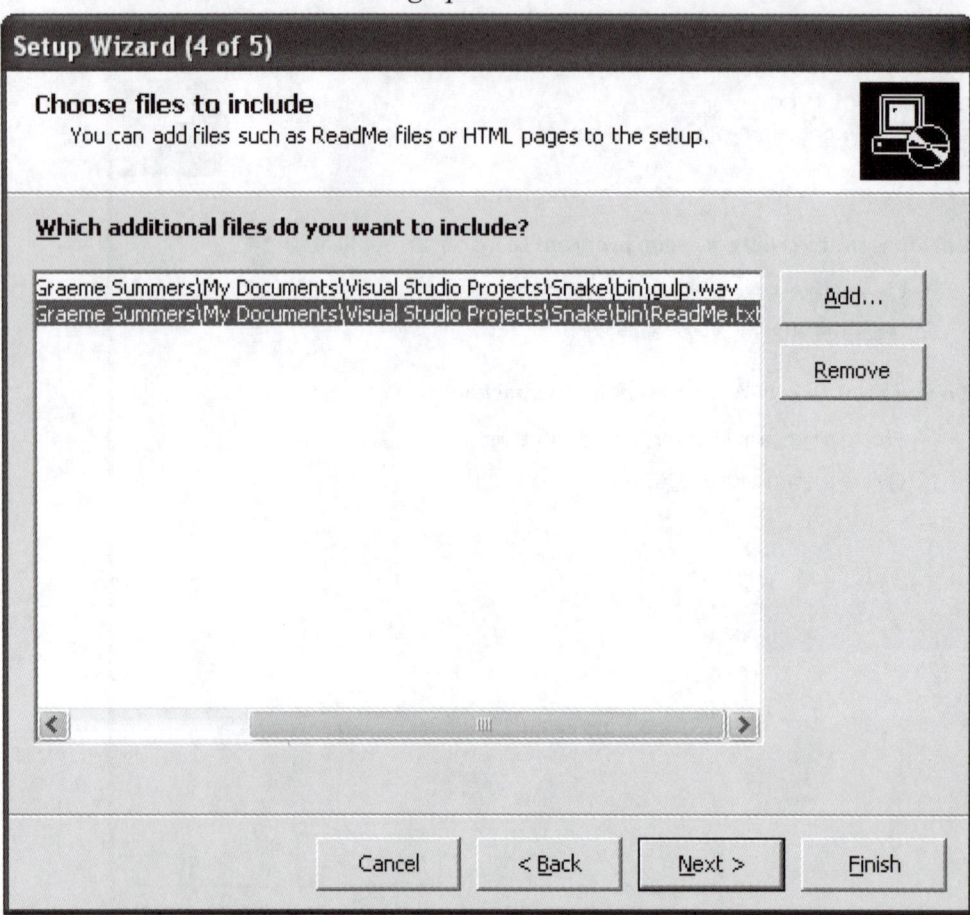

- Proceed to the final step of the wizard that creates the project.

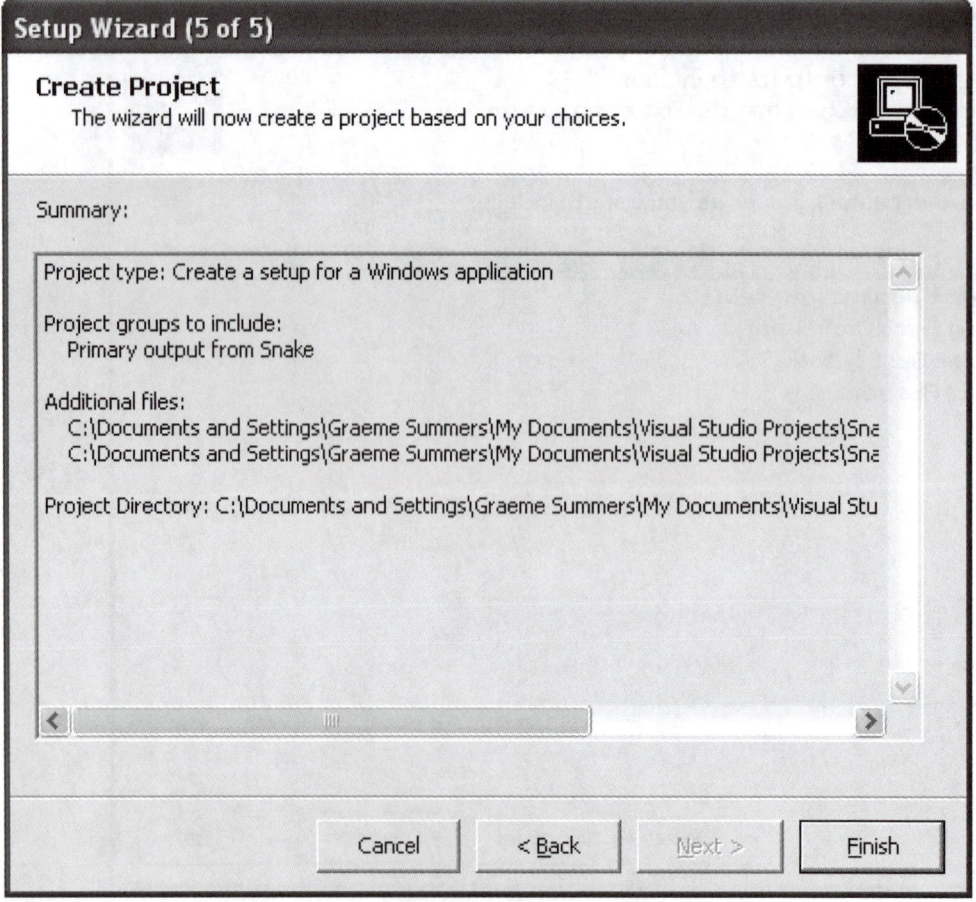

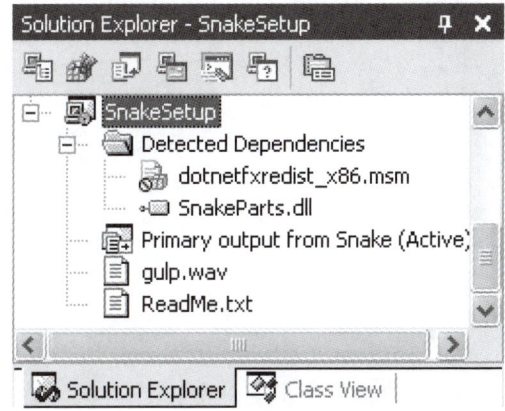

- As well as the new project appearing in the Solution Explorer the **File System Editor** will also appear.

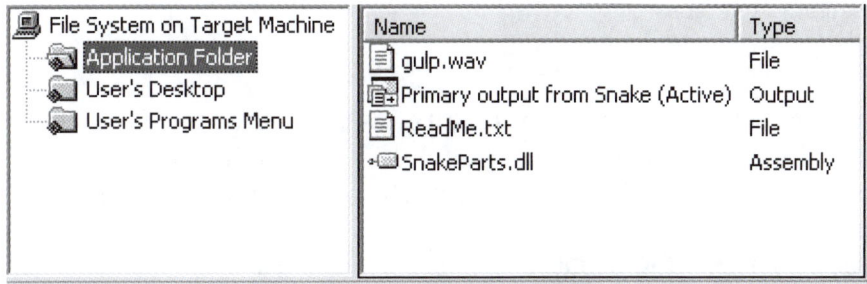

Initially the File System Editor shows you what will be installed in the **Application Folder**, the User's **Desktop** and the User's **Programs Menu**. You can use the File System Editor to add other items to the deployment project and where they will be located during installation. For example, we will use it to create an application shortcut for the User's Programs Menu:

- In the Application Folder right click on 'Primary output from Snake' and create a shortcut.

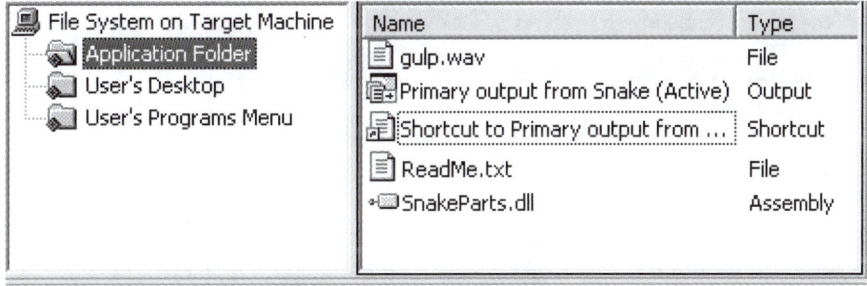

- Rename the shortcut to Snake, then drag it to the 'User's Programs Menu' folder.

■ There are a number of properties of the new project that you may want to set:

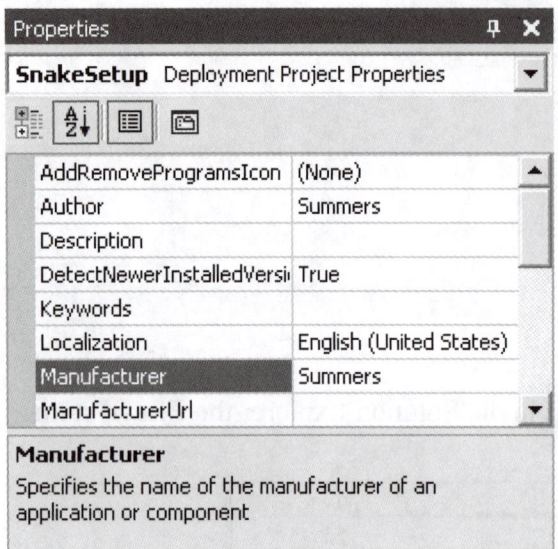

■ You should at least set a value for **Manufacturer** as this is used to construct the default path for the application under Program Files. If you'd like to offer support the SupportPhone and SupportUrl properties should be considered.

Building the deployment package

■ From the Build menu choose Configuration Manager.
■ Select Release as the Active Solution Configuration. This is presuming that no more debugging is required for *Snake*, and it is ready for the building of a deployment package.

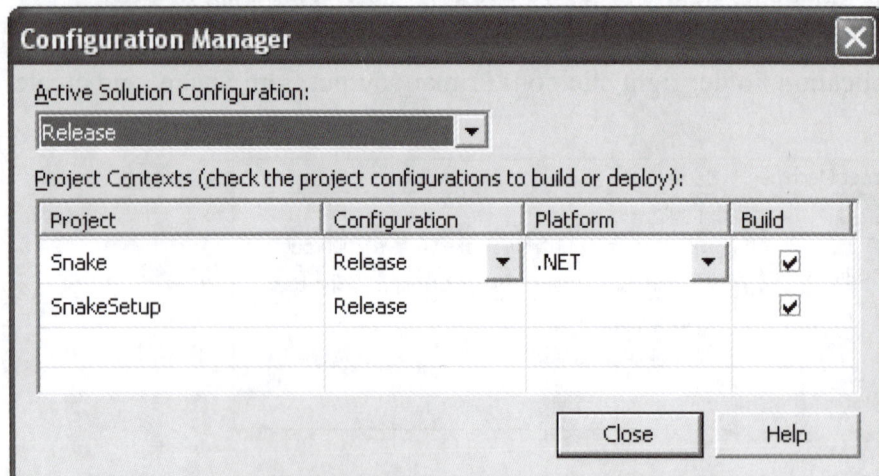

■ Make sure both **Build** check boxes have been checked.
■ Select Build the Solution from the Build menu. A progress bar will show activity followed by a 'Build Succeeded' message in the status bar.
■ The deployment package is now neatly contained in a folder named *Release* in the *SnakeSetup* folder.

■ Snake can now be installed by launching the Setup application and following the instructions given by the wizard.

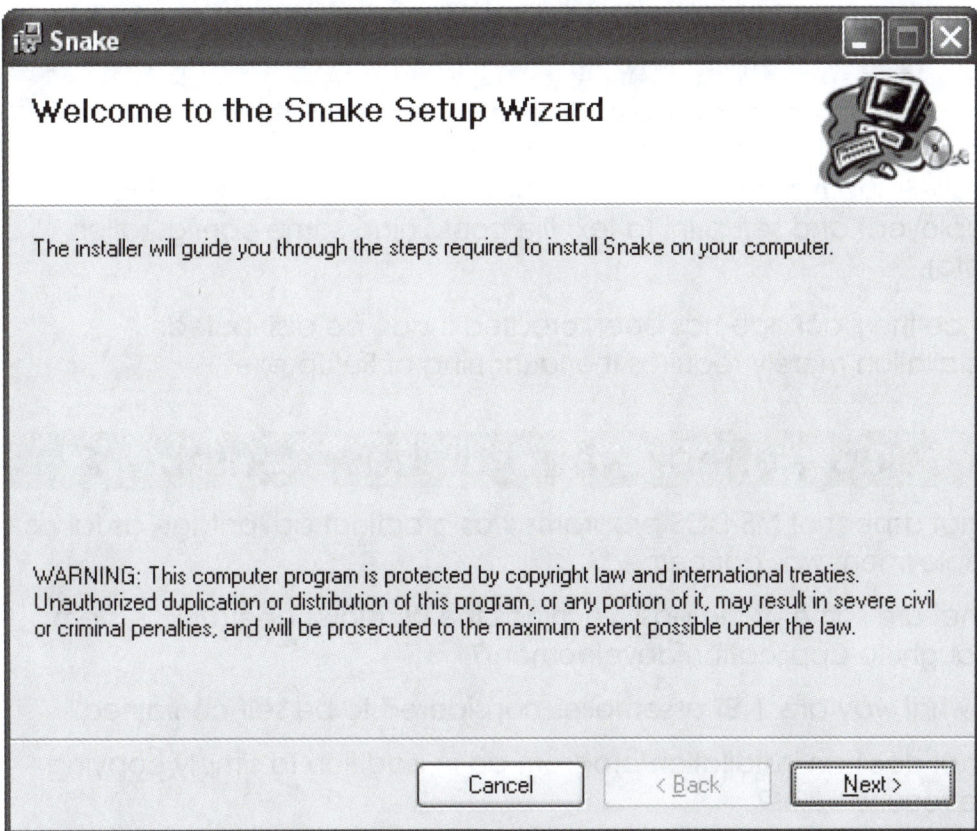

SnakeSetup – points to note

■ **Installation programs** make Windows 'aware' of the new application as well as copying the necessary files. The new program appears in the menu system, it may have a shortcut on the desktop and has an easy uninstall from the Control Panel.

■ A **deployment project** is a project that has been added to a solution for the purpose of creating a deployment (or setup) package.

■ The EXE file created for an application is referred to as the **primary output**.

■ Additional files like **ReadMe** text files may also be included in the package.

■ When the deployment project is created the **File System Editor** shows what will be installed in the application's folder, what will appear on the desktop and what will appear in the Programs menu. The editor allows you to do your own fine tuning.

■ The **Manufacturer** property of the deployment project is a part of the default installation path. Some of the other properties of the deployment project provide the opportunity to give **support** information and contact details.

- By default the active solution configuration is **Debug** while the application is still in development. Once everything has been finalised this is changed to **Release** for the building of the deployment package.

- The deployment package consists of three files: **Setup.exe** (an application that is provided for all deployment packages), **SnakeSetup.msi** (the actual package for the application being deployed) and **setup.ini** (a text file containing some configuration data).

- Once the package has been created it can be distributed. Installation merely requires the launching of Setup.exe.

SnakeSetup – check what you have learnt

1   What aspect of MS-DOS programs was a distinct advantage as far as deployment was concerned?

2   What are some of the positive things the Windows operating system brought to application development?

3   In what way are .NET assemblies considered to be self-contained?

4   What does an installation program do in addition to simply copying the required files?

5   What type of editing is possible with the File System Editor?

6   Why is it important that the Manufacturer of the application be given a name?

7   What is the difference between setting active configuration to Release rather than Debug?

8   Give some examples of the types of files you would include as additional files in the setup.

9   What is a shortcut?

10 ⌨ Use what you have learnt from this example to create deployment projects for some of your favourite programs that you have written.

Appendix 1: Code modules

Collision.vb

```
Module Collision

    Public Overloads Function Collision(ByVal Obj1 As Object, ByVal Obj2 As Object,_
    Optional ByVal HorizTolerance1 As Integer = 0, Optional ByVal VertTolerance1 As_
    Integer = 0, Optional ByVal HorizTolerance2 As Integer = 0, Optional ByVal _
    VertTolerance2 As Integer = 0) As Boolean
        If Obj1 Is Nothing Or Obj2 Is Nothing Then
            Return False
        Else
            Return (Obj1.Top + Obj1.Height - VertTolerance1 >= Obj2.Top + _
            VertTolerance2) And (Obj2.Top + Obj2.Height - VertTolerance2 >= Obj1.Top _
            + VertTolerance1) And (Obj1.Left + Obj1.Width - HorizTolerance1 >= _
            Obj2.Left + HorizTolerance2) And (Obj2.Left + Obj2.Width - _
            HorizTolerance2 >= Obj1.Left + HorizTolerance1) And Obj1.Visible _
            And Obj2.Visible
        End If
    End Function

    Public Overloads Function Collision(ByVal Rect As Rectangle, ByVal Obj As _
    Object, Optional ByVal HorizToleranceRect As Integer = 0, Optional ByVal _
    VertToleranceRect As Integer = 0, Optional ByVal HorizToleranceObj As Integer _
    = 0, Optional ByVal VertToleranceObj As Integer = 0) As Boolean
        If Obj Is Nothing Then
            Return False
        Else
            Return (Rect.Top + Rect.Height - VertToleranceRect >= Obj.Top + _
            VertToleranceObj) And (Obj.Top + Obj.Height - VertToleranceObj >= _
            Rect.Top + VertToleranceRect) And (Rect.Left + Rect.Width - _
            HorizToleranceRect >= Obj.Left + HorizToleranceObj) And (Obj.Left + _
            Obj.Width - HorizToleranceObj >= Rect.Left + HorizToleranceRect) _
            And Obj.Visible
        End If
    End Function

    Public Overloads Function Collision(ByVal Rect1 As Rectangle, ByVal Rect2 As _
    Rectangle, Optional ByVal HorizTolerance1 As Integer = 0, Optional ByVal _
    VertTolerance1 As Integer = 0, Optional ByVal HorizTolerance2 As Integer = 0, _
    Optional ByVal VertTolerance2 As Integer = 0) As Boolean
        Return (Rect1.Top + Rect1.Height - VertTolerance1 >= Rect2.Top + _
        VertTolerance2) And (Rect2.Top + Rect2.Height - VertTolerance2 >= Rect1.Top _
        + VertTolerance1) And (Rect1.Left + Rect1.Width - HorizTolerance1 >= _
        Rect2.Left + HorizTolerance2) And (Rect2.Left + Rect2.Width - _
        HorizTolerance2 >= Rect1.Left + HorizTolerance1)
    End Function

    Public Overloads Function Collision(ByVal Loc As Point, ByVal Obj As Object, _
    Optional ByVal HorizTolerance As Integer = 0, Optional ByVal VertTolerance As _
    Integer = 0) As Boolean
        If Obj Is Nothing Then
            Return False
        Else
            Return Loc.X >= Obj.Left + HorizTolerance And Loc.X <= Obj.Left + _
            Obj.Width - HorizTolerance And Loc.Y >= Obj.Top + VertTolerance And _
            Loc.Y <= Obj.Top + Obj.Height - VertTolerance And Obj.Visible
        End If
    End Function
```

```vb
Public Overloads Function Collision(ByVal Loc As Point, ByVal Rect As _
    Rectangle, Optional ByVal HorizTolerance As Integer = 0, Optional ByVal _
    VertTolerance As Integer = 0) As Boolean
        Return Loc.X >= Rect.Left + HorizTolerance And Loc.X <= Rect.Left + _
        Rect.Width - HorizTolerance And Loc.Y >= Rect.Top + VertTolerance And Loc.Y _
        <= Rect.Top + Rect.Height - VertTolerance
    End Function

End Module
```

Bearing.vb

```vb
Module Bearing

    ' The positive Left direction is an angle of 0
    ' The positive Top direction is an angle of 90 degrees or Pi/2 radians
    '***********************
    '*   OUTPUT IN RADIANS   *
    '***********************
    Public Overloads Function DirnRad(ByVal FromObj As Object, ByVal ToObj As _
    Object) As Double
        ' Calculated in radians
        Dim DirnCalc As Double
            Dim FromCentre As New Point(CInt(FromObj.Left + FromObj.Width / 2), _
            CInt(FromObj.Top + FromObj.Height / 2))
            Dim ToCentre As New Point(CInt(ToObj.Left + ToObj.Width / 2), _
            CInt(ToObj.Top + ToObj.Height / 2))
            Dim HorizDist As Integer = ToCentre.X - FromCentre.X
            Dim VertDist As Integer = ToCentre.Y - FromCentre.Y
            DirnCalc = Math.Atan2(CDbl(VertDist), CDbl(HorizDist))
            If DirnCalc < 0 Then
                DirnCalc += Math.PI * 2
            End If
            Return DirnCalc
    End Function

    Public Overloads Function DirnRad(ByVal FromPoint As Point, _
    ByVal ToPoint As Point) As Double
        ' Calculated in radians
        Dim DirnCalc As Double
        Dim HorizDist As Integer = ToPoint.X - FromPoint.X
        Dim VertDist As Integer = ToPoint.Y - FromPoint.Y
        DirnCalc = Math.Atan2(CDbl(VertDist), CDbl(HorizDist))
        If DirnCalc < 0 Then
            DirnCalc += Math.PI * 2
        End If
        Return DirnCalc
    End Function

    Public Overloads Function DirnRad(ByVal FromPoint As Point, _
    ByVal ToObj As Object) As Double
        ' Calculated in radians
        Dim DirnCalc As Double
        Dim ToCentre As New Point(CInt(ToObj.Left + ToObj.Width / 2), _
        CInt(ToObj.Top + ToObj.Height / 2))
        Dim HorizDist As Integer = ToCentre.X - FromPoint.X
        Dim VertDist As Integer = ToCentre.Y - FromPoint.Y
        DirnCalc = Math.Atan2(CDbl(VertDist), CDbl(HorizDist))
        If DirnCalc < 0 Then
            DirnCalc += Math.PI * 2
        End If
        Return DirnCalc
    End Function
```

```vbnet
Public Overloads Function DirnRad(ByVal FromObj As Object, _
ByVal ToPoint As Point) As Double
    ' Calculated in radians
    Dim DirnCalc As Double
    Dim FromCentre As New Point(CInt(FromObj.Left + FromObj.Width / 2), _
    CInt(FromObj.Top + FromObj.Height / 2))
    Dim HorizDist As Integer = ToPoint.X - FromCentre.X
    Dim VertDist As Integer = ToPoint.Y - FromCentre.Y
    DirnCalc = Math.Atan2(CDbl(VertDist), CDbl(HorizDist))
    If DirnCalc < 0 Then
        DirnCalc += Math.PI * 2
    End If
    Return DirnCalc
End Function

'***********************
'*   OUTPUT IN DEGREES  *
'***********************
Public Overloads Function DirnDeg(ByVal FromObj As Object, _
ByVal ToObj As Object) As Double
    ' Calculated in degrees
    Dim DirnCalc As Double
    Dim FromCentre As New Point(CInt(FromObj.Left + FromObj.Width / 2), _
    CInt(FromObj.Top + FromObj.Height / 2))
    Dim ToCentre As New Point(CInt(ToObj.Left + ToObj.Width / 2), _
    CInt(ToObj.Top + ToObj.Height / 2))
    Dim HorizDist As Integer = ToCentre.X - FromCentre.X
    Dim VertDist As Integer = ToCentre.Y - FromCentre.Y
    DirnCalc = Math.Atan2(CDbl(VertDist), CDbl(HorizDist)) * 180 / Math.PI
    If DirnCalc < 0 Then
        DirnCalc += 360
    End If
    Return DirnCalc
End Function

Public Overloads Function DirnDeg(ByVal FromPoint As Point, _
ByVal ToPoint As Point) As Double
    ' Calculated in degrees
    Dim DirnCalc As Double
    Dim HorizDist As Integer = ToPoint.X - FromPoint.X
    Dim VertDist As Integer = ToPoint.Y - FromPoint.Y
    DirnCalc = Math.Atan2(CDbl(VertDist), CDbl(HorizDist)) * 180 / Math.PI
    If DirnCalc < 0 Then
        DirnCalc += 360
    End If
    Return DirnCalc
End Function

Public Overloads Function DirnDeg(ByVal FromPoint As Point, _
ByVal ToObj As Object) As Double
    ' Calculated in degrees
    Dim DirnCalc As Double
    Dim ToCentre As New Point(CInt(ToObj.Left + ToObj.Width / 2), _
    CInt(ToObj.Top + ToObj.Height / 2))
    Dim HorizDist As Integer = ToCentre.X - FromPoint.X
    Dim VertDist As Integer = ToCentre.Y - FromPoint.Y
    DirnCalc = Math.Atan2(CDbl(VertDist), CDbl(HorizDist)) * 180 / Math.PI
    If DirnCalc < 0 Then
        DirnCalc += 360
    End If
    Return DirnCalc
End Function
```

```vb
Public Overloads Function DirnDeg(ByVal FromObj As Object, _
    ByVal ToPoint As Point) As Double
        ' Calculated in degrees
        Dim DirnCalc As Double
        Dim FromCentre As New Point(CInt(FromObj.Left + FromObj.Width / 2), _
        CInt(FromObj.Top + FromObj.Height / 2))
        Dim HorizDist As Integer = ToPoint.X - FromCentre.X
        Dim VertDist As Integer = ToPoint.Y - FromCentre.Y
        DirnCalc = Math.Atan2(CDbl(VertDist), CDbl(HorizDist)) * 180 / Math.PI
        If DirnCalc < 0 Then
            DirnCalc += 360
        End If
        Return DirnCalc
    End Function

End Module
```

Positioning.vb

```vb
Module Positioning

    Public Overloads Sub CentreOn(ByVal ObjOnWhichToCentre As Object, ByRef _
    ObjToCentre As Object)
        ' Centre on an object
        Dim WidthDiff As Integer = ObjOnWhichToCentre.Width - ObjToCentre.Width
        Dim HeightDiff As Integer = ObjOnWhichToCentre.Height - ObjToCentre.Height
        ObjToCentre.Location = New Point(ObjOnWhichToCentre.Left + WidthDiff \ 2,_
        ObjOnWhichToCentre.Top + HeightDiff \ 2)
    End Sub

    Public Overloads Sub CentreOn(ByVal PointOnWhichToCentre As Point, ByRef _
    ObjToCentre As Object)
        ' Centre on a point
        ObjToCentre.Location = New Point(PointOnWhichToCentre.X - ObjToCentre.Width _
        \ 2, PointOnWhichToCentre.Y - ObjToCentre.Height \ 2)
    End Sub

    Public Function InSightsVert(ByVal Attacker As Object, ByVal Target As Object) _
    As Boolean
        ' in a vertical line above or below
        Return (Target.Left >= Attacker.Left And Target.Left < (Attacker.Left + _
        Attacker.Width) Or Attacker.Left >= Target.Left And Attacker.Left < _
        (Target.Left + Target.Width)) And Attacker.Visible And Target.Visible
    End Function

    Public Function InSightsHoriz(ByVal Attacker As Object, _
    ByVal Target As Object) As Boolean
        ' in a horizontal line to the left or right
        Return (Target.Top >= Attacker.Top And Target.Top < (Attacker.Top + _
        Attacker.Height) Or Attacker.Top >= Target.Top And Attacker.Top < _
        (Target.Top + Target.Height)) And Attacker.Visible And Target.Visible
    End Function

End Module
```

PlayWave.vb

```vb
Module PlayWaveModule

    Private Enum PlaySoundFlags
        SND_SYNC = 0
        SND_ASYNC = 1
        SND_FILENAME = &H20000
        SND_RESOURCE = &H40004
    End Enum
```

```
Private Declare Function PlaySound Lib "winmm.dll" (ByVal fileName As String, _
ByVal hmod As IntPtr, ByVal flags As PlaySoundFlags) As Integer

Public Sub PlayWaveFile(ByVal FileName As String)
    PlaySound(FileName, IntPtr.Zero, PlaySoundFlags.SND_FILENAME Or _
    PlaySoundFlags.SND_ASYNC)
End Sub

End Module
```

FormBackground.vb

```
Module FormBackground
    Public Enum WhichWay
        Right = 0
        Down = 1
        Left = 2
        Up = 3
    End Enum

    Public Sub ScrollBackground(ByVal WhichForm As Form, ByVal InputBitmap As _
        Bitmap, ByVal PixelInc As Integer, ByVal Direction As WhichWay)
        Static Y As Integer = 0, X As Integer = 0
        Dim DWidth As Integer = WhichForm.DisplayRectangle.Width
        Dim DHeight As Integer = WhichForm.DisplayRectangle.Height
        Dim SelectedBitmap As New Bitmap(DWidth, DHeight)
        Dim objBack As Graphics = Graphics.FromImage(SelectedBitmap)
        Static objRect As Rectangle
        If WhichForm.BackgroundImage Is Nothing Then
            WhichForm.BackgroundImage = InputBitmap
        Else
            Select Case Direction ' to scroll the background image
                Case WhichWay.Up
                    If InputBitmap.Height >= DHeight + (Y + PixelInc) Then
                        Y += PixelInc
                        ' define part of image to see
                        objRect = New Rectangle(X, Y, DWidth, DHeight)
                        objBack.DrawImage(InputBitmap, 0, 0, objRect, GraphicsUnit.Pixel)
                    End If
                    WhichForm.BackgroundImage = SelectedBitmap
                Case WhichWay.Down
                    If Y - PixelInc >= 0 Then
                        Y -= PixelInc
                        ' define part of image to see
                        objRect = New Rectangle(X, Y, DWidth, DHeight)
                        objBack.DrawImage(InputBitmap, 0, 0, objRect, GraphicsUnit.Pixel)
                    End If
                    WhichForm.BackgroundImage = SelectedBitmap
                Case WhichWay.Right
                    If X - PixelInc >= 0 Then
                        X -= PixelInc
                        ' define part of image to see
                        objRect = New Rectangle(X, Y, DWidth, DHeight)
                        objBack.DrawImage(InputBitmap, 0, 0, objRect, GraphicsUnit.Pixel)
                    End If
                    WhichForm.BackgroundImage = SelectedBitmap
                Case WhichWay.Left
                    If InputBitmap.Width >= DWidth + (X + PixelInc) Then
                        X += PixelInc
                        ' define part of image to see
                        objRect = New Rectangle(X, Y, DWidth, DHeight)
                        objBack.DrawImage(InputBitmap, 0, 0, objRect, GraphicsUnit.Pixel)
                    End If
                    WhichForm.BackgroundImage = SelectedBitmap
            End Select
        End If
    End Sub
End Sub
```

```vbnet
Public Sub RotateBackground(ByVal WhichForm As Form, ByVal InputBitmapArray()_
As Bitmap, ByVal PixelInc As Integer, ByVal Direction As WhichWay)
    If WhichForm.WindowState <> FormWindowState.Minimized Then
        Static J As Integer = 0
        Static X As Integer = InputBitmapArray(0).Width * -CInt(Direction = _
        WhichWay.Left)
        Static Y As Integer = InputBitmapArray(0).Height * -CInt(Direction = _
        WhichWay.Up)
        Dim DWidth As Integer = WhichForm.DisplayRectangle.Width
        Dim DHeight As Integer = WhichForm.DisplayRectangle.Height
        Dim CompositeBitmap As New Bitmap(DWidth, DHeight)
        Dim objBack As Graphics = Graphics.FromImage(CompositeBitmap)
        Dim Last As Integer = InputBitmapArray.GetUpperBound(0)
        Static objRect(Last) As Rectangle
        Select Case Direction
            Case WhichWay.Up
                If Y < DHeight Then ' two parts to the background
                    ' upper part of background
                    objRect(J) = New Rectangle(0, InputBitmapArray(J).Height - Y, _
                    DWidth, Y)
                    objBack.DrawImage(InputBitmapArray(J), 0, 0, objRect(J), _
                    GraphicsUnit.Pixel)
                    ' lower part of background
                    objRect((J + 1) Mod (Last + 1)) = New Rectangle(0, 0, DWidth, _
                    DHeight - Y)
                    objBack.DrawImage(InputBitmapArray((J + 1) Mod (Last + 1)), 0, _
                    Y, objRect((J + 1) Mod (Last + 1)), GraphicsUnit.Pixel)
                Else    ' whole background from one image
                    objRect(J) = New Rectangle(0, InputBitmapArray(J).Height - Y, _
                    DWidth, DHeight)
                    objBack.DrawImage(InputBitmapArray(J), 0, 0, objRect(J), _
                    GraphicsUnit.Pixel)
                End If
                WhichForm.BackgroundImage = CompositeBitmap
                ' move on PixelInc pixels
                Y -= PixelInc
                If Y <= 0 Then ' reached the end of image, have to rotate
                    J = (J + 1) Mod (Last + 1)
                    Y = InputBitmapArray(J).Height
                End If
            Case WhichWay.Down
                If Y < DHeight Then ' two parts to the background
                    ' upper part of background
                    objRect((J + 1) Mod (Last + 1)) = New Rectangle(0, _
                    InputBitmapArray((J + 1) Mod (Last + 1)).Height - Y, DWidth, Y)
                    objBack.DrawImage(InputBitmapArray((J + 1) Mod (Last + 1)), 0, _
                    0, objRect((J + 1) Mod (Last + 1)), GraphicsUnit.Pixel)
                    ' lower part of background
                    objRect(J) = New Rectangle(0, 0, DWidth, DHeight - Y)
                    objBack.DrawImage(InputBitmapArray(J), 0, Y, objRect(J), _
                    GraphicsUnit.Pixel)
                Else    ' whole background from one image
                    objRect((J + 1) Mod (Last + 1)) = New Rectangle(0, _
                    InputBitmapArray((J + 1) Mod (Last + 1)).Height - Y, DWidth, _
                    DHeight)
                    objBack.DrawImage(InputBitmapArray((J + 1) Mod (Last + 1)), 0, _
                    0, objRect((J + 1) Mod (Last + 1)), GraphicsUnit.Pixel)
                End If
                WhichForm.BackgroundImage = CompositeBitmap
                ' move on PixelInc pixels
                Y += PixelInc
```

```
                If Y >= InputBitmapArray((J + 1) Mod (Last + 1)).Height Then
                    ' reached the end of image, have to rotate
                    Y = 0
                    J = (J + 1) Mod (Last + 1)
                End If
            Case WhichWay.Left
                If X < DWidth Then ' two parts to the background
                    '  left part of background
                    objRect(J) = New Rectangle(InputBitmapArray(J).Width - X, 0, _
                    X, DHeight)
                    objBack.DrawImage(InputBitmapArray(J), 0, 0, objRect(J), _
                    GraphicsUnit.Pixel)
                    '  right part of background
                    objRect((J + 1) Mod (Last + 1)) = New Rectangle(0, 0, _
                    DWidth - X, DHeight)
                    objBack.DrawImage(InputBitmapArray((J + 1) Mod (Last + 1)), X, _
                    0, objRect((J + 1) Mod (Last + 1)), GraphicsUnit.Pixel)
                Else     ' whole background from one image
                    objRect(J) = New Rectangle(InputBitmapArray(J).Width - X, 0, _
                    DWidth, DHeight)
                    objBack.DrawImage(InputBitmapArray(J), 0, 0, objRect(J), _
                    GraphicsUnit.Pixel)
                End If
                WhichForm.BackgroundImage = CompositeBitmap
                ' move on PixelInc pixels
                X -= PixelInc
                If X <= 0 Then ' reached the end of image, have to rotate
                    J = (J + 1) Mod (Last + 1)
                    X = InputBitmapArray(J).Width
                End If
            Case WhichWay.Right
                If X < DWidth Then ' two parts to the background
                    '  right part of background
                    objRect((J + 1) Mod (Last + 1)) = New _
                    Rectangle(InputBitmapArray((J + 1) Mod (Last + 1)).Width - X, _
                    0, X, DHeight)
                    objBack.DrawImage(InputBitmapArray((J + 1) Mod (Last + 1)), 0, _
                    0, objRect((J + 1) Mod (Last + 1)), GraphicsUnit.Pixel)
                    '  left part of background
                    objRect(J) = New Rectangle(0, 0, DWidth - X, DHeight)
                    objBack.DrawImage(InputBitmapArray(J), X, 0, objRect(J), _
                    GraphicsUnit.Pixel)
                Else     ' whole background from one image
                    objRect((J + 1) Mod (Last + 1)) = New _
                    Rectangle(InputBitmapArray((J + 1) Mod (Last + 1)).Width - X, _
                    0, DWidth, DHeight)
                    objBack.DrawImage(InputBitmapArray((J + 1) Mod (Last + 1)), 0, _
                    0, objRect((J + 1) Mod (Last + 1)), GraphicsUnit.Pixel)
                End If
                WhichForm.BackgroundImage = CompositeBitmap
                ' move on PixelInc pixels
                X += PixelInc
                If X >= InputBitmapArray((J + 1) Mod (Last + 1)).Width Then
                    ' reached the end of image, have to rotate
                    X = 0
                    J = (J + 1) Mod (Last + 1)
                End If
        End Select
    End If
  End Sub

End Module
```

RotateImage.vb

```vb
Imports System.Math

Module RotateImage

    Public Function Rotate(ByVal ImageSource As Image, ByVal DegAngle As Single) _
    As Bitmap
        Dim InputBitmap As New Bitmap(ImageSource)
        Dim RadAngle As Single = DegAngle * PI / 180
        ' starting width and height
        Dim W1 As Single = InputBitmap.Width
        Dim H1 As Single = InputBitmap.Height
        ' Set starting vertices with (0,0) at centre
        Dim Vertex(3) As Point
        Vertex(0) = New Point(-W1 / 2, -H1 / 2)
        Vertex(1) = New Point(W1 / 2, -H1 / 2)
        Vertex(2) = New Point(-W1 / 2, H1 / 2)
        Vertex(3) = New Point(W1 / 2, H1 / 2)
        ' Calculating the new width and height
        Dim W2 As Single = Abs(W1 * Cos(RadAngle)) + Abs(H1 * Sin(RadAngle))
        Dim H2 As Single = Abs(W1 * Sin(RadAngle)) + Abs(H1 * Cos(RadAngle))
        ' Rotate vertices  through the given angle
        ' and translate so X >= 0 and Y >=0 for all vertices
        Dim I As Integer, X, Y As Single
        For I = 0 To 3
            X = Vertex(I).X
            Y = Vertex(I).Y
            Vertex(I).X = X * Cos(RadAngle) + Y * Sin(RadAngle) + W2 / 2
            Vertex(I).Y = -X * Sin(RadAngle) + Y * Cos(RadAngle) + H2 / 2
        Next I
        ' Create an output Bitmap and a Graphics object
        Dim OutputBitmap As New Bitmap(CInt(W2), CInt(H2))
        Dim OutputGraphics As Graphics = Graphics.FromImage(OutputBitmap)

        ' DrawImage only requires an array of three vertices
        ReDim Preserve Vertex(2)
        ' Draw the rotated image onto the output Bitmap
        OutputGraphics.DrawImage(InputBitmap, Vertex)
        Return OutputBitmap
    End Function

End Module
```

Appendix 2: Dynamic link libraries

Maze.dll

```
Public Class MazeBlock

    Inherits System.Windows.Forms.PictureBox

    Dim X As Integer = 0, Y As Integer = 0
    Dim EOpen, SOpen, WOpen, NOpen As Boolean

    Sub New()
        SizeMode = PictureBoxSizeMode.AutoSize
    End Sub

    Property GridX() As Integer
        Get
            Return X
        End Get
        Set(ByVal Value As Integer)
            X = Value
        End Set
    End Property

    Property GridY() As Integer
        Get
            Return Y
        End Get
        Set(ByVal Value As Integer)
            Y = Value
        End Set
    End Property

    Property OpenEast() As Boolean
        Get
            Return EOpen
        End Get
        Set(ByVal Value As Boolean)
            EOpen = Value
        End Set
    End Property

    Property OpenSouth() As Boolean
        Get
            Return SOpen
        End Get
        Set(ByVal Value As Boolean)
            SOpen = Value
        End Set
    End Property

    Property OpenWest() As Boolean
        Get
            Return WOpen
        End Get
        Set(ByVal Value As Boolean)
            WOpen = Value
        End Set
    End Property
```

```
            Property OpenNorth() As Boolean
                Get
                    Return NOpen
                End Get
                Set(ByVal Value As Boolean)
                    NOpen = Value
                End Set
            End Property

    End Class

    Public Class Dot

        Inherits System.Windows.Forms.PictureBox

        Dim X As Integer = 0, Y As Integer = 0
        Dim A As Reflection.Assembly = Reflection.Assembly.GetExecutingAssembly

        Sub New()
            Image = New Bitmap(A.GetManifestResourceStream("Maze.dot.bmp"))
            SizeMode = PictureBoxSizeMode.AutoSize
            Width = 32
            Height = 32
        End Sub

        Property GridX() As Integer
            Get
                Return X
            End Get
            Set(ByVal Value As Integer)
                X = Value
            End Set
        End Property

        Property GridY() As Integer
            Get
                Return Y
            End Get
            Set(ByVal Value As Integer)
                Y = Value
            End Set
        End Property

    End Class
```

BoardSquares.dll

```
    Public Class BoardSquare

        Inherits Windows.Forms.PictureBox

        Dim I As Integer = 0, J As Integer = 0, ThisSquare As Integer = 0

        Sub New()
            Me.Height = 32
            Me.Width = 32
        End Sub

        Property SquareIndex() As Integer
            Get
                Return I
            End Get
            Set(ByVal Value As Integer)
                I = Value
            End Set
        End Property
```

```vbnet
   Property GoToSquare() As Integer
      Get
         Return J
      End Get
      Set(ByVal Value As Integer)
         J = Value
      End Set
   End Property

   Property Markers() As Integer
      Get
         Return ThisSquare
      End Get
      Set(ByVal Value As Integer)
         ThisSquare = Value
      End Set
   End Property

End Class
```

Bullets.dll

```vbnet
Public Class Bullet

   Inherits Windows.Forms.PictureBox

   Dim M As Boolean = False
   Dim I As Integer = 0
   Dim A As Reflection.Assembly = Reflection.Assembly.GetExecutingAssembly

   Public Enum Classification
      Friendly = 0
      Enemy = 1
   End Enum

   Dim T As Classification = Classification.Friendly

   Sub New()
      Image = New Bitmap(A.GetManifestResourceStream("Bullets.whitebullet.bmp"))
      SizeMode = PictureBoxSizeMode.AutoSize
      Visible = False
   End Sub

   Property BulletIndex() As Integer
      Get
         Return I
      End Get
      Set(ByVal Value As Integer)
         I = Value
      End Set
   End Property

   Property BulletType() As Classification
      Get
         Return T
      End Get
      Set(ByVal Value As Classification)
         T = Value
      End Set
   End Property

   Property Moving() As Boolean
      Get
         Return M
      End Get
      Set(ByVal Value As Boolean)
         M = Value
      End Set
   End Property

End Class
```

PlayingCards.dll

```
Public Class PlayingCard

    Inherits Windows.Forms.PictureBox

    Public Enum PlayingCardSuit
        NotDetermined = 0
        Clubs = 1
        Diamonds = 2
        Hearts = 3
        Spades = 4
    End Enum

    Public Enum PlayingCardValue
        NotDetermined = 0
        Ace = 1
        Two = 2
        Three = 3
        Four = 4
        Five = 5
        Six = 6
        Seven = 7
        Eight = 8
        Nine = 9
        Ten = 10
        Jack = 11
        Queen = 12
        King = 13
    End Enum

    Dim I As PlayingCardSuit, J As PlayingCardValue, K As Integer = 0

    Property Suit() As PlayingCardSuit
        Get
            Return I
        End Get
        Set(ByVal Value As PlayingCardSuit)
            I = Value
        End Set
    End Property

    Property CardValue() As PlayingCardValue
        Get
            Return J
        End Get
        Set(ByVal Value As PlayingCardValue)
            J = Value
        End Set
    End Property

    Property CardIndex() As Integer
        Get
            Return K
        End Get
        Set(ByVal Value As Integer)
            K = Value
        End Set
    End Property

End Class
```

SnakeParts.dll

```
Public Class Segment

    Inherits Windows.Forms.PictureBox

    Dim I As Integer = 0

    Sub New()
        Width = 8
        Height = 8
        BorderStyle = BorderStyle.FixedSingle
        BackColor = Color.LawnGreen
    End Sub

    Property SegmentIndex() As Integer
        Get
            Return I
        End Get
        Set(ByVal Value As Integer)
            I = Value
        End Set
    End Property

End Class
```

Answers

Chapter 1 – Serious fun

page 4

1 Zoologists believe that when young animals play they are practicing the skills they will need in their adult life.
2 The young animals are learning social bonding and communication skills.
3 Plato believed that (selected) toys would help children learn the skills they need for adult life.
4 Games reflect society in the types of rules they have, their settings, the symbolism of their components and the types of winning strategies they encourage.
5 Viewing television and videos are passive forms of entertainment.
6 *Group discussion*
7 *Group discussion*
8 *Group discussion*
9 *Group discussion*
10 *Group discussion*

Chapter 2 – Let's get it started

Viper cycle page 9

1 **a** btnStart **b** lblScore **c** imlCards
2 .Left = 48, .Top = 120
3 picRocket.Left -=8
4 They are not visible on the form while the application is running.
5 Every $^2/_{10}$ s or 5 times per second.
6 Enabled
7 Comments assist in the documentation.
8 The LocationChanged event is raised when the Location of an object changes.
9 .Left < 0
10
```
If picRocket.Top >= Me.Height Then
    picRocket.Top = -picRocket.Height
End If
```

Spaceship page 12

1 Image lists are used to store a collection of images.
2 The unit of measure for Location and Size is the pixel.
3 **a** 256, 256 **b** 16, 16
4 A zero-based collection has a first index of 0.
5 The KeyPreview property should be set to True.
6 The two arguments are sender and e.
7 e.KeyCode
8 **a** Two way branching means there are two possible courses of action.
   b Multiple branching means more than two possible courses of action.
9 Object names should be descriptive. They should suggest the purpose of the object.
10 See *Spaceship2* on the accompanying CD.

Fairy flying page 15

1 ImageSize and TransparentColor
2 The first index is 0, the last index is 7.
3 Camel casing breaks the name into its parts by highlighting the starting letter.
4 **a** 4 **b** 6 **c** 0
5 0, 1, 2, 3, 4, 5, 6, 7, 8.
6 Integers are whole numbers along with their negative opposites.
7 The Tick event is the default event of a timer.
8 If an object's Left property is negative its left side is beyond the left border of the form.
9 The top left corner of the object is in the top left corner of the form.
10 See *Fairy flying2* on the accompanying CD.

Explode

1   **a**   To make an object disappear set its Visible property to False.

      b   To make an object reappear set its Visible property to True.

2   The default event of an object is the event that most commonly occurs.

3   The two most important events for a timer are Start and Stop.

4   Name, Enabled, Location, Size, Visible.

5   The other name for an event handler is event procedure.

6
```
If Frame = 10 Then

End If
```

7   The condition is Frame = 10. This is either True or False.

8   The next time the explosion starts it will do so at Frame 0.

9   **a**   100   **b** $^1/_{10}$ second

10   An explosion sound, some smoldering left where the explosion occurred.

Chapter 3 – Heading in the right direction

Tank aimimg

1   A colour can be specified by its RGB composition. A number in the range 0-255 is given for each.

2
```
CInt(Direction / 360 * 32) Mod 32
= CInt(128 / 360 * 32) Mod 32
= CInt(11.377777) Mod 32
= 11 Mod 32
= 11
```

3   The two properties are Image and BackgroundImage.

4   The ImageSize and TransparentColor properties must be set.

5   AppStarting, Arrow, Cross, Default, Ibeam, No, SizeAll, SizeNESW, SizeNS, SizeNWSE, SizeWE, UppArrow, WaitCursor, Help, HSplit, VSplit, NoMove2D, NoMoveHoriz, NoMoveVert, PanEast, PanNE, PanNorth, PanNW, PanSE, PanSouth, PanSW, PanWest, Hand.

6   e.X and e.Y specify the position of the cursor.

7   Variables declared at form level can be used in any procedure on the form. Local variables declared in a procedure can only be used in that procedure.

8   Modules can be reused in multiple applications. Having useful procedures and functions in a module reduces the code required on the form.

9   When Mod 32 is applied the only possible results are the integers from 0 to 31.

10   See *Tank aiming2* on the accompanying CD.

Follow me

1   The functions Sin and Cos, and the constant PI are from the namespace System.Math.

2   **a**   0 and 180   **b**   90 and 270

3   360 ÷ 32 = 11.25

4   180°

5   Radians is the only unit of angular measurement accepted by the trigonometric functions.

6   240 ÷ 180 × 3.14159 = 4.19

7   Greater than 180° and less than 270°

8   CInt rounds an number to the nearest integer.

9   The overloads of a function are the different versions offering a different set of arguments.

10   See *Follow me2* on the accompanying CD.

Chapter 4 – Meet and greet

1   A splash form is used to give a bright and flashy introduction to an application, allow time for startup information to be loaded, display registration and copyright information.

2   A splash form should display the name of the application, the name of the developer(s) and the version number. It should be displayed long enough for the user to read the information given.

3   An entry form is used to gather information from the user that will be required later in that session.

4   An entry form could collect the name and password of the user. An unauthorized user could be prevented from progressing any further.

5   PassWrd is the variable, TextBox is the class.

6   The startup object could be Form1, Form2 or Sub Main.

7   ShowDialog displays a modal form. A model form must be closed before another form can gain focus. When a form is displayed with the Show method there is no such restriction.

8   The value of the Interval property of the timer on the splash form determines how long it will be displayed.

9   The code is executed after the period of time determined by the value of the Interval property.

Chapter 5 – Controlling the bugs

Wolf running   page 40

1   The transparent colour on an image should be one that has not been used anywhere else in the picture.

2   **a**   Picture boxes, forms and printers.

    b   `ObjCanvas = picPaint.CreateGraphics`

3   A graphics object must be created after a form has loaded. The Paint event does occur after loading.

4   **a**   The DrawImage and FillRectangle methods are used in this example

    b   Other methods are DrawEllipse, DrawLine, DrawRectangle, DrawCurve, FillEllipse, FillPolygon.

5   GDI+ provides more effective layering and overlapping.

6   FillRectangle uses a Brush object that produces a solid rectangle. DrawRectangle uses a Pen object that produces a rectangle outline.

7   The DrawImage method requires arguments to specify the image and the X and Y coordinates specifying where the image is to be drawn on the graphics object.

8   `Dim MyArea As New Rectangle(72, 48, 112, 64)`

9   See *Explode2* on the accompanying CD.

10   See *Elsa walking* on the accompanying CD.

Flying insects   page 45

1   The butterfly changes its image every $^3/_{10}$ second.

2   `objCanvas = Me.CreateGraphics    ' create graphics object on form`

3   Both these variables need to retain their values for the next time the procedure is called (the next tick).

4   **a**   Goes up 30 pixels   **b**   stays at same height   **c**   Goes down 30 pixels

5   If DragonflyMove = 5
```
(DragonflyMove + 5) Mod 10
= (5 + 5) Mod 10
= 10 Mod 10
= 0
```
If DragonflyMove = 0
```
(DragonflyMove + 5) Mod 10
= (0 + 5) Mod 10
= 5 Mod 10
= 5
```

6   The butterfly would leave a trail of its old images.

7   From ¼ of the form height to ¾ of the form height.

8   An overload of a method is another version of a method with a different set of arguments. For example the DrawImage method has thirty overloads.

9   **a**   The butterfly has seemingly erratic movements, dancing up and down. The dragonfly stays almost level with a very fast wing motion, pausing and hovering.

    b   Random numbers have produced varying erratic changes in the butterfly's coordinates. The dragonfly was given a set Y coordinate so that it flies at the same level. The Interval of the times varied to produce different wing speeds of the insects. An additional timer produced the pausing of the dragonfly.

10   See *Rally car race* on the accompanying CD.

Chapter 6 – Sound advice

page 55

1   Background sound sets the mood while sound effects add realism to the actions.

2   PlayWaveFile is restricted to wave files. These sounds are limited to a few seconds in length.

3   The default flags are: the name is a file name, play asynchronously and silence if the sound is not found.

4 The constant vbNullString is an empty string. If PlayWaveFile encounters an empty string it results in silence.

5 **a** The Reset procedure makes all the settings necessary ready to play another sound.

    b It is needed in a number of places in the application so it has been written as a general procedure.

6 **a** The AudioVideoPlayback module is used in this application.

    b Other modules are for graphics, handling input and communication.

7 **a** End of the file   **b** 0

8 The AutoStart property is set to False.

9 Event procedure arguments in .NET are always sender and e. With COM objects the event procedure arguments can vary event to event.

Chapter 7 – Collision decisions

Space   page 62

1 A bat hits a ball, a car hits another car, and arrow hits the bull's eye, a missile collides with a spacecraft, a player lands on a platform.

2 You would check for a non-collision if an object loses contact with another or if an object misses something it was headed for.

3 One timer moved the UFO, another moved the missile and a third controlled the sequence of the explosion.

4 The method Start turns a timer on, the method Stop turns a timer off.

5 There are 11 images, each taking $^1/_{10}$ second. The whole explosion takes 1.1 s.

6 Mod 11 can only result in integers 0 to 10.

7 A Rectangle with an object, a Rectangle with a Rectangle, a Point with an Object and a Point with a Rectangle.

8

9 Alter the speed of the UFO and/or the missile. Have the UFO fire at the spaceship.

10 See *Space2* on the accompanying CD.

Leap and land   page 65

1 The three constants represent the Top property of the character in three different states: at base level, on the platform and at the top of his leap.

2 There is a multiple branching structure in this procedure. What actions are taken depends on which key is pressed down.

3 CurrentState is one of the form level variables that is declared. It is used in more than one procedure.

4 LeapDist appears in every procedure.

5 `WhichImage = (WhichImage + 1) Mod 3 ' must be 0 to 2`

6 When LeapDist is +4 the Top property is increased, hence a downward movement. When LeapDist is –4 the Top property is decreased, hence an upward movement.

7 `If picChar.Top = PLATFORMTOP And Not Collision(picChar, picPlatform) Then`

8

9
```
Case Keys.Space
    If CurrentState <> Movement.Leaping Then
        CurrentState = Movement.Leaping
        LeapDist = -4 ' on way up
        tmrLeap.Start() ' start a leap
    End If
```

10 See *Leap and land2* on the accompanying CD.

Paddle ball
page 70

1   `picBall.Location = New Point(XPos, YPos)`
2   The DisplayRectangle.Width is slightly less than the Width. Given the size of the ball this small difference would be noticed.
3   If both IncX and IncY are negative then both the Left and Top are being reduced. The ball is moving up the form towards the left.
4   If IncX is multiplied by –1 it will reverse the horizontal direction. If IncY is multiplied by –1 it will reverse the vertical direction.
5   When the ball goes off the bottom of the form it means somebody missed. For example
      `If lblGreenPaddle.Visible Then    ' Green missed`
6   If the ball goes off the form the timer is stopped:
      `If YPos > Me.Height Then    ' ball off form, somebody missed`
        `tmrBall.Stop() ' stop ball`
7   `XPos = Int(Rnd() * MaxX)    ' random start`
8   The Not operator toggles a Boolean value. True goes to False, False goes to True.
9   The code in Swap_Paddles and Restart is required several times, so it is better placed in separate general procedures.
10   See *Paddle ball2* on the accompanying CD.

Chapter 8 – An array of hope

Enemy attack
page 75

1   `Dim RallyCar(7) As PictureBox`
2   The first index of all arrays is 0. They are zero based.
3   The use of arrays both simplifies and reduces the amount of code.
4   Irrespective of the size of an array, a loop will require the same amount of code.
5   Me.Controls is the collection of controls on a form.
6   The array was instantiated (or populated) in the Form Load procedure, then applied in the timer procedure. Because it was used in more than one procedure it had to be declared at form level.
7   AndAlso in the condition is not checked if the first part of the condition is found to be False. So if the control is a label its Tag would not be checked.
8   The set of integers is 0, 1, 2, … 9
9   WhichEnemy is declared with Dim because it takes on a new value each time the procedure is called. It does not need to keep its last value.
10   See *Enemy attack2* on the accompanying CD.

Double trouble
page 78

1   The controls in the Controls collection may come from a number of classes. The class Object is a general class that all other classes can belong to. So picture boxes, labels, buttons etc can all be assigned to a variable from the Object class.
2   Tag belongs to the Object class. So anything can be assigned to a Tag. This gives a developer the freedom to use the Tag property in a variety of ways.
3   The PictureBox arrays are declared at form level because they are instantiated in one procedure (Form Load) and applied in another (timer Tick).
4   Zero-based refers to arrays. Their first index is always 0.
5   The PictureBox arrays won't be able to be used until they are instantiated (populated). So this needs to be done at the very start of the application.
6   The expression `Int(Rnd() * 4)` will produce integer values from 0 to 3.
7   `Dim Enemy(19) As PictureBox ' an array of 20 picture boxes`
      `Dim WhichShip As Integer = Int(Rnd() * 20) ' random number 0-19`
8   J is initialized with the value 0. So the first element of the array instantiated is Missile(0). Then J has to increase by 1 for each subsequent element.
9   To slow down a moving object either increase the Interval of the timer or decrease the increments in the Left or Top properties (or all three).
10   See *Diagonal cars* on the accompanying CD.

Chapter 9 – I see the Earth move

Helicopter patrol page 83

1 The joining edges of the images must have a seamless match.

2
```
For Each obj in Me.Controls
    If TypeOf obj Is PictureBox AndAlso obj.Tag > "" Then
        I = obj.Tag
        ObjBit(I) = obj
    End If
Next obj
```

3 Arrays help reduce code, but in this case the use of a procedure from a code module has greatly reduced the code that had to be written.

4 `ScrollBackground(Me, objBit, 4, WhichWay.Up)`

5
```
Select Case e.KeyCode
    Case Keys.Up
        ScrollBackground(Me, objBit, 4, WhichWay.Down)
    Case Keys.Down
        ScrollBackground(Me, objBit, 4, WhichWay.Up)
    Case Keys.Left
        ScrollBackground(Me, objBit, 4, WhichWay.Right)
    Case Keys.Right
        ScrollBackground(Me, objBit, 4, WhichWay.Left)
End Select
```

6 The object would appear to be moving at a speed of 40 pixels/s to the right.

7 `(Frame + 1) Mod 3`
$$= (2 + 1) \text{ Mod } 3$$
$$= 3 \text{ Mod } 3$$
$$= 0$$

8 When declarations in *Formbackground.vb* are Public the enumeration and the procedures are available to all procedures on all forms in an application.

9 The object needs to have its own animation to have it appear that it is really moving.

10 See *City rambler* on the accompanying CD.

Endless road page 89

1 The functions Sin and Cos and the constant PI are from System.Math.

2 36 degrees
$$= 36 \times 3.14159 \div 180 \text{ radians}$$
$$= 0.628 \text{ radians}$$

3 $180 \div 16 = 11.25$

4 The Cos function is used to calculate the horizontal movement
`picCar.Left += PIXELMOVE * Cos(11.25 * WhichCar * PI / 180)`

5 Abs – absolute value, Log – natural logarithm, Round – rounds to nearest whole number, Sqrt – the square root.

6 a `imlCars.Images.Item(0)`

   b `imlCars.Images.Item(16)`

   c `imlCars.Images.Item(8)`

7 As the mouse moves over the picture the three labels change in the values they display. The labels show the RGB value of the pixel located at the cursor.

8 The condition is checking if any part of the car is protruding beyond the right side of the form.

9 $5760 \div (384 \times 3)$
$$= 5760 \div 1152$$
$$= 5$$

10 See *Endless road2* on the accompanying CD.

Chapter 10 – Telephones and tophats

Power of 2 page 98

1 $2^6 = 64$

2 $1 \times 2^0 + 0 \times 2^1 + 0 \times 2^2 + 1 \times 2^3$
$$= 1 + 0 + 0 + 8$$
$$= 9$$

3 $2^8 \times 2^8 \times 2^8$
$$= 2^{24}$$
$$= 16,777,216$$

4 `Dim RainbowCol() As String = {"Red", "Orange", "Yellow", "Green", "Blue", _`
`"Indigo", "Violet"}`

5 **a** `Int(Rnd()* 6)` **b** `Int(Rnd()* 6) + 1` **c** `Int(Rnd()* 11) + 2`

6 `Dim MyLoc As New Point(Me.Width \ 2, Me.Height \ 2)`

7 Any value that is a factor of 360 would be unsuitable as this would result in some rotations looking identical.

8 You need to be certain that the squares are in the order you intend. The most reliable way is for the squares to be given the indexes you want them to have.

9 `picCard.Image = Rotate(picCard.Image, 15)`

10 Open to your ideas.

Snakes and ladders   page 104

1 With the snakes there is a total loss of $(18 + 20 + 20 + 44 + 22 + 3 + 18 + 22 + 10) = 177$ squares. With the ladders there is a total gain of $(37 + 10 + 38 + 39 + 63 + 19 + 16 + 19 + 22) = 263$ squares. So there is more good fortune than misfortune.

2 The randomness of the die is assured with no physical obstacles. There is no possibility of cheating or error with the movement of the markers.

3 The ImageSize and TransparentColor properties must be set before adding to the Images collection.

4 You would leave the TransparentColor Transparent if you were using transparent GIFs or if you didn't require any transparency.

5 The random numbers produced with Rnd are pseudo random numbers. The Randomize statement ensures you don't get the same set with any two runs.

6 The code for Winner or Next_Player would have to be repeated twice each in other procedures. Having them as general procedures means their code only has to be written once. So it's about reduction of code and greater simplicity.

7 The code in *RotateImage.vb* is complex and long. It is very convenient to apply it in one line.

8 Only move it the 'StopAt' square is up to 100. If over 100 progress to the next player.

9 Group discussion.

10 See *Snakes and ladders2* on the accompanying CD.

Chapter 11 – Blocks and dots

Mouse maze   page 113

1 Special additional characteristics were required for a maze block.

2 **a** True or False **b** $2^4 = 16$

3 Enumerations are sets of numbers with descriptive names. This adds to the clarity of the code.

4 The number of elements $= 7 \times 4 \times 6 = 168$

5 **a** 1 **b** 3 **c** 5

6 If the condition is never met the loop will continue to repeat.

7 `WhichImage = (WhichImage + 1) Mod 9 ' 0-8 range of values`

8 The mouse moves 2 pixels per tick = 80 pixels per second.

9 See *Mouse maze2* on the accompanying CD.

10 See *Random maze* on the accompanying CD.

Dot eater   page 122

1 You don't have to move your hand from the keyboard to the mouse.

2 **a** A flag is a Boolean variable (usually) that indicates something has happened.

b `GameOver`

c Its value is set when the DotEater runs out of lives or eats all the food. The DotEater cannot eat more food if GameOver is True

3 The choice for MessageBoxButtons is from AbortRetryIgnore, OK, OKCancel, RetryCancel, YesNo and YesNoCancel. The choice for MessageBoxIcon is from Asterisk, Error, Explanation, Hand, Information, None, Question, Stop and Warning.

4 **a** Keys.Space **b** Keys.Escape **c** Keys.ControlKey

5 Wave files should be placed in the Bin folder, with the EXE file.

6 If the food is not eaten, the game is not over and the game hasn't been paused then …

```
7    For I = 0 to 4
        For J = 0 to 7
            Occupied(I, J) = False
        Next J
     Next I
8    For I = 0 to 4
        For J = 0 to 7
            Occupied(I, J) = Not Occupied(I, J)
        Next J
     Next I
```
9   If possible the ghost will try to move towards the doteater. Only if this is not possible will the ghost make a random move.

10   Your own ideas.

Chapter 12 – How to be sharp

Want a hand?   page 127

1   The two Integer divisions are \ and Mod.
2   **a**   Queen of Clubs   **b**   Two of Hearts   **c**   Eight of Spades
3
```
For I = 1 To 200
    Reserved(I) = False
Next I
```
4   `WhichCard = Int(Rnd() * 13) + 13 ' random Heart 13 to 25`
5   Enabled
6   Two cards have not been dealt.
7   The condition is tested at the end of the loop. The loop actions will occur at least once.
8   The default value of a Boolean variable is False.
9   `Dim Player(3) As TextBox`
10   See *Want a hand2* on the accompanying CD.

Pontoon   page 139

1   Images collection of an image list, Items collection of a combo box and the Panels collection of a status bar.
2   A rich text box allows the formatting of its Text and the inclusion of grahics.
3   The HandResult enumeration gives a clear description of its value. For example
     `If PlayerResult = HandResult.Bust Then`
4   The relative value of the members is the order of value of the hands.
5   ExtraTen flags whether the player has chosen to give an Ace a value of 11. PlayerAce and BankerAce flag if an Ace has been dealt.
6   The sender is the object that raised the event.
7   Mod 2 will only return values 0 or 1.
8   If adding 10 to the bankers total will beat the player without busting …
9   The banker must win. He is paid single if the player has a five card trick otherwise double.
10   See *Concentration* on the accompanying CD.

Chapter 13 – Objects on the fly

Snake   page 147

1   `Dim Participant() As String`
2   Declaration (creation), added to the parent's control collection, properties assigned, used in the application, disposed of.
3
```
Dim SnakePart() As Segment ' the segments of the snake are an array
ReDim SnakePart(Last)    ' array starts with 0 to 20
ReDim Preserve SnakePart(Last)   ' increase elements in the array
```
4   Preserve ensures that all existing elements remain intact.
5   The KeyDown event of the form and the Tick event of the timer.
6   `picTarget.Location = New Point(200, 180)`
7
```
For I = 21 To Last  ' dispose of additional segemts
    SnakePart(I).Dispose()
Next I
```
8   `mnuSound.Checked = Not mnuSound.Checked`

9 If the leading segment moves to a new location then its old location is lost and the segment behind it will not 'know' where to go. So the segment behind moves first on top of the one in front, then the one in front moves.

10 See *Snake2* on the accompanying CD.

Tetraminos page 157

1 **a** Shortcut keys are key combinations or function keys that are the keyboard equivalent of a mouse click.

    b An access key is a chosen letter from the Text property of certain controls that allows Alt key access. They are also the equivalent of a mouse click.

2 $15 \times 15 = 225$

3 The picture boxes are added to the Controls collection of the panel.

4 The shape is an L.

5 The pivot square remains stationary, the others rotate about it.

6 The code is dropping a part of a shape out of sight.

7
```
Dim SquareColour(6) As Color
SquareColour(0) = Color.Red
SquareColour(1) = Color.Blue
SquareColour(2) = Color.Green
SquareColour(3) = Color.Violet
SquareColour(4) = Color.Black
SquareColour(5) = Color.Brown
SquareColour(6) = Color.Lime
```

8 If there is more than one file open the file handle identifies which file is being operated on.

9 OpenMode.Append, OpenMode.Input, OpenMode.Output.

10 See *Tetraminos2* on the accompanying CD.

Chapter 14 – Space hero

page 167

1 The CentreOn procedure and the InSightsVert function are used in this application.

2
```
If obj.BulletType = Bullet.Classification.Friendly Then ' hero bullet
    I = obj.BulletIndex
    HeroBullet(I) = obj
```

3 The Initialise procedure is called in Form Load and lblLives_TextChanged.

4 It is a convention that helps distinguish variables from constants.

5 Altering the declaration of LASTBULLET.

6 `If sender.Top >= Me.Height Then     ' enemy gone below form`

7 When the last frame is reached the Stop method is applied to the timer.

8 It is possible for the bonus to be off, or partly off, the form.

9 Most often it is only one object that has raised an event.

10 Open to your ideas.

Chapter 15 – Deployment benefits

page 176

1 Deployment with MS-DOS programs was often simply a case of copying a few files.

2 Windows provides common services like the user interface, printing and clipboard functions

3 .NET assemblies are considered self-contained in that they can be installed by copying to a computer that has the .NET framework.

4 As well as copying files, an installation package registers the application and may place shortcuts in the menu system and on the desktop.

5 The File System Editor allows the developer to decide what will be in the application's folder, what will appear on the desktop and what will appear in the Programs menu.

6 The Manufacturer property of the deployment project is a part of the default installation path.

7 Debug is the setting while the project is still being worked on. The Release setting is used when everything is ready for deployment.

8 Additional files might be HTML files, ReadMe help files, sound files, data files.

9 A shortcut is a file that simply points to an application (or another file) in a different location. It is possible for an application to have several shortcuts.

Index

A

Abs function 88
access keys 156
Add method 144, 155
Add New Item 31
Add Windows form 30
ampersand (&) 138, 156
And operator 74
AndAlso operator 74
animation 2, 61
Anticipation 3
application folder 173
argument 12, 20, 23, 26, 40, 57, 61, 81,
     133
arrays 71, 74, 76, 82, 98, 112, 116,
     125, 126, 156
assemblies 169
AutoSize setting 8, 21, 85, 115
AutoStart property 51, 54

B

BackColor property 22
BackgroundImage property 21, 23, 45,
     79, 94, 100, 160
base class
benefits of games 2
binary number 91
Bitmap class 81
BMP files 161
board games 1, 91
BoardSquare class 92, 97
Boolean data type 70, 125, 126, 156
BorderStyle property 49
Branching
     Multiple 59, 64, 83, 87, 113, 117, 144,
          150
     two way 8, 52, 54, 68, 76, 81, 83, 164,
          167
Build configuration 174
Bullet class 159, 166
button control 50, 51, 52, 96, 101, 133, 135

C

camel casing 15
Case keyword 11, 12
Checkers 1
Check box control 49
Checked property 52, 149, 156
CheckedChanged event 53
Chess 1
CInt function 22, 23, 27, 52
class 35, 77

Click event

button 96, 125, 126, 133, 135
menu 119, 155
Closed event 34
Cluedo 1
code module 20, 22, 31, 47, 57, 61, 67, 80, 93,
     95, 100, 166
collision detection 57, 61, 65, 70, 143, 164,
     165
Color class 150
COM component 51, 54
combo box control 128, 138
comments 54, 65, 89
common services 169
component tray 5, 7, 11
concatenation 96, 101, 103, 104, 135, 138
conditional loops 112, 113
Configuration Manager 174
Const statement 63, 65, 86, 102, 103, 161,
166
Controls collection 72, 74, 141, 146
Cos function 19, 24, 25, 27, 86, 88
counted loop 119, 121, 125, 126, 127,
     143, 147, 150, 154
CreateGraphics method 38, 39, 43
CurrentPosition property 52, 54
cursor keys 12
Cursor property 21

D

Debug configuration 175, 176
decimal numbers 91
declaring variables 27, 44, 71
deployment package 169, 175
DeskTop 173
DialogResult enumeration 51
dice 92
DisplayRectangle 67, 146
Dim statement 38, 74
DirectX 47, 54
Dispose method 147
DLL 47, 169
Do Loop statements 112, 113, 124, 126, 163
Dock property 131, 138
Dominos 1
Donkey Kong 1
Doom 1
Double data type 23, 26
DrawEllipse method 40
DrawImage method 37, 39, 45
DrawLine method 40
DrawRectangle method 40
Dung Beetles 107

Duration property 52, 54

E

e argument 12, 23, 81, 117, 144, 152
elements of an array 71
Enabled property 8, 51, 127
End statement 145, 155
Ending event 53, 55
entry form 29
enumeration 63, 69, 86, 110, 112, 116, 120,
    131, 136, 138, 149, 156
EOF function 155, 157
event handlers 12, 17, 45, 167
event procedures 12, 17, 45, 167
events 47
EXE files 47, 171
exponentiation operator (^)

F

File System Editor 173, 175
FileClose statement 155, 157
FileName property 51
FileOpen statement 155, 157
FillEllipse method 40
FillPolygon method 40
FillRectangle method 38, 40
Filter property 49, 54
Final Fantasy VII 1
flag 120, 139
For Each loops 72, 73, 76, 88, 95, 110, 116,
    125, 132, 141, 143, 162
For Next loops 119, 121, 125, 126, 127, 143,
    147, 150, 154, 161, 167
form
    BackColor 22
    BackgroundImage 42, 160
    Cursor 21
    FormBorderStyle 30, 94, 148
    Icon 148
    MaximizeBox 100
    StartPosition 30
form level variable 22, 26, 38, 45, 63, 67, 86,
    132, 143, 149
Form Load event 14, 76, 77, 81, 95, 110, 116,
    125, 132, 141, 143, 162
Format function 155
FreeFile function 155
functions 57

G

GDI+ 37, 39, 98
general procedures 51, 54, 67, 69, 96, 101,
    104, 117, 132, 134, 139, 146, 149, 153,
    161, 166
GetPixel method 86, 89
GIF files 16, 81, 85, 109
graphics object 38, 39, 43
GridSize property 108, 109, 111
GUI 169

H

Handles keyword 134, 140, 164, 167
HatchBrush object 40
Hide method 34
history of games 1
humanise opponent 3

I

If Then Else statement 8, 52, 54, 68, 81,
    136, 137, 145, 162
ImageList control 10
Image property 23
Images collection 10, 13, 14, 20, 25, 92,
    95
ImageSize property 11, 13, 16, 21, 25, 82
Imports statement 25, 51, 54, 88, 95, 100,
    110, 125, 131
Index 71
InputBox 150, 156
Installation 175
instantiation 27, 44, 81, 95, 101, 125
Int function 43, 44, 70, 74, 76, 77, 93, 98,
    123, 146
Integer data type 15, 18, 22
integer division (\) 110, 112, 123
internal documentation 54
Interval property 8, 14, 44, 103
Items collection 130, 138

J

K

KeyCode property 11, 38, 81, 87, 117, 121,
    144, 152
KeyDown event 11, 12, 38, 59, 65, 81, 87, 89,
    117, 121, 144, 152, 162
KeyPreview property 12, 38, 142, 148
Keys enumeration 11, 38

L

Label
    BackColor 67, 85, 115, 160
    BorderStyle 67, 85, 115, 125, 142,
        160
    Font , 85, 115, 129, 142, 160
    ForeColor 67, 85, 115, 129, 160
    Size 67
    Text 67, 85, 115, 125, 129, 142, 160
    TextAlign 67, 85, 115, 160
Left property 5, 7
levels 3
LineInput function 155, 157
list box 148
literal 104
Load event 14, 76, 77, 81, 95, 110, 116
LoadFile method 137
local variables 45
Location property 5, 7, 19, 118, 145
LocationChanged event 6, 7, 8, 60, 69, 165
Log function 88
Loops 71, 112

M

MainMenu control 115, 116, 128, 148, 149
Manufacturer property 174, 175
MaximizeBox property 49, 81
MazeBlock class 107
mazes 107
Me object 38, 72, 73, 76, 88, 95, 110, 116,
    125, 132, 141, 143
Messagebox 69, 104, 119, 135, 137, 145, 164
MiddleCenter setting 49
modal forms 35, 139
Mod operator 14, 15, 23, 38, 40, 43, 81, 110,
    116, 117, 123, 162
modules 20, 22, 31, 47, 57, 61, 67, 80, 93, 95,
    100, 166
Monopoly 1
MotoGP 1
MouseMove event 22
movement 5, 70
MUD 2
multidimensional arrays 112
multiple branching 11, 12, 59, 64, 68, 83, 113,
    136, 150, 162
music 2

N

namespaces 25, 26, 100, 110, 125
nested loop 119, 121
New keyword 51, 144
NewState argument 53
Not operator 69, 70, 119, 121, 147, 155, 156
Nothing object 119, 134
Now function 155
null string 52

O

Object class 77
object naming conventions 15
OpenFileDialog control 49, 54
OpenMode. enumeration 155, 157
overloads 20, 26, 40, 57, 61

P

Pac Man 1, 107
Paint event 38
Panel control 148, 156
Panels collection 130, 138
parent control 155
PasswordChar property 35
Pen object 40
PI constant 86, 89
Pinball 1
Plato 1
Play method 49, 54
playing cards 123
PlayingCard class 124
PlaySoundFlags 47
PlayStateChange event 53, 55
Point class 22, 68, 95, 101, 145
Preserve keyword 144, 146
Primary Output 171

PrintLine statement 155, 157
Programs menu 173
Public statement 82

Q

Quake 1

R

Radian 21, 27, 89
RadioButton control 49
    Checked 51
    Text 50
Randomize statement 43, 74
randomness 3, 70, 74, 76, 77, 93, 98
ReadMe file 172, 175
ReadOnly property 131
Rectangle class 38, 40, 43
ReDim statement 144, 146, 149
reference 48-50
Release configuration 174, 176
Remainder division (Mod) 14, 15, 23, 38, 40,
    43, 81, 110, 116, 117, 123, 162
Return statement 133, 136, 139, 154
rewards 3
RGB setting 14, 22, 38, 39, 89, 94
RichTextBox control 131, 138
Rnd function 43, 44, 70, 74, 76, 77, 93, 98,
    123, 146
Round function 88

S

Scrabble 1
Segment class 141
Select Case statement 11, 12, 59, 64, 68, 87,
    113, 117, 144, 150, 162
sender argument 12, 140, 164, 167
shortcut keys 116, 131, 156
ShortCut property 116, 149
Show method 34, 35
ShowDialog method 51, 139
ShowPanels property 129
Sign function 70
Sim City 1
Sin function 19, 24, 25, 27, 86, 88
SizeMode property 8, 21, 85, 94, 115, 142,
    160
Snakes and Ladders 1, 99
SolidBrush class 40
solution explorer 10, 32, 173
sound effects 2
splash form 29, 35
Sqrt function 88
Start button 7
Start method 8, 17, 18, 121, 161
StartPosition property 30, 148
startup object 32, 35
Static statement 14, 15, 18, 38, 43, 74, 81
StatusBar control 128, 138
Stop method 8, 17, 18, 49, 52, 121, 161
StretchImage setting 142
String data type 51, 98

subclass 92, 97, 111, 124, 141, 146, 159, 166
Sub Main 32, 35
Super Mario Bros 1
system events 47
System.Math namespace 25, 26, 70, 86, 88

Z

zero-based, collections and arrays 11, 23, 71, 77

T

Tag property 71, 76
Tan function 88
test first loop 155, 157
test last loop 112, 113, 124, 126, 163
Tetris 1
TextAlign property 49
TextChanged event 69, 87, 89, 119, 126, 145, 164
text files 155, 157
TextureBrush object 40
Tick event 6, 17, 60, 73, 81, 102, 117, 162, 163
Timer control 6, 17, 60, 61, 73, 81, 102, 117
    Interval 8, 14, 44, 103
Title property 49
Toolbox 108, 159
ToolTipText property 130
Top property 5, 7
TrackBar control 105
TransparentColor property 13, 14, 16, 21, 25, 38
Trigonometry 89
Trivial Pursuit 1
two-way branching 8, 52, 54, 68, 76, 81, 83, 136, 137, 145, 162, 164
TypeOf keyword 72, 73, 77, 95, 110, 116, 132, 141, 162

U

Ultima V 1
underscore character 7, 8
Unreal1 1
URL property 49, 54
user defined function 133, 136, 139, 154, 156

V

variables 14, 15, 18, 35, 45, 77
vbCr 137
vbLf 150
vbNullString 52
View Code button 10
Visible property 17, 70, 88

W

WAV files 47, 59, 68, 120, 143, 149, 152, 165, 167
wildcard character 54
Windows API 47
Windows Media Player 47, 48, 51
WindowState property
WithEvents 51, 55
Wolfenstein 3D 1